WILD HORSES
OF THE
SUMMER SUN

A MEMOIR OF ICELAND

TORY BILSKI

PEGASUS BOOKS
NEW YORK LONDON

WILD HORSES OF THE SUMMER SUN

Pegasus Books Ltd.
148 W 37th Street, 13th Floor
New York, NY 10018

First Pegasus Books cloth edition May 2019

Interior design by Maria Fernandez

Library of Congress Cataloging-in-Publication Data is available.

ISBN: 978-1-64313-064-4

10 9 8 7 6 5 4 3 2 1

Printed in the United States of America
Distributed by W. W. Norton & Company
www.pegasusbooks.us

For Matthew, for all the reasons

CONTENTS

PREFACE

THE WILD HORSE IN US

—⟨oᴐᴐo⟩—

"Blame it or praise it, there is no denying the
wild horse in us."

—Virginia Woolf

I am out of control, my preferred way of being. I am on horseback, my
preferred mode of transportation. I am cantering, my preferred gait. Even
after a long, cold trek to get here, I can't tamp down the spirit of this mare
when we finally reach the sea. It's like she breaches.

All the horses get wilder here, their blood filled with the wind and the
waves of the Arctic waters. I can't really stop her now, so I let her go, let her
run to her heart's desire, which becomes my desire. I am part of her rhythm
and speed, galloping along the densely packed sand, sea-spray splattering my
face, breaking an imagined barrier. The whole world becomes what I can see
through the space between her ears, her wind-parted mane. She is fast and
sleek; like a ship she is yar. I don't think of falling or stopping, I only think
which one of us—horse or rider—will tire first. I am wildly free, giddily so,
the long-forgotten impulses of my youth awakening and leaving my heart in
flight mode.

I am known around my hometown as the woman who goes to Iceland to ride horses. At parties or at our local coffee shop, I get introduced as, "This is Tory. I told you about her. She goes to Iceland every year to ride horses."

If this once-a-year gig is part of my identity, I'll take it. I prefer identities that aren't tethered to either DNA or to the happenstance of birth. I'm American, whatever that all means; my father's Polish ancestry is written in my face, though the connection to the culture has long been lost; my mother's side has contributed a jumbled concoction of Northern European from Scottish to Estonian.

And as far as identities we make ourselves, I check the usual boxes: mother, wife, worker bee, suburbanite. But being the woman who rides horses in Iceland—that gives me, at least in my own mind, a bit more panache than, say, being the president of the PTA (a title I once held). It at least makes me worthy of another glance. If someone is about to politely pass me by, taking in my looks (hey there! I say) or my age (hey again!), and can only muster a ho-hum interest, this sometimes give them pause . . . *Huh?* I mean it's not polar bear tracking in Greenland (I wish) or reindeer herding in Lapland (oh please, oh please), but it pulls up a close third.

We are what we venture.

Why Iceland, why horses, why me? Because I was in my office, bored at my desk job—in boredom begins adventure—and had one of my first forays into "surfing the web" as it was so quaintly called those days, circa 1999, when Google was new and not yet a slouchy verb. I was only a few years out from my graduate degree thesis on Viking invasions of England, where I looked at the cultural influences those invasions may have had on Anglo Saxon life. I studied the Norse settlements in Yorkshire and Lincolnshire, never thinking about the Norse settlements in Iceland. But the clicks down those new Google steppingstones finally led to the official page of the Icelandic horse. I stopped and stared at the page for a long time. I had found something I didn't know I was looking for.

On my screen was a dark bay horse standing alone on a misty hill of green tussocks. It's hard to say why certain topics, objects, or places resonate with certain people. Why some people may gravitate toward the African continent, or, say, all things Italian.

But with that first glance of the pixelated Icelandic horse, I was nothing short of obsessed, a girl again, smitten. It was a well-muscled horse with a noble head, a compact body, flaring nostrils, and a Fabian black mane swept back from the wind. I knew it was a stallion; he had that tough-guy look to him. It was a horse that I felt some past kinship with, a memory of, a familiarity of place and time (I know, I know . . .). Usually I don't believe in past lives until my third glass of wine, but there I was, midday and procrastinating at work, staring at this dark horse that stared right back at me. We reconnected. It had been centuries.

So the dream began. This place: Iceland; that horse: Icelandic.

Once the North got in my psyche, it didn't let go. Iceland was not on the tourist grid back then. It was hanging off the map of Europe. If people knew anything, they knew that Erik the Red had intentionally switched around the idea that Iceland was green and Greenland was covered in ice. Maybe people had heard of Björk. Or if they were really in the know, they knew of Sigur Rós and the burgeoning music scene of Reykjavík. Maybe they knew of the cheap flights to Europe with a pit stop at Keflavík. It was mostly known as a flyover country on the way to London or Paris.

I got laughed at by a cousin when I expressed my desire to go: "You want to go *where*? To do *what*? That sounds like hell."

It wasn't just her. I knew no one, neither family nor friend, at the turn of our last century, who had the slightest interest in Iceland. Or their national horse.

My husband discouraged it. Mishaps always happened when I was gone: the basement flooded, the roof leaked, the dog got sick, the kids missed school, as if I were the household lucky charm. He couldn't get his work done. "Why can't you fall in love with a horse around here?" he asked. "What's the matter with Connecticut horses?" He was suspicious I was some kind of horse racist.

One friend did encourage me to go, wondering aloud if it was my version of a midlife crisis and instead of falling in love with someone else, I fell in love with some*thing* else, a horse, a particular kind of horse. On deeper reflection, she said, "Oh, Tory, you have to go," settling all matter of conflicting discourse. She was a social worker with Jungian training, who dabbled in desert vision quests. She grabbed my arm with an urgency I could not dismiss: "This is your spirit animal calling. Your totem. You have no choice but to meet it, greet it."

My digital, mythical, totemic horse called, and I had to answer. I set my compass north, to a remote ice rock of an island in the northernmost sea so I could throw myself on the back of a horse and gallop to land's end, to drum out the humdrum, and wake up the dormant desire, and fear, of a fast horse.

It wasn't my first equine affair. I was a horse-crazy young girl. I did the riding lessons and summer horse camps, and the fastidious grooming, fussing over the mane of a thousand-pound animal the way some girls fuss over their dolls. But by age eleven, I had lost my fervor.

On the cusp of puberty, my solitary horse love was usurped by a newfound girl clique. The tribal need to belong took precedence and there wasn't a horse-lover among them. We girls all lived in the same neighborhood, took the same bus home. Our houses edged a thousand-acre forest, in which we roamed every day after school. We tested our derring-do on trestle tracks, or with makeshift hockey games on frozen streams full of jutting roots and rocks, or played with matches, flicking them into stalks of dried grass that lit (oh shit!) too quickly. On the remains of old army barracks, we made a pact to return when we were older, which we swore we would keep, though "down we forgot as up we grew." We talked incessantly. We ate Twizzlers and drank Yoo-hoo. We tested out cigarettes, trying various methods of inhalation and exhalation, often pretending we had a cocktail in our hands at a swanky party.

Such were the joys.

Sometimes life circles back and gives us a chance to recreate ourselves, to revisit some prior incarnation. So, thirty-odd years later, I was traveling in a van in Iceland with a pack of women, new friends. Only this time the common bond was the pursuit of Icelandic horses. And we didn't plan on making a pact to return every year—but nonetheless, we did. Each June, we left our ordinary life behind, full of work and routine and all the troubles and concerns of adulthood, and ran with the horses in Thingeyrar, so to speak. Our time in Iceland was not a vacation, but our temporary vocation. We rode our horses through lupine fields and black volcanic sandbanks. We crossed rivers and lakes and came back, covered in dirt and mud, to our guesthouse in Thingeyrar. We talked incessantly. We ate cake and drank beer. We grew older together; we kept each other young.

Such, such were the joys.

BOOK I
THE WALK (FET)

———— ✺ ————

A slow and natural four-beat gait, during which two hooves always touch the ground and all hooves move forward at an even pace.

2004

Getting Lost

First time, right off the bat, years before the technical advantages of GPS or iPhones, we get lost.

Within thirty minutes of leaving Reykjavík we are at a fork in the road and, putting all our collective navigational skills to work, we take the wrong turn. It takes about an hour before we realize it. We are nine women stuffed in a van, three layers deep, with luggage on our laps and at our feet—four teenagers, four middle-agers, and Sylvie, who defies age-related genres. The teenagers sit in the back of the van and tune out on their iPods.

Bags of cheese-filled pretzels and chocolate-covered cookies get passed around. Eve's driving, and the rest of us grown-ups, at least Sylvie, Maggie, and I, are supposed to be navigators. We are armed with a map, the unwieldy fold-up variety sold at gas stations and tourist centers. Our index fingers dutifully, if erroneously, follow the map. We take turns passing it around every few minutes or so, occasionally interrupting our stream of conversation to weakly feign interest in the directions, saying something helpful like, "We should be in Smorgasbordafjordur any minute now." After making such a declaration, we crumple the map back up and pass it on, as if to say, "My job's done, pass those McVitie's."

Sylvie does most of the talking. Her conversation ranges from her enthusiasm for her newfound yoga instructor, Rodney Yee (Eve agrees, "He's a god") to Pema Chödrön (Eve again, "A goddess") to Sartre (dead silence on that one) to Shakespeare, which is my only safe entry into the conversation. I can talk Titania, Iago, King Lear.

Sylvie squeals and pushes Eve's seat from behind. "See, that's why I invited her, I need a literary companion." Eve, I presume, is her spiritual companion.

I barely know these two women who have organized the trip; the other women and the teenage girls, I know not at all. We are going to Helga's farm, a person and place I don't know, either. But I am in a place that I love: Iceland. They love what I love: Icelandic horses.

Sylvie is the connection to Helga: "We became friends when we drove to Saratoga together to look at a horse. We couldn't find the stables and we drove around for hours and got lost in the dark, but we found our friendship."

Sylvie is possessive and boastful of her friendship with Helga. "She invited me and said I could invite others. We are the only people she does this for. She doesn't open her guesthouse up usually. She is doing this for me and whoever I decide to bring."

Before this trip, I had met Sylvie a few times, and Eve maybe twice up at her horse farm in the Berkshires, the closest Icelandic horse farm to me. The trip was one hour and forty-five minutes; I could make it up and back in a day. I found out from Eve's stable manager about their trip to Iceland, and I wrote a lengthy email to Sylvie asking if there was any room for me. She wrote back: "Van crowded. Wheel hub seat over heater avail." I took it as a yes, soon to learn that while Sylvie is verbally expressive, her written skills are curt, truncated missives open to all kinds of interpretation.

So I am the last to join, the odd woman out, one up from a hitchhiker. Perched, as promised in that email, up on the wheel hub with my head bumping the top of the van. Soft bags and pocketbooks are stuffed between every available space. My seat is literally the hot seat—June in Iceland can still require heat, and it is pouring out of the side door.

Eve slows down to look at a road sign. "Can anyone find that town on the map?"

Maggie has the map and squints at the road sign, not the map. "I think so."

Satisfied enough with her answer, we drive on. Looking in the rearview mirror at the teenage girls, Eve tries to engage them. "Should we play Earl?"

"Yes, Earl," Maggie says, "Put on Earl." She has hardly spoken at all, except to weigh in with utter surety that we should take a right instead of a left at what turned out to be a critical crossroad.

"Should we play Earl?" Eve repeats, gathering support and enthusiasm.

"Earl," Sylvie demands.

One of the teenagers takes out her earbuds, and looks through her bag to pull out a CD.

I am not in on the joke, whatever Earl is, but soon it is blasted from the audio player up front. I don't know the song at all, don't quite get all the words to it, but I get the sentiment. Goodbye, Earl, Earl's gotta die. A woman's revenge song. Eve chimes in at the chorus. Earl is dead. I sit back and relax. These women, girls, are okay. But also, someone's mad at her husband.

After a few more Dixie Chicks songs, I hear Eve murmur to herself, "Mmm, we're supposed to go through a tunnel at some point."

But the landscape has changed from a few horses in the fields—when Sylvie irrepressibly shouts out, "Horsey!"—to hundreds of horses in the fields, with herds of fecund mares and knobby-kneed colts. "Babies!" It's a horse-lover's dream. All the Icelandic horses the eye can behold in all the Icelandic greenery. We give up on the map and pick up our cameras, haphazardly dangling them out the window to click away.

And it's more the grownups in the car than the teenagers who revert to childhood at the sight of these horses. I am forty-six and Sylvie is going on sixty-six; Maggie is Eve's negligibly older sister and Eve, I'm guessing, is about fifty-two. To this day I don't know Eve's real age. If the topic comes up, she diverts attention away from it. I know many women like this. They don't like to be pigeon-holed by their age, and that's fair. If we live in an era where people can be gender fluid, I think we can be age fluid as well. We can say it's a spectrum, and we can go back and forth in age at will. When challenged, we can say: Why be so dogmatic about the biology of age? Hanging out the window, cooing at all the horses, we are ten again.

Eve does her best to get on with the purpose of getting us to our destination. She pulls over to a road sign, squinting at the town name and asking, "Does that look like anything on the map?" In the back seat, Sylvie and I collectively put our heads together and pretend to study the map again. "Mmm, sort of."

Sylvie gives up and holds the map out. "Who's good at navigating?"

Maggie and I don't volunteer. Sylvie rattles the map in my face. "Here you navigate."

I take the map with no real conviction, singularly focused on the fields of horses in the green tussocks, running freely all over the hills and dales. It's a visual feast. I do not know if I am recalling an early childhood episode or if it's paleo-genetic memory, but nothing lowers my blood pressure, nothing stimulates my hippocampus and alights my dopamine receptors, like the sight of herds of horses. Peace, tranquility, and, incongruently, excitement possess me all at once. The map flops limply in my hands as Eve drives on.

Sylvie is chatting away about her husband, who hasn't moved with her and still lives in Connecticut and is "Frankly, a drag, he acts like an old man. He doesn't want to do anything."

Eve slows down to almost a stop. "Folks, we've been on a dirt road for miles. There's no highway in sight."

This alarms Sylvie, who with that exaggerated intake of air, says dramatically, "We're lost. Pull over." She covers her face with her hands.

I didn't know what all of Sylvie's anxieties were at this early stage of our travels, but I know the signs when people fear being lost. My husband has this fear. There are no palliative words to calm these people down.

Eve pulls off the road at a juncture with a gravel lot and below us is the watery landscape of a mesmerizing blue fjord. It is not just blue, but a royal cobalt blue that shimmers in metallic pointillism and leaves golden spots on the backs of my eyelids. It's a blue I've only ever seen in Iceland. A northern-sea blue. A color so rich it makes you contemplate the meaning of color, and the physics of light in creating color.

Eve is unperturbed over losing our way, as am I. I don't mind being lost as long as I have time on my hands and I know I'm not in danger. And June in Iceland is all daylight. It might dim a little from clouds, but night won't get dark. And even in a worst-case scenario, we have enough junk food in our car to last us a few days. I can't see us picking each other off for the last package of McVitie's anytime soon. I do worry, though, about Sylvie's fear of being lost, and also that my navigational credentials will be forever ruined with this group. (As it turns out, this is a legitimate fear: every year we come to the tunnel's crossroad and every year we wind up discussing how we got lost the first year and who was at fault. Since Maggie never came with us again, the blame defaults to her.)

Meanwhile, the hitherto mute teenagers unplug from their earbuds. "What's going on?" they ask.

"I think we missed the turnoff to the tunnel," Eve says, full of bewilderment though masking it in good cheer.

"We're completely lost," Sylvie bleats. "Who was supposed to be navigating?"

The evidence, the map, is still on my lap. But many miles back at the crossroads, Maggie was the one who said to go right where I thought we should go left.

"We're fine," Eve says, looking at the shores of the fjord. A family of about ten—what looks like grandparents, parents, and children—are digging for mussels. "Maybe they can help us."

Sylvie grabs the map from me and gets out of the car. She hitches her jeans up before strutting down to the shoreline.

"Look at her go," Eve says.

She walks like a cowboy with her skinny, slightly bowed legs. Her curly red hair is only partially tamped down with a multicolored Peruvian wool beanie. She wears red round-rimmed Harry Potter glasses and, around her neck, a dash of more color from a Bali-made scarf. On her feet, Australian Blundstone paddock boots. Somehow this international fashion panoply works well on Sylvie; she swaggers with sartorial confidence.

Approaching the natives, she waves the map over her head, and gives them her signature greeting, "Yoohoo, yoohoo."

At first they look as if they will ignore her. It is a truism that the older a woman is the more she is ignored. But it is hard to ignore Sylvie. She tramps down the hill closer to them. We hear her ask, "Hello, does anyone speak English?"

Out of earshot, we watch the gesticulating communication from the safe distance of our van, until Eve says, "I have to pee." Which starts many murmurings of "oh, yeah, me, too, I'm dying." Eve says, "There's some rocks over there."

The teenage girls express their disdain by saying, "I would rather die than pee outside." To which I voice the wisdom that is earned from many decades of full bladders: "I'd rather pee outside than pee in my pants. There's not a toilet around for hours."

Eve, Maggie, and I tumble out of the car and surreptitiously look for a suitable rock to duck behind. Practically in sync, we each find our own private boulder to crouch down behind, pee, and pull up our pants as quickly as possible. But that, for some reason, gets the Icelanders attention, at least their steely stares. Did we offend? Did we act like a pack of territorial dogs, sending out a scout to divert attention while the rest of us mark our territory?

Sylvie makes her way up the hill looking discouraged, leaving the foraging family behind her, looking slightly relieved. "We're way off track. We missed the tunnel."

For the first time, I take a serious look at the map and see our mistake. "When we missed the tunnel we must have gone all the way around this fjord, Hvalfjörður. This bump in the land where we are now, must be this bump in the map here."

Eve is listening to me and following along, but Sylvie is lost in her thoughts. She looks down to the beach and the mussel-digging family. "I don't think they liked me very much." We assure her that they just didn't understand her.

Eve toots the horn and waves to the family on the beach, yelling out, "Thank you, thank you, thank you," before driving away.

Eve says, "See? The universe provides. I'll call Helga at our next stop and tell her we'll be a bit late." Eve is the only one with a cell phone and it's impressive. A Blackberry, and it works, though reception is temperamental. She has to hold it halfway out the window or stand in a meadow or lean against a wall.

The mere mention of Helga and the farm revive Sylvie with a renewed giddiness. She squeals, "And she'll have horses for us!"

The grownup women in the car are much more excited than the teenagers. And Sylvie, the most "grown," is the most excited of all.

Oh, and then there is the woman in the back seat, Dora.

I've ignored her in the story thus far, because I believe she wanted to be left alone.

She doesn't take part in any conversation, even when, on occasion, she opens her eyes. The rest of the time she feigns sleep, or for all I know, is asleep. It's like a homeless person who camps out next to an outdoor cafe; you're eating and drinking and having fun, but she's there, minding her own business but serving as a reminder that everyone, even in your cloistered van, is not having a good day.

Not that Dora looks impoverished in any way. But she doesn't look like the rest of us, either. She doesn't dress for Iceland by wearing Polartec or a parka, heavy sweaters, and paddock boots. She wears expensive jeans, a silk blouse, a dressy white jacket with fur trim, and Tory Burch flats. A heavy dose of perfume permeates the car—another thing the rest of us wouldn't think of wearing on our way to a horse farm. The only thing that seems to be amiss is that her hair is dirty, stiff, and unkempt, and an overly golden-dyed blonde. Generally speaking, her whole hue is gold. Her wrists are covered in gold bangle bracelets, and so are her fingers, neck, and pierced ears. She has tanning-bed colored skin with an overlay of bronzer, and very Cleopatra made-up eyes, lined in black with metallic gold eyelids. I know it's often said that women dress for other women, but I don't get that from her. She is dressing for someone who's not there.

Eve looks in the rearview mirror every so often at her. When she does, Sylvie rolls her eyes indicating her displeasure with this passenger accompanying us. Maggie pretends Dora isn't there, and I'm waiting to hear the story of why she is on this trip.

In Search of the Perfect Pylsur (Hot Dog)

Back on the Ring Road and heading in the right direction, Eve talks about being on a dairy-free diet and feeling better than ever. "Jack and I have given it up. It's so toxic, lactose. Humans are not meant to consume dairy."

Sylvie sort of agrees. She works at a macrobiotic health store part-time and says it took her a long time to accept rice milk in her coffee every morning. "But I'm not completely miserable. Not completely."

I ask them, "Are you lactose intolerant?"

They both answer no, but Eve expounds. "All humans are lactose intolerant to a degree. Lactose is making us sick. Our bodies can't break it down and it leads to disease."

Cheese and anything creamy and dairy-based are the mainstay of my diet; they never make me sick. In fact, consuming fatty dairy products makes me feel good. I'd go as far as to say that they make me feel loved. But I am susceptible to dietary pressures, and I briefly reconsider my love of cheese and ice cream, though Iceland doesn't seem the right place to give it up.

"I'm getting hungry," Sylvie says, the discussion of dangerous lactose clearly firing up her appetite.

"Me, too," Eve says.

Despite the steady car diet of cookies, pretzels, and licorice, it is at long last lunchtime.

Eve begins innocently enough with the idea of getting a hot dog. "The last time I was in Iceland . . ."

This is not Eve's first trip to Iceland. She has been twice before with her husband, Jack, to buy horses to stock their Icelandic farm in the Berkshires.

"I had this hot dog at one of these gas stations. It was somewhere around here, at one of these N1 stops. Oh, it was so good," she says mistily, like a hot dog at a gas station was the best thing in her life.

"I remember it just had this certain snap to it, and these crunchy onions and the bun was perfect." Eve takes one hand off the steering wheel and her fingers give that little kiss sign at the end of the sentence.

As I said, I am susceptible to food fads and diets. So, I don't necessarily hold it against Eve for doing this to me; she doesn't know how food obsessive I can be. But that day she starts me on the long circuitous path to finding the perfect Icelandic hot dog.

She repeats that dead-on detail—the snap of the hot dog as your teeth break the skin. She describes the kind of day it was: cold and rainy, the fog forcing them to stop at the gas station and wait out the weather. They were on their way to purchase a horse.

That is the happiness trifecta in my view: a journey with purpose—horse buying; a physical challenge—stormy weather; and unexpected great eats—a hot dog.

"Are they boiled or pan fried, these hot dogs?"

"They're in one of those hot dog rollers. You know, it warms and crisps them."

"What kind of roll?"

"Just a regular white bun, the soft and mushy ones."

"Ketchup or mustard?"

"Neither, they have these two rémoulade sauces: a white one and a yellow one."

Every answer to my questions sets my urges loose. "Are they beef, pork?"

"Supposedly they're lamb and pork. And they come with a topping of potato salad."

Potato salad?! I am about to die from hot dog desire. And I'm not usually a big hot dog lover. In fact, it's one of my least favorite foods. I think of it as composite garbage meat, what gets done with the entrails and offal and ground up ear bones of poor old dairy cows. It's one of those meat concoctions that could turn me into a vegetarian. But I know that in Iceland the meat is organic. The lamb and cows are free-range out of tradition, out of necessity, and out of practicality.

"We have to find this place," I tell her.

We cross a narrow isthmus surrounded by a tidal bay where the sand and water are gray. No sun now to speak of, but there is a thin light coming from behind a cloud, giving the brackish water a hint of glitter.

We have entered Borgarnes. "Is it in this town?"

Eve looks carefully at the cheery red symbol of the gas station and pulls in to a parking space.

"Is this the place?" I ask her.

She hesitates, "I think so."

I bustle her out of the car and into the N1. Since so much of Iceland is rural, gas stations are where people often meet and eat. They serve as a quick mart where you can buy everything: woolen hats, maps, milk, yogurt. But they also provide a bakery, an expansive penny variety candy counter, a soft serve ice cream stand, and a café that serves up meat soup, fried fish, or hamburgers with fries. And then near the register are the hot dog rollers and condiments.

I jump in line and wait not so patiently. When my turn comes, the fresh-faced young girl speaks to me in Icelandic. At a quick glance, I'm white enough and blonde enough to pass as a local. And there is always a moment when you want so badly to pass, to pretend you're someone who can speak the language, that you persuade yourself you can pull it off. I knew the word for hot dog, had seen it in downtown Reykjavík and had invested a few days on Icelandic language tapes, which left me with a shaky grasp of counting to five.

"Einn *pylsur?*" I ask, questioning my own request. And then comes the long list of Icelandic questions and my moment of shame. I am forced to give up my fake identity. "Ummm, can I have a hot dog with onions and the two sauces and potato salad?"

There was a time, way back in the early 2000s, when once out of Reykjavík, people's English skills were limited, so language misunderstandings were common, but always calm and unemotional. After all, this is the country that hosted the Reagan-Gorbachev summit; this is a country where people can make peace and disarm nuclear escalations.

The girl at the counter decides it's too much for her and asks a coworker for help with English. Another fresh-faced young person steps in and bails her out. I explain to him, and point. "I want a hot dog with that and that and that. The works."

And then we go through the pointing game. "This? No that. This? Yes, that." His English is no better than hers, but he's stuck with me now. My hot dog is half-constructed and he can't pass me off to someone else.

It seems to take forever. The local people behind me, if they can speak English, don't offer up help. Icelanders at that time were not used to tourists and didn't seem particularly interested in them, so if anyone knows English, no one is helping us out, but neither are they getting impatient. Good thing, too, because Eve's behind me and they have to wait as she goes through the same order again.

Finally, the precious, lusted for, linguistically fought for hot dog with all the trimmings is in my hands. A paroxysm of joy. I can't decide whether to stand at one of the plastic tables to eat it or take it outside to a picnic table. But outside is cold with the lashing wind and rain of late June. I eat it standing up in three bites. The crunch of the onions and the soft roll are perfect. The meat itself is not as garlicky as American hot dogs, probably because they don't have so much offal to cover up.

Eve is just starting hers. "What do you think? Is this the place?" I have loved my three bites, but I need her assent.

She chews thoughtfully before saying, "It's great, isn't it?" Eve's first impulse is always to be positive. But then on reflection she says, "But it doesn't quite have the right snap. I don't think this is the place. That place must be farther down the road."

Oddly, I'm happy about that. For there it is, that mythical destination "down the road." The only thing better than finding the perfect pylsur is having to keep looking for it and knowing that any gas station in Iceland could be my Rosslyn Chapel. It's the perfect quest. And I will eat many hot dogs in pursuit of it.

The Land of Oz

Sylvie, Eve, and I are back in the car, but everyone else is still in the gas station buying yogurt, ice cream, coffee, and *kleinur* (donuts), stocking up in fear of another wrong turn, another delay before we get to Helga's.

Outside, Dora is smoking a cigarette, hunched on the side of the building, avoiding the wind, avoiding us. She stubs it out, looks around, reaches into her pocket, pulls out a box, and shakes out a Tic Tac, or maybe a pill.

Eve explains Dora. "Her husband died about a year ago. He came in from a run and dropped on the kitchen floor from a massive heart attack at thirty-eight. After that, she wound up spending a lot of time at Guild Acres. She was in such a rut. I told her, 'You need to come to Iceland with us.'"

"Funny, you didn't tell me she was at Guild Acres," Sylvie says.

"It wasn't that much time. I was hoping she'd join in more with us. We need to bring her out a little."

Sylvie clucks. "Well, if she was in Guild Acres she has addiction issues and most likely depression issues. And, just a wild guess, but I'd say she probably has socialization issues. That's a lot for us to work on. And this is my first trip to Iceland. I'm on vacation."

"She'll figure it out. Oh, Sylvie, we're all on our own journey."

Sylvie mutters something about how Dora is "actually on our journey."

"I think Iceland will heal her. It's good for your soul, this place. Look how beautiful everything is here. It's magical!"

At the moment, dark clouds have moved in and the rain has turned briefly into snow. The wind blows hard on the van, rattling the doors. Dora turns her back against the wind to light another cigarette.

In years to come, there will always be "a Dora" on our trips, someone Eve decides needs her help. Eve's modus operandi is trying to save people, always thinking that taking them down the Yellow Brick Road to Iceland will heal what hurts them, give them back their hearts, their minds, their courage.

Sylvie mentions how Dora slipped on the floor in the airport bathroom, how there was a *kerplunk* and she looked over to see Dora sprawled out under the stall, with her legs sticking out from underneath the door.

"See, she's manifesting grief and depression. It's the law of attraction, she's attracting falls and accidents. She is bringing herself down, literally. She needs to manifest health and life.

"This trip will be good for her, you'll see. She needs this. And the horses. They will heal her. Horses have a way of healing," Eve says.

Sylvie agrees on this point only. "It's true. Horses can save you. They can."

No doubt I was in the company of a couple of new age spiritualists. Most of my friends at home are professionals like lawyers who want rational arguments, or doctors who want evidence-based findings, or social workers who believe we have childhood issues to work out. And I have spent the last eight years working at Yale for political economists who are devoted to data crunching. I spend my days listening to them talk about hot deck imputations, weighted variances, and smoothing random effects. I edit their academic journal, assiduously checking citations, grammar, and the Chicago Manual of Style's arcane hyphenation rules on papers with titles such as, "The Indirect Effects of Downstream Experimental Analysis: Cost-Effectiveness of Randomized Field Experiments."

I don't own one self-help book, and have never gotten farther than two pages into any book about a new age philosophy. So the language is strange to me and rings untrue.

Law of attraction? No, just an overproduced way of saying "like likes like." The universe will provide? Sorry, fate is fickle, no overarching plan here. Manifestation of grief? Good god, give the woman a break—her husband dropped dead in front of her.

I don't "journey," I travel. I don't "heal," I get over things.

But the idea that horses can save you, that this big beautiful animal with a wild heart and an over-reactive flight instinct can teach you, connect deeply to your soul, mirror your intent, and lead you into an I-Thou relationship?

Oh, man. I was all in.

Horse History

Y ou've been to Iceland before?" Eve asks me.
"Yes, in 2001. I signed up with an Equitour company. I had no idea
what I was doing. I just knew I had to come to Iceland."

"Wow, you were really called to these horses," Sylvie says.

"Isn't that funny how that happens?" Eve says. "Jack and I were riding
Lusitanos and we were going to go to Brazil to buy some and start our horse
farm, when someone said we should check out the Icelandic horses in upstate
New York. And that was it, there was something about them. We never went
to Brazil, we started our Icelandic farm. We never looked back."

I finally had validation from these women. I am understood. My calling
is their calling.

We take turns explaining our horse history, which is a lot like explaining
our lives. Sylvie tells us that she was a high school English teacher who took an
early retirement at fifty-nine, moved up to the Berkshires, and started taking
riding lessons. "I didn't know I loved horses until then." Her first foray into the
equine world was with big horses, English Hunter style, and was disastrous.
"My riding instructor was so mean, she said I was hopeless. She called me
'hopeless'! Can you believe that?"

Eve says she was always horse crazy. She grew up in Ohio and used to ride
the pigs on a nearby farm and pretend they were horses. Her sister, Maggie,
nods, confirming it was true. "She was always begging for a horse, but we
didn't have the room in our yard."

"Or the money," Eve says.

I tell them my horse history, how, yes, I was a horse-crazy young girl, but
how desire bubbled up in me soon after turning forty and I started taking lessons at a local barn. Once a week I rode Charlie, a 21-year-old Thoroughbred,
around and around the ring. Walking and trotting, fine, but I could rarely
get him to canter. I loved the big, old gelding, but in a pitiable way because he
had his freedom broken early in his life and he was deadened and shut down
to humans. He was once an abused racehorse, now he was an overused school
horse. I didn't want to tax him too much. I took my lesson but spent most of
the time grooming him, as if he were the most important horse in the world,
as if he had won the race. But some days I would get to his stall and he was

standing in pee-soaked sawdust with his body bumpy from infected fly bites or other horse bites. Old horses get picked on—it's enough to break your heart.

Each one of our horse histories, our searches, ends with: "And then I found Icelandics." But finding these horses, we would learn, was only the beginning.

"They are complicated horses, with all of the gaits," Eve says. "There is so much to learn."

Sylvie agrees emphatically with an audible intake of air, and on the exhale she says, "They're *sooo* complicated. I spent my first two years just learning the walk and the collected walk."

"So you went alone, without knowing anyone?" Eve goes back to my original trip.

"I had to ride these horses, nothing else would do, and I didn't know anyone who wanted to go with me." I wish I had known them.

———

After finding the Icelandic horse on the internet, I spent the next two years working myself into a tizzy over them, dying to meet one. But there were none close to me. I made a trip to an Icelandic farm in northern Vermont to test drive one shortly before I embarked on my first Iceland trip. As I expected, it only fed my obsession, because age bestows peculiarities of taste, eccentricities of desire. Or to paraphrase the duplicitous Woody Allen, "The heart does want what it wants," and this one wanted these horses. Nothing else.

I randomly chose an Equitour company and specifically chose the longest and most difficult trip they offered. I was not much of a rider, mind you. But that didn't concern me. I only thought of my mythical horse and the galloping we would do together.

I flew into Keflavík, took the bus to the national airport and a prop plane to Akureyri, completely bypassing Reykjavík. I waited for a couple of hours at the Akureyri Airport to be picked up by someone from the farm. It was a one-room terminal and after the first few minutes, I was the only person there. I read *Being Dead*, a novel by Jim Crace, which goes into great detail about how a corpse rots after a couple gets robbed and bludgeoned and left for dead. I looked up every so often for my ride, and thought, *What am I doing here? I flew all the way here to read a book in a deserted airport?* It hardly felt like the appropriate beginning to an adventure. I should have chosen a northern-bound book, too, a Shackleton tale, at least. But this is what happens when you are bored at work and let your daydreams get the better of you. *What if this whole trip turns out to be a dud?* I thought. After two hours, a young woman showed up, an intern at the farm, and she gave no excuses for her lateness—my first experience with "Icelandic time," which is well intentioned, but noncommittal.

But the trip was hardly a dud. On the contrary, the riding was more challenging than I expected. We started out with twelve riders. One, a young woman from Chichester who embodied everything I loved in an English-woman (cheery, chubby, with a trilling laugh), got thrown the first day and dislocated her shoulder. Her trilling laugh turned to whelps of pain, lasting until an ambulance, which took an inordinate amount of time coming since we were in the hinterlands, drove her away. It was a bad start and then there were eleven . . . .

Two Americans, a couple from Arizona, were the next to drop out. She was a big blonde, and he was her lanky cowboy-looking husband, an army vet who worked in the defense industry. After the second day of riding, Ms. Arizona, lowered her voice and said, "That's it for us, after what happened to the English girl. I'm fifty-nine, I can't bust myself up like that."

I spent the remaining six days with nine Germans, of all different ages. They were jolly and laughed a lot, and during dinner would translate their jokes for me and then I would throw my head back and laugh, like them, feeling like a jolly German. But unlike me, they were all experienced riders. In Germany equestrian courses are offered in high school.

And then there was Jonki, our tour guide, a big, young, bald, Icelandic fellow, who ignored all his foreign charges because he was busy romancing his pretty girlfriend, who he had brought along for the ride. When he paid attention to us, I wished he hadn't. He was one of those laughing sadists—when I told him I was nervous about riding over a narrow mountain pass or a high bridge without a railing crossing a rushing river, he clucked at me and picked up the pace. He took us through thrown-up ground—frost heaves, a moorland of tussocks. We never slowed down. We would stop only to give the horses a rest.

One day, he handed me the reins of two horses to pony alongside me so he could go off to smooch with his girlfriend in the back of the line. At first, I was flattered. He thought I was a good enough rider to pony horses. So I didn't hesitate. I took the long lead ropes of the unsaddled horses, and along with my horse's reins, held all three pairs in my hands. I did my best to keep them from tangling and keep the ponied horses in some semblance of a line off my right side and slightly behind my horse. I understood ponying more in theory than in practice—it should look like half a V formation—and for a while I kept it all together. When we cantered downhill, though, I lost my stirrups and lost my seat, and struggled not to lose the horses. It was hard work, out-of-my league riding, baptism by fire, but I was in my glory riding like a cowgirl.

On the last day of our journey, out on the tip of the Eyjafjörður peninsula, we turned the horses toward home. My horse decided to run home and for a few miles, I led the team or left them unintentionally in the dust behind me. Not of my doing, or desire, of course—I had no idea how to stop the horse. When they caught up to me, Jonki was smiling. "Now you want to go in a hurry?"

I feared I had spent most of my good fortune and fessed up: "This horse has gotten the better of me." I switched over to the pack horse, who had two gaits—a plodding walk and a slow gallop—a true pack horse, no matter what country he lived in. After twenty miles of riding like this, I got off for the last mile and walked the horse back to the farm. I was sore and relieved, proud and happy. I could do it, I *did* do it. And I couldn't wait to go back.

But I did wait. It took a couple of years to find Eve's farm in the Berkshires. And it took another year before Helga invited Sylvie to Thingeyrar, and for me to invite myself, and for Sylvie to say, in effect, hop on board.

Arrival in Thingeyrar

B ack on the road, Eve asks me what I do. I tell them about Yale and my job editing the journal. It sounds so dry and dusty. I picture my office in the third-floor attic of a Victorian-era house. I see myself in third person, a woman sitting alone, in a semiautonomous job. Taking a break from tedious proofing with its arcane editing shorthand in the marginalia, she dreams of riding horses in Iceland again. Her desktop computer makes it too easy to leap into other worlds, which includes not only Iceland but places like

Greenland and the reindeer country in Lapland. Maybe if she had a more outgoing, social type of job, she would not have the time or need to fantasize about far-flung cold places. But then she wouldn't be in the back of this van in Iceland.

They ask me about my children and I tell them my son, who is going on fifteen, studies classical piano and jazz guitar. My daughter, who is eleven, is at ballet camp. "She only likes classical ballet."

"They sound wonderful," Eve says.

And they are, and my life revolves around them and my husband at home. We're like four limbs of a body. I can't go to sleep at night until I know we are all home in our beds, though with my son, now that time gets later and later. He has hit an age where he has emotionally detached from us, and it's an odd estrangement. He has attached himself to a pack of five guys; they move together on the sly like a pack of wolves. It's normal, I tell myself, but he drifts away in front of us. I suspect he comes home high or drunk, though it's hard to tell how much and how often. He knows how to hide things.

Until asked, I have not thought of my family since I entered the van. And I realize that I barely thought of them in Reykjavík, except to send off a few emails from the hotel's computer. The very act of traveling and always having to take the temperature of a new place and unknown people is completely consuming. Maybe I'm assuaging my guilt here, but traveling requires at least a small amount of survival skills by navigating language, people, and places, and keeping your eyes on what's up ahead.

Thingeyrar is what's up ahead. After nearly six hours of food stops and getting lost, we turn off the Ring Road where the sign tells us it is just six kilometers down a dirt road. The rain and snow and wind have stopped. The sun is high. We pass one farm after another, each spaced out every couple of miles, with hundreds of grazing sheep and horses.

At the end of the road there is an iron gate that says THINGEYRAR on top.

"This is it." Sylvie is squirmy with excitement. "We're actually here! Look at all her horses! Oh! Look at all those babies."

Maggie gets out and opens the gate. We drive through and she closes it. In front of us is our farm for the week, at the end of the road, with a 360-degree view of the green valleys, the glacial mountains, two rivers that converge, and a large lake with black sandbanks that empties into the sea.

At the end of the driveway, we park next to what must be Helga's house, a modern two-story duplex, and what must be our guesthouse, an older house, behind which looms a large black stone church.

Someone comes walking up from the barn to greet us—it must be Helga. She is stunningly beautiful in a way that is mundane in Iceland. Light, almost white, blonde hair, ruddy cheeks, dazzling blue eyes, high cheekbones, flawless skin. She looks to be in her early thirties, though I know she is closer to my age.

"So we're here. Did you think we'd actually come?" Sylvie says.

"Well, I didn't know, but here you are." She laughs at Sylvie and hugs her. "Good to see you, my friend."

Sylvie beams, as if this is all she's ever wanted, to be Helga's friend. And I find myself emotionally reverting back to middle school, oddly envious of their friendship, as if Sylvie hooked the cool girl in school to be best friends with.

<hr />

An hour later, we're down at the barn. Dora does not join us because she has a headache, which is a relief to me and Sylvie. As much as I want to ignore Dora, her quiet presence is still a presence, and it's troubled.

Eve says, "Maybe it's best she doesn't ride with us anyway, in her state, you know." Eve doesn't have to fill in the rest: People who are down attract calamity, and we would all be riding with her and, hence, we'd all fall down or fall off. It's very easy for this thinking to devolve into superstition.

Disa, a young woman from the equine college Holar, is at the barn to help us. She will ride sweep while Helga rides in the lead. She is twenty-six and even more beautiful than Helga: her cheekbones are higher, her hair is thicker and parted into two long golden braids, her eyes are deep set and cat-shaped. She is all this, plus cheery, outgoing—she says everything with half a laugh and a big smile. In Eve-speak, she beams radiant light, attracts positive energy. Her teeth are even dazzlingly white. At six-feet tall, thick and powerfully built, Disa dwarfs Helga and the rest of us. She exudes an Amazonian size and strength, like she could easily throw an average-sized man over her shoulder. Hell, she looks like she could wrestle a bear and come out a smiling victor.

Disa hands me the reins to a pretty chestnut mare named Perla, and has me test her out in a nearby paddock. When I first get on a horse, if I haven't

20

ridden for a while, I'm always looking for the seatbelt. I want to strap myself on, though I know that would be worse. I know it would be much better if I learned how to fall, which is what jockeys and event jumpers learn how to do.

As I walk my horse around the paddock, Helga tells me Perla is five, but very steady, and that the Holar interns trained her this winter. "She's a very good horse and you look good on her."

I want to tell Helga, don't be fooled. I'm not such a good rider. And five is green for an Icelandic horse. Even in the paddock I can sense that Perla is too much horse for me. I feel as if I'm atop a revved-up motorcycle that will explode when we ride out from these fences. Eve backs Helga up though, and says that I look "great" on Perla, and tells Helga that I've ridden in Iceland before and that I'm a pro. So, of course, I don't mention my fears. I'd rather look great on a pretty horse than risk looking like a wimp in front of these women.

"And for you, my friend . . ." Helga turns to Sylvie. "Let's put you on . . ."

Sylvie looks as if she's going to collapse from fear and starts babbling: "Remember the kind of horse I ride at home, the kind of horse I'm used to. Remember, I ride Hátið [pronounced "How-teeth"]. That's the level of horse I'm used to, remember? Hátið is so old she's practically toothless. You know Hátið. That's my level, Helga."

"Yes, I know. I'm going to put you on Thoka, she is my very special old mare. She is the horse I take when I'm going to the neighbor's and I know I'm going to be drinking a lot of beer with my girlfriends. Thoka just takes me home."

Thoka is a small, white mare. Her coat is still shaggy from the winter, and it makes her look older, bedraggled, and docile, like a kid's pony at a birthday party.

Sylvie uses a mounting block to get on. She plops down heavily on Thoka's back and sucks in air. "This horse scares me."

Sylvie knows a lot more about horses than I do. She rides daily at home, while I ride maybe a few times a year, if that. But having someone to worry about takes my own worries away. "You okay?" I ask her.

"I'm okay, but I'm not okay. I took half a Valium, so once that kicks in I should be fine."

"Is that safe to do?"

"My doctor says it's fine. Oh, I'm crazy, didn't I tell you that?"

Now we both have to wait in the saddle, in the paddock, for everyone else to mount. My horse gets antsy and I walk her around in circles. Sylvie talks to her horse, "Whoa, whoa, shh, shh," but her horse is standing stock still with closed eyes, basically napping.

When all eight of us are up, we wait for Helga and Disa to saddle up. This is it. This is what we've come all this way to do: ride. This is what I sit in my office all year long dreaming about—being in Iceland, riding. But I know something Sylvie doesn't know but obviously senses: that riding in Iceland is much more rigorous than riding Icelandics in the Berkshires, where we plod along, purposely keeping them slow and safe.

"Everybody ready?" Helga asks.

"Alright," Sylvie says. "Let's get this over with!"

"You came all the way to Iceland just to get it over with?" Helga asks.

"Oh, that is so Sylvie," Eve says as a way of explaining to Helga.

And off we go, out through the main gate to the outer lands. The horses pick up the pace immediately. They vie to be in the front of the pack. This is what horses are like in Iceland because they aren't coddled like pets. They are brought up under semi-feral conditions: the young and the mares are set free for many months, driven into the mountains to live off the land with no human care. Since they are left to forage for food and water on their own and figure things out for themselves, they grow to be healthy, sturdy, and, for the most part, sane. If a horse is not right in the head, Icelanders have no compunction about putting it down. Or selling it to Americans.

Traveling in a pack of ten as we are, the horses bunch up together, like they would in their herd. I am knee-to-knee with Maggie, who is bouncing around a lot in the saddle, but she doesn't complain. Eve has a big smile on her face ("Isn't this great!"). Two of the teenage girls are very good riders and they know how to slow their horses down, turning them in circles to get back in line. I envy that ability. My horse is passing everyone and wants to be in front. She is young and has no manners, and my skills are too limited, my reactions not reflexive yet.

Perla catches up with Helga's lead horse and at first Helga thinks I mean for this to happen. "Don't let Perla get in front of me," she says. She then starts chatting with me, asks me where I am from, how I know Sylvie. I get out a few words and then admit to Helga that my horse is getting away from me.

She cuts a sideways glance at Perla and says in Icelandic, "Fet, Fet," and her horse and mine magically slow down to a fast walk. It is clear from the start of this ride that my first trek in Iceland three years ago was old school. We rode farmers' horses with a local farmer as our guide. There was little concern for our safety or our riding level—it was get on your horse and go. Helga is new school, a Holar graduate and a Holar instructor, who wants horse and rider safe. She wants the experience to be mutually beneficial. She trusts her horses, but she sees we have varying degrees of riding ability and confidence.

When the rest of the horses catch up to us, everyone checks in on Sylvie, who has been in the back of the line under Disa's watchful eye.

"How are you doing, Sylvie?" Eve asks.

"Sylvie, you okay?"

Helga is most concerned about her friend and says to me, "Maybe this is too much for her."

"I'm alright," Sylvie finally peeps up. "But this is not like riding my horse at home. We do a lot of walking on the trail. Can we just walk for a while? I like to walk."

So we walk for a while, but the horses are straining to go faster. Much like the Arabian horse and the harsh desert environment they sprang from, Icelandics have been bred for endurance in formidable weather and rough terrain. Iceland's roads are a fairly new luxury. The main ring road around the country was not completed until 1974, and there have never been trains in Iceland. The horses needed to serve as long-distance carriers and most of the getting around pre-automobile was done on well-worn sheep trails. While the rest of Europe spent centuries breeding their horses to be larger and heavier for war or pulling carriages, or larger and leggier for sport racing, Iceland never had a standing army, had few serviceable roads for carriages, and never had the leisure time to use horses as sport. Instead, they purposely kept their horses small, quick, and hardy. And the *tölt* gait was key for comfortably riding long distances.

After a few minutes, Helga calls out, "Sylvie, do you think you can tölt some more?"

Reluctantly she admits that she's up to more tölting. And we're off again at a fast clip, through fields of lupine that graze our thighs, through dry paths where the hooves kick up yellow dust in our faces. I get used to Perla and am no longer just a passenger who can't control the brakes. My legs fit comfortably around her girth, and after riding for an hour or so, I am beginning to use my leg yields and lighten up on my reins. I consider myself a novice rider because I am. I never ride consistently. I ride in fits and spurts. But when I'm on a long trail ride, I have time to do more than simply react to the horse. There is time to experiment with small cues and aides, to put together everything that I have learned.

A proper tölt should have a steady four beat footfall, similar to a walk but at a much faster speed. It is often said that each sequence, every four beats, should sound like "Black and Decker, Black and Decker." To get a horse to tölt, it helps if the rider first collects the horse, that is, lightens up the front end so that the propulsion comes from the hindquarters. It seems like a contradiction in cues to collect a horse: you press your leg on the horse which tells it to go forward and faster, but then you give the reins a half halt to tell it "not so fast." The idea is the horse will need to collect itself and instead of pulling forward from the front, it will rebalance its weight so that the power comes from underneath and the hind end when the muscles are engaged.

It's like when I go out for a run: sometimes I flop around out there lazily with my stomach loose and leading the way, shifting my weight side to side, hip to hip, and it's difficult. After the first mile, I want to quit. But then I remember to pull up my sternum and suck in my belly, and by doing that I engage my running muscles and my step changes. Horses can be like that, too. If not ridden properly, they can resort to being a lazy runner.

So I wiggle her into a smooth four-beat tölt by leaning an inch or two back to take the weight off the front, giving her shoulders room to lift her front hooves and her head up.

Perla has a smooth tölt. The trick is to keep my legs still but my hips loose in the seat so that I follow the cadence of her movement. Icelandics are ridden with a slightly longer stirrup so that there is less bend in the knee, which helps in tölt but not necessarily in trot. When the ground is too rough, I move her back to a trot by giving her more rein and sitting slightly forward in a light seat. Tölt, trot, tölt, trot: I find the rhythm more than I lose the rhythm—that's a good ride for me.

I check frequently on Perla's ears to see if they are flat back annoyed at me or eagerly pointing forward. Horses' ears are the barometers of their mood. But Perla's are somewhere in between, not easily decipherable. They do get twitchy when she senses another horse might pass her, and I feel her power tick up a bit, as she wants to race against the other horse. I give her some rein and let her keep her lead.

This is what I am here for: full concentration on the horse's gait, mood, speed, collection. My mind clears of all else to focus on the ride: staying on, staying balanced, feeling the horse's rhythm, looking ahead at the path, the rocks, the lupine, the tufted grass, the burry calls of the terns flitting in front of me. I can ride Icelandic horses in the States at Eve's farm, but it is contained. It is a completely different experience to ride here in this endless treeless expanse, to ride in the place these horses come from, where they have been birthed, where their ancestors have run for a millennium on this rough terrain. It's like nowhere else on earth.

When the Norse first arrived in Iceland in the late 800s, it was uninhabited by people, though there are saga accounts of hermitic Celtic monks living on the island. And it was uninhabited by other mammals, too, except for the arctic fox and the stray polar bear taking a ride on a wandering ice floe. So the settlers brought all the people and animals with them. The settlement era occurred at the height of the Viking era. In other places where the Vikings seized power, they mixed and assimilated into the country and intermarried. Think of the French Normans (they were the raiding Norsemen a century earlier) who in 1066 invaded the Danelaw borough of England, which had been settled by Vikings from the previous century.

But in Iceland there was no one to seize power from, no one to assimilate with or marry. And though some women from Norway also came to settle this new land, the early population was mostly men who picked up women from Ireland and the Scottish islands en route to Iceland. (Iceland's deCODE, a genomic biobank, collected DNA from every Icelander in the 1990s, and found the women were 63% Celtic, the men 80% Norwegian.) And by "picking up" women, I mean stopping off to buy women on the slave market. Dublin was established during the Viking Era as a slave trading post. The profits from selling captured men, women, and children from the British Isles and Eastern Europe enriched and established many Viking chieftains' power.

Horses were traded, too. The Icelandic horse is a DNA map of the Vikings pathways and conquests. The breed is a genetic mix of the Norwegian Fjord horse, the Shetland pony, the Irish Connemara, and the Fell and Dales Ponies of Yorkshire. There is even a dab of Mongolian horse in it.

The difficult journey these horses took in the boats, and their lives in the new harsh land, culled out the weak and left only the hardiest and healthiest horses to survive and interbreed in isolation in Iceland. Like the Yakut horse in Siberia, it quickly evolved into a breed with a second winter coat, a thick mane, stout trunk, short thick legs, a low set tail, and the ability to survive without shelter. In 930, the Althing, the early Icelandic parliament, did something unusual: they passed a law banning all other horses from coming into the country. And any horse leaving the country could not be brought back. These laws are still in effect today, making this a breed that has remained isolated on this island for over a thousand years.

The Guests in the Guesthouse

The guesthouse is a small two-story, but it also sprawls. The older part was built in the early 1900s, and a new addition was tacked on in the 1960s. It has four bedrooms on the first floor, all with multiple beds. The three bedrooms in the front of the house all face south. The small bedroom in the back of the house is dark and paneled with a window covered by a dark curtain that blocks out the light. Dora takes that room immediately and no one questions her need for privacy. She goes in, shuts the door, and except for coming out for a smoke every hour, we don't see her much.

"She's getting a lot out of this trip," Sylvie says.

In the back of the house is an old-fashioned parlor room with a couch, but it's also big enough for a full dining room table. In this parlor room/dining room there are four built-in bed cubicles, about as long as I am, five feet six inches. Each cubby comes with a floral curtain you can draw close. The house was built for large families that lived in close quarters. It looks like the old *baðstofas* in the Icelandic turf houses from a century ago, which look like the old bed-boxes in the recreated Viking longhouses of a millennium ago.

The kitchen is large enough for a table that sits ten. The view from the kitchen window is of the church and the church's graveyard. But also, much closer to the guesthouse is a curious cluster of gravestones slammed up against each other, way too close to each other to be actual grave sites. And someone thought it important to fence these gravestones in, as if to prevent them from wandering around at night and bothering the clothesline next to it.

In the refrigerator, we find *nýmjólk* (pasteurized milk), *súrmjólk* (like kefir), *AB mjólk* (like sweeter kefir), *skyr* (like Greek yogurt), bland cheese (like Emmentaler), lamb salami (like nothing else), soft yellow apples, hard-boiled eggs, flat hearth-baked bread, brown sweet bread, peat-smoked salmon, pale hothouse tomatoes, and *smjör* (sweet butter). Also, two six packs of Gull, Icelandic beer (like Coors). This is my diet for the week, and no food makes me happier.

The pantry is stocked with coffee from Denmark, Harrods tea bags, sugar, muesli from Germany, chocolate covered raisins, a box of Franzia red wine, and mismatched dishes, cups, and mugs. The big gray phone box hangs on the kitchen wall next to a fire extinguisher.

The stairs leading up to the second floor are narrow, the treads and risers each only about four inches, so you need to turn your foot and body sideways to go up and down. Two doorless bedrooms are upstairs, and both have deeply pitched eaves, so we can only stand up straight in the middle of the rooms. Once we check out the upstairs, no one wants to sleep there, no one ever wants to go up there again.

We choose our rooms without any fuss. I take the bedroom with two twin beds. It has two large windows, each covered with sheer white curtains. One window looks south out onto the barn and the pastures, the other west. The beds in this room, in this house, and pretty much everywhere in Iceland, even the hotels, come with just a fitted bottom sheet and a comforter, folded in half lengthwise. And one pillow. No more, no less. No complaining.

The four teenage girls take the large room with a set of bunk beds across the hall from me. Eve, Maggie, and Sylvie sleep in the room on the other side of the girls.

The first night we all turn in around eleven P.M. The sun is bright and the sheer curtains don't block out any of the light. What use do these curtains serve? It feels like two in the afternoon in my bedroom. Even when I put my blackout mask over my eyes, I can feel the sun from the western window, keeping me awake.

It is impossible to sleep. I read for a while, put the book down, cover my eyes again with the mask, and try to fall asleep again. But the teenagers have decided that it's a good time to run in and out of the house. I put my earplugs in. But they get more boisterous. I try wrapping my pillow over my ears. They start slamming doors, stomping down the hallway to the kitchen, laughing, and in general making a regular racket. Four girls can sound like twenty in the middle of the night.

They didn't seem to be rowdy types. They have been easy to travel with, if easy means they stick close to each other in an age-linked pod, oblivious to everything else, but sensitive to each other's approval. So far, they have been mild mannered fourteen-year-olds. I chalk that up to Brittany being from a small town—she lives down the road from Eve and keeps her horse at the farm—and Eve's nieces being from Ohio, and what I know about Ohio is zilch. Less than zilch. But in general, horsey girls tend to be their own breed, resilient and introspective. At their age, you seek in horses what you can't get in humans. Maybe that's at any age.

So even though they have been quiet and considerate all day long, they choose midnight to get rambunctious. Maybe I don't remember fourteen that well. I don't want to seem like an ogre, and I don't want to ruin their fun. It's the midnight sun, the summer solstice, why shouldn't they run around and party all night?

Except that we are getting up early to ride. And I need my sleep. The scenario that keeps replaying in my head is that if I don't sleep I'll make stupid mistakes in the saddle. I'll fall and hurt myself and it will all be because the teenage girls kept me awake. In Eve-speak, I'm thinking negatively down, not positively up.

I toss, turn, and silently fume about how much racket they are making. I debate with myself: How much time should I give them to settle down? How much of a spoil sport do I want to be? But the door keeps slamming and their feet keep stomping, like they are kicking mud or snow off their boots every time they re-enter the house, and they keep laughing uproariously as they run up and down the hallway.

Finally, I take my earplugs out and my eye mask off, get up and storm into the hallway, sure I'll encounter them coming in and out of the house. I'm ready to roar at them, but the hallway is empty and quiet. Their bedroom door is slightly ajar and I peak in. Brittany is lying on the top bunk, reading quietly with a bedside lamp on. The others are all in their beds, sleeping or half-asleep.

"Have you all been here the whole time?

"What do you mean?" Brittany asks.

"You weren't just running up and down the hallway, slamming doors, going inside and out?"

"What??" she says.

"I heard this racket, like you were all running up and down the hallway, having a party. You've been in your beds the whole time?"

"Yessss," she says.

"You didn't hear anything?"

"Oh my God," she says, and the other girls hear her.

"What's going on?" They want to know.

She points at me, like I'm a witch. "She heard the ghosts!"

"What do you mean, the *ghosts*?"

"You heard the ghosts! We were warned that there were ghosts in this house!" Brittany and the other girls scream but in a hoarse whisper, so as not to wake up the others, or alert the ghosts, or because they've scared themselves so much they can't get their louder screams out. It's like they're in a horror movie and they're afraid their heads are going to be lopped off.

I can't calm them down, and I'm sure of what I heard. I was awake; I wasn't dreaming. I hadn't even lapsed into the jumbled mind of pre-sleep. I heard a racket, the doors slamming, feet stomping, and lots of voices, like they were muffled in scarves.

The next morning, Helga blithely confirms that of course there are ghosts in the house. "Oh yes, they are in the front of the house. In the old section. But they don't bother anyone."

It's funny how some cultures just accept things other cultures scoff at. Maybe because Iceland's scenery is starkly beautiful and otherworldly, it lends itself to the supernatural. Icelanders talk about the elves and the trolls as they would talk about someone they know, like their cousins or neighbors. I'm never sure if they're trying to hoodwink tourists or not. Or if they're trying to hoodwink themselves, to keep the folklore alive. I notice that they never completely confirm or deny it.

But if you spend enough time in the country, in the grassy, misty moors, in the boulder fields of volcanic rock, in the actively steaming areas that bubble up mud and sulfur like a cauldron in Mordor, you might start seeing things, too.

Anyway, I heard ghosts.

Where I Want to Be

At the end of Laugavegur, the main shopping street that runs through the heart of Reykjavík, Sylvie and I head toward the wharves. The rest of our group has left, but I booked my flight home a day later because it was significantly cheaper, and Sylvie booked her flight home three days later to see the sights of Reykjavík, though there aren't many sights to speak of. There is no glam, no glitz, nothing fancy, nothing luxurious. No grandeur—definitely no Versailles. The country has a history of colonial rule and natural disasters that never allowed it to accumulate immense wealth. When wealth finally came to the island, the government did a good job of spreading it equally through the population, and democratic socialism is said to flourish more easily in small populations that all share the same culture, religion, and ancestors. Hence, the modest cities, modest homes.

Sylvie and I find a bar near the wharves without giving it a whole lot of thought. It's four in the afternoon and it's open—that's good enough for us. The place is dimly lit, cavernous, and empty, except for the bartender, who is drying glasses and stacking them on mirrored shelves. The bar has floor-to-ceiling smoky glass windows that make the overcast Reykjavík skies look even dimmer. Almost all of Reykjavík's buildings are modest two stories. Because wood is scarce and expensive, the buildings are almost all made of cement, with a rough finish and painted gray, beige, or mushroom brown. It seems as if in every window I pass, the same eyelet white curtains hang, with plastic flowers and a cat lazing on the windowsill. Though the city is said to be getting popular, it's hard to see how or where. True, I'm not up late enough to witness the music scene or the unbridled pub crawls that end in the wee hours of the morning. During the annual music festival, the place is apparently crawling with New York A&R agents looking for new talent.

The bartender motions for us to sit anywhere, and we take a tall table with stools at the front window and order Thule beer. On medieval European maps, "Thule" signified a distant place "beyond the borders of the known world," and it specifically referred to the far northern regions hanging off the edge of the map: Orkney, Shetland, Iceland, and Greenland.

And Reykjavík in 2004 still has vestiges of that version of Thule. It has an edge-of-the-world feel to it, that gull-crying mourn of desolation. The minute you roam away from downtown you are reminded you are in a port town on the northern tip of the world, facing Greenland. Here be dragons.

After a week up north riding on Helga's farm, Sylvie and I are happy and self-satisfied. We rode for miles through dunes to the Greenland Sea, through fields of lupine to a place called "the valley of the horses." We raise our beer glasses and say, "Cheers."

"Those horses were fast."

"Yeah, and we rode them."

"Do you *believe* it?" she squeals.

"We outdid ourselves."

"It was beyond my expectations."

"There is nothing like riding in Iceland."

The bartender puts on music and I'd like to think he did so for us, that he notices we are there and that he has found this way to communicate with us.

A manly baritone voice whisper-sings in my ear:

"The ponies run, the girls are young, the odds are there to beat.
You win a while and then it's done, your little winning streak."

The voice is familiar, yet I can't place it. "Who is this?" I ask Sylvie.

"It's, it's . . . oh, it's . . ." But she can't come up with the name, either.

I interrupt the bartender, who is reading a book behind the bar. "Who is this singing?"

He puts his book down, ducks under the bar, and holds up the CD case for me to see. "Leonard Cohen," he says. "*Ten New Songs.*"

I haven't listened to Leonard Cohen in years; I know him mainly through my guitar-playing husband and his guitar-playing friends who often pick out his earlier classics. It's been so long since I've heard Cohen sing Cohen that I forget how subversively seductive his voice is, and now that he is older it is even more so.

"I remember reading that Cohen became a Buddhist monk and spent years in a monastery. I wonder if this is his first album out after that."

Sylvie tells me about her forays into yoga and meditation, traveling to Asia–Bhutan, India, Bali. She goes with a yoga group, but once she went alone for a month to study under a guru in northern India. "There's something over there that you can't get here in the West. It has to do with how one lives believing in fatalism. The West has lost that. In the Middle Ages, they had the Wheel of Fortune. You spun the wheel and the goddess Fortuna decided your random fate."

I know only a little about one small slice of early medieval history, the two hundred years of Viking attacks and settlements in England. "The Vikings had what they called the three 'wyrds': That which we can see, that which we can become, that which we should become. 'Wyrd' was synonymous with fate, destiny. Maybe the unexpected outcome of our destinies is how 'wyrd' became the word 'weird.'"

"So is that your first connection to Iceland, Viking history?" Sylvie asks me. "I figured it was the sagas."

"No, I have only read the Vinland sagas, and only because they're short."

"You'll wind up reading them all."

"My first connection was finding a picture of an Icelandic horse on Google. I looked at it every day and I couldn't think of anything else."

"You had that immediate connection, that deep horse love. It's so powerful."

There is one side of Sylvie that plays to the audience as the queen bee, always the center of attention, hamming it up with her zaniness. During the week at Helga's farm, Sylvie somehow created an atmosphere where everyone wound up making sure she was happy, where nothing got done without her approval. One night Helga brought in a layer cake for dessert, and Sylvie said, "For me? I guessed you figured it out—I like to be treated especially special."

Helga considered all of this with friendly bemusement. "You do, don't you? You are like a queen, I suppose."

But we all have multiple selves. Sylvie flutters from one self to another, deftly and interestingly. She is much different away from the group, at least with me at the bar down on the wharves. When she quiets down, she is thoughtful and wise. She listens closely to what you say and then thinks more about it and how it applies to who you are. Friendships demand not only equality of interest or flattering mutual self-reflection, but also new expectations of self. So much of the time we are too wrapped up in our own narrative, the same old story in our head, that we need new people to break through the fog, and show us a new story of ourselves, one that is slightly different and one that we have to live up to.

I'm watching two boats in the harbor: a whale watching boat and a cruise ship to Greenland, the idea of which excites me. Imagine a place even more farther north, more desolate, more Thule-like.

"Do you have any desire to go to Greenland?" I ask Sylvie.

"I might be up for that someday," Sylvie says.

This brings up my current literary obsession, Jane Smiley's book, *The Greenlanders*, which to my surprise Sylvie has read. "I've read it three times," I admit, "and I'm just waiting a little while before I start it again."

"I get that," she says. "It's my favorite Jane Smiley book, and in my mind, it's an underrated masterpiece."

In my mind, people who have read this book and love it are my spiritual kin.

I am cautious with people and don't open myself up too quickly. At heart, I am a solitary soul, perfectly able and at peace to spend time alone, even to travel alone. My husband is the extrovert who does all the social planning in our family. I sometimes think I got married and had children so I would have people to love on this earth to act as ballast to keep me from floating away, to save me from going from a solitary soul to a lonely soul. And because I have my family and am grounded in my own worth and importance to them, I don't seek the love or approval of many others. I don't make friendships fast and I don't make them easily. Most of my friendships have been hard earned, and as a result I don't take them for granted.

I want to cultivate Sylvie's friendship. Eve's, too, but Eve has a busier life. And from what I can tell from the few visits I've made to the Berkshires, Eve's horse farm creates a hub, and Sylvie keeps it buzzing. Eve provides the space and activity; Sylvie provides the connectivity. Sylvie is nearly twenty years my senior and her grandchildren are my children's age. So often we segregate into friend groups by age, but Sylvie attracts a multigenerational following, as does Eve.

I've never been clubby, or a joiner, a member of a tribe. The one and only time I belonged to a clique were those brief years when I belonged to that roaming band of preteen girls who ran in the woods, those years that bridged the freedom of childhood to the rumored glories of puberty.

But now I want to belong to Sylvie's group—the women who run with Icelandic horses. I want in with Sylvie and Eve and their quirky Icelandic horse club back home, and also to be able to return to what I've seen and experienced with Helga and Iceland. This is the club I want to be a member of, the perfect complement, or foil, to my ordinary life.

When the bartender comes by to pick up our empty glasses, we ask for a second round. He is like so many Icelandic men I have met: emotionally low-key, not unfriendly exactly, but not warm and welcoming, either. I don't mind that. I can live without that cringeworthy bartender line: "What can I get you ladies next?" And I'd prefer for him to get back to his book.

Over our second beer, Sylvie says, "She invited us back for next year . . . Helga. She thought maybe a smaller number of us, like five or six. I need to make a list of the people who I really want to come, not just the ones Eve feels she has to save."

I knew Dora was the primary tension between Eve and Sylvie during the week, though in her own way Dora came around. She joined us for dinner one night, albeit a bit wobbly at the table as if she had spent too much time lying down. She even took a short ride with us one day, though she fell off her horse while standing still and claimed the horse had slipped. Before we left, she wrote in the farm's guestbook an effusive, heartfelt note bestowing praise on Helga, the horses, and the life-changing restorative power of the Icelandic lavender skies that put my "thanks for your hospitality" note in the guestbook to shame. Eve summed it up by saying, "See, we all bring something different to the trip. We all take away something else."

"So I am making my A-list. The selected few. Are you interested in coming next year?"

"Absolutely. Put me on the list." I say this calmly, belying a growing excitement that I am having difficulty containing. I want to return as many times as Helga will have us. But I don't want to appear too needy to Sylvie, too take-me, take-me, as if I am a stray that needs to be saved. I don't want to invite myself along every year, I want to *be* invited. This is where I belong.

Staring out at the boats on the harbor, Sylvie says, "This is what I want to do for now, this is where I want to be, what I'm drawn to do. I don't know for how long, but this is the place for now."

"I feel the same."

Our conversation pauses as we let Leonard Cohen's voice caress us. His pull is hypnotic, and we go silent to listen more fully to him:

"So come, my friends, be not afraid, we are so lightly here."

Over the years, I will never tire of listening to this CD. While driving up to the Berkshires, it becomes my Route 8 soundtrack. If I were to form a religion, I would base it on Leonard Cohen's songbook. I heard it's a cult. Through constant repetition of the CD, I wind up committing the entire album to memory—every word, every note, every balalaika beginning and every balalaika ending. And without fail it brings me back to that bar down by the wharves, back to the beginning of our twelve-year sojourn.

We finish our beers at about the same time Leonard Cohen stops singing. The bartender puts on some other music that breaks the spell. More people come in and he's forced to put his book under the bar. We get up to leave.

Outside again, we walk aimlessly. We're done talking. We're lost in our own thoughts that we no longer have an urge to share. She waves me off, saying she is going to do a bit more exploring on her own. Like me, she is comfortable traveling alone. Like me, there are times when she probably prefers it.

I walk down to the piers, close to all the large vessels with their engines thrumming, pumping bilge out of their sterns. Kittiwakes mob the fish being hauled in and fulmars fret over the garbage. It only takes two beers in the afternoon to make me deliriously happy, but also I'm exactly where I want to be—on the coast of Iceland, east of Greenland, and facing the fathomless North Atlantic. I'm hanging off the northern edge of a medieval map: the geographies of Thule.

2005

---❦---

Repeat after Me: Hvammstangi

I t's raining when I land in Keflavík. The light is tin-colored from the cloud cover. It's six thirty A.M. Iceland time, two thirty A.M. New York time. Since my flight from New York gets in before the Boston flight, I have to wait for my traveling companions. Keflavik is tiny for an international airport, so small and efficient that my luggage is on the belt by the time I get to the baggage claim. In 2005, the airport serves only Icelandair flights; other airlines are allowed to land at the airport only in the summer months. It is also a popular landing spot for planes in trouble. My mother was once on a flight back from Greece when the pilot had to make an emergency landing in Keflavík. She stayed overnight at the airport and I'd like to think Iceland saved her life by letting the plane land.

My mother was fiscally cheap, the kind that made you pay her back $3.39 when she picked up a box of tampons for you (pennies counted). Her only indulgence was travel, and she always brought me numerous and expensive gifts from her trips. From Greece, she brought me a gold chain necklace and pearl-drop earrings. From Iceland, she brought two Icelandic sweaters from the airport store, the most luxurious sweaters I'd ever seen: one, a silk-lined zip up jacket of white angora wool with a geometric brown band, and the other, also white angora, a pullover of even whiter wool and a petal softness. I wore them both for many winters, and when I'd meet up with a boyfriend on a snowy evening, I'd put up the loose hoods to frame my twenty-year-old face. At that age, I couldn't pass a mirror without marveling at myself. ("Vanity, vanity," my mother would say, "thy name is Victoria." She liked to use my full name when pointing out my flaws.) But the way the wool fell over my body and draped my head, the thought of the wintry island and the sweet lamb that shed its wool for me, the happenstance or higher power that brought my mother to land there, transformed me into a fairy snow princess with magical power. I thought, with all the surety of youth, *who could not fall in love with me?*

That was my first introduction to Iceland: those two sweaters that I wore for a few years and then eventually lost in the dozen or so moves I made in my twenties, amidst falling in and out of love.

Iceland and its people are still a novelty for me. While waiting for the plane from Boston to arrive, I watch a couple greet each other. I had already noticed her on the flight from New York, because she is a young woman who knows how to draw attention to herself, another version of myself in a different time and different place, and instead of being an American wearing Icelandic sweaters, she is an Icelander wearing American clothes. She has on a cowboy hat, cowboy boots, a short green skirt, and a black leather bomber jacket. Along with her regular luggage, she carries a DKNY shopping bag.

Her boyfriend, who's been waiting among the twelve people in the arrivals section, springs forward upon seeing her and the two of them fall on each other, playful as puppies. They kiss extravagantly and intimately, diving into each other's mouths like adolescents, though they are probably in their late twenties. He's dressed like a rock musician, skinny jeans and short sweatshirt jacket, piercings, tattoos. His hair is a crested wave that must be held up with gel. He kisses her so much he kisses her cowboy hat off her head. She has to hold it in place for some one-handed kissing. They stop kissing only to talk quietly and to press far enough back from each other so they can stare at each other's face. But not for long. They dive into each other again, kissing, nuzzling, whispering, two bodies in symbiosis in the middle of the airport, either oblivious or uncaring about the people passing by them. Their physical attraction is like a force field no one else can enter but everyone can watch. Or at least I can. No one else bothers.

This is not the first time I've seen such an open display of a couple's intimate fondness for each other—I'm thinking of Jonki and his girlfriend snogging on the trail as they left me haphazardly wrangling the reins of three horses. Maybe passionate public affection is the cultural norm. Though Iceland has had a thousand years of Christianity, most of it typically sexually repressive, I can't help but wonder if this public display doesn't contain the vestiges of the earlier pagan days where, all things considered for era and place, women had more equitable status, and sexuality was forthright and did not evolve from original sin.

The Sagas of Icelanders are like the Bible of Iceland, oral history written down, and no doubt interpreted, by monks in the thirteenth century two or three hundred years after the events. The eight-hundred-year-old tales are taught in Icelandic schools as literature, with modern interpretations of characters' personalities, moralities, and power struggles, and also as a look into the historical social structure of the times they relate. Some sagas are blood-soaked revenge tales, not all that different from video games where a modern kid wracks up points for kills. And in some sagas, the women take on an equally vengeful role.

Njal's saga features the particularly interesting Hallgerd. She is tall and beautiful with a voluminous head of hair: "so much hair she could hide herself in it." She is also, fortunately for her, "hard-tempered." Her first two marriages are arranged with her initial consent, but they go quickly awry. Her first husband slaps her when she talks back to him, so she incites her axe-wielding foster father to kill him. Ditto with her second husband—he slaps her and . . . he's a dead man.

She chooses her third husband, Gunnar, for his good looks and fighting prowess. He is a lifelong friend of Njal's, after whom the saga is named. But Hallgerd is no friend of Njal's wife, Bergthora. At a winter feast they fight over a prime spot on the cross bench—it's a you-can't-sit-here, this-seat-is-taken scene—and Hallgerd is incensed. She and Bergthora hurl insults at each other. Thus begins a long trail of killings. Hallgerd sends a servant to kill Bergthora's servant—Bergthora then retaliates by having another servant kill one of Hallgerd's servants. They go at each other this way, avenging each household death, always making their servants do the killing and dying, until they've made a severe dent in the local servant population. Hallgerd's mother-in-law wryly notes: "Hallgerd does not let our servants die of old age." After each ordered hit, their husbands settle the deaths by paying compensation in court (the Althing).

Then during a time of famine, Hallgerd orders her slave to steal food from a neighbor. Her husband Gunnar catches wind of the plan, and steps in to make financial amends to the neighbor for his wife's behavior. Later, when he gets into an argument with Hallgerd over her plans to steal the food, he . . . slaps her face. In public. People witness her humiliation. She vows she will repay him for that. And, as we know by now, it never ends well for slapping husbands.

The women in this saga only account for a minor fraction of the violence, and all of it is hired or incited, while the men go on to personally commit a dizzying number of revenge killings. Toward the end of the saga, we catch up with Gunnar and Hallgerd. Their house is surrounded by enemies and Gunnar is valiantly making every attempt to withstand the attacks. He has wounded eight, killed two. He is armed with arrows, and he asks his wife for a few strands of her famous hair to fix his broken bowstring. She refuses, saying, "I call to mind that slap you gave me." He dies soon afterward from battle exhaustion.

It's hard to reconcile those sagas with modern day people. The country consistently rates high as one of the most peaceful. Icelanders are quiet people in general. Daily conversations are more whispered than spoken. I never hear the Icelandic language shouted, though I don't go to their soccer games. Since modern Icelandic is pretty close to the old Norse spoken by the Viking settlers 1,200 years ago, one expects the language to be brutally harsh and guttural, an invader's pugilistic rampage baked into its DNA. But the language has a lilting Scandinavian brogue with variations of "th." It has lifts and falls and breathiness. It's a lullaby language with nursery tale tonality, and the general sentence pattern often ends in an up-phrase.

Of course, I don't understand a word of it. It's not an easy language to learn. Not that I have a flair for languages anyway. I suffer from typical American foreign language disability. I speak high school Spanish, restaurant French, and now my newly acquired Icelandic place-names, which are built on compound nouns. So I know that *stadir* means farmstead and *hvoll* is a mound; a *nes* ending indicates a peninsula, an *a* at the end means it's a river. *Dalur* means dale, *vatn* means water, a *foss* is a waterfall, *falla* a mountain, *jokull* a glacier, *hraun* a lava field, and *laugur* steamy water.

Meaning is one challenge, pronunciation is another. One must beware of treacherous blended consonants. A little knowledge can be a dangerous thing. When I say a place name like "Hvammstangi" to an Icelander, they look quizzically at me. I have to explain, "It's in Iceland. It's a town around here." Oh, no, no, and they repeat the town's name back to me. The "Hvamm" is said in a way my tongue won't curl, with a "pwhoo," a "vrrrm," and a lilt and a whisper that confirms the futility of my ever really learning to speak the language.

But at home . . . no one knows that. I can fake it. It's a neat trick and I sort of sound like I'm speaking the elf language from Middle Earth. At parties, I sometimes throw out wicked Icelandic place names, just for the fun of the reaction I can get. "When I was in Hafnarfjörður. . ." I slip in casually while dipping into my mother-in-law's canapés.

Invariably, someone will ask me, "What, where? Say that again?"

Well, okay, if I must. "Hafnarfjörður, it's a town near Reykjanesbaer." I like to toss in Helga's place, "Thingeyrar." Thanks to my high school Spanish, I can roll the "r." And if I am really trying to impress, I do the whole "Thingeyrarkirja," which simply means the church at Thingeyrar. It's not like they can correct me.

Place name obsession is like a mildly pleasant compulsive disorder. I can't pass a road sign without mumbling it to myself. I share it with the people in the car. "Hvalfjörður. That means whale's fjord. They must have done some whale hunting around here, or maybe it is where whales breed."

"Listen to you, you're getting good at Icelandic," Sylvie says. She's humoring me.

Brittany, now fifteen, is in the back seat with me. She is doe-eyed and quiet, as usual. I am at the stage in life where I think about other kids in relation to my own children. My son is a year older than Britt. Maybe they could date? She would be good for him—a horse-loving, sensible, thoughtful, independent girl. And he? One-fifth of a wolf pack who has perfected this teenage guy thing of not moving his lips when he talks. It could work. It is never too early to start planning your child's future. But Britt has other plans.

"Britt is interested in attending Holar when she graduates high school," Sylvie says.

"Oooh, Holar," I say, which is the only appropriate remark when someone mentions Holar. In some crowds, you mention Harvard or the Sorbonne to signify life's glories and achievement. In this crowd—the Icelandic horse crowd, which when I travel becomes *my* crowd—you mention Holar.

"If I get in," Britt offers up.

"It's very hard to get in," Sylvie explains. "And you have to know Icelandic pretty well. Everything is taught in Icelandic. But Britt here is our best hope."

"You will be only the second American ever to go to Holar," I toss out, tapping into my limited knowledge of the Holar horse world, even though she knows it. Everyone knows that there is only one person, a young woman from California, who has ever gotten into and graduated from Holar. And in this crowd, this very small Icelandic horse community from the States, she has become a legend, inspiring awe.

"I have Icelandic language tapes you should start with," Sylvie tells her.

"There's a couple of online programs to learn Icelandic, too." I offer this up, though I have tried them and doubt their efficacy.

Sylvie says, "The language has more declensions than Latin. For instance, the word for horse is *hestar*. But there are nine variations of it according to case, gender, number, and whether you put an article in front of it."

"It's impossible to learn unless you live in the country," Eve says.

"Let's face it, it's an aggravating language," Sylvie says, putting the matter to rest.

Britt remains mute as we barrage her with all our advice only to end on a disparaging note about the Icelandic language. When she's sure we are done talking, she pulls out her iPod and pops in her earbuds.

Eve's Life

S ince my first visit to Iceland a year ago, I have made an effort to visit Sylvie and Eve in the Berkshires. I have stayed overnight at Sylvie's. I have had my morning coffee with rice milk at her house. I have ridden on the trails with her and others at Eve's farm, though hardly ever with Eve, who usually says that she has too much work to do. She and her husband, Jack, run their business out of their house, though their business is a mystery to me. From what I can tell, they appear to be entrepreneurs who sell? distribute? produce? spa products and exercise cycles that sell on QVC. They have a New York apartment, an office in London, business partners in Atlanta, and Chinese investors. And they have their Berkshire horse farm.

If Helga's farm at Thingeyrar is the dream farm of Iceland, Eve's farm is idyllic by American standards, though on a completely different scale. Helga has hundreds of horses on her farm, hundreds of acres of land; Eve has only a dozen Icelandic horses and forty acres. Yet Eve has a brand-new barn, several paddocks, an outside tölting track, and an indoor arena with the latest high-tech surface: geotextile footing for the horse—a mixture of ground-up leather, recycled tires, wax, and silica sand. A horsey version of Astroturf.

When I visit the farm, Eve and Jack are the consummate hosts. They gather everyone into their fold, offering you a place to stay, horses to ride, an "in" to their ever-growing crowd of friends. Neither Eve nor Jack comes from money and their relationship to it is nouveau riche spiritual. Eve says, "It's there to spend, to give away, otherwise I have no reason to want to make money in the first place. I make it to give it away." Though that will eventually get her and Jack into some financial difficulties.

Their house and farm is upscale communal. They hire lots of people: gardeners, house cleaners, barn help, pet-sitters, and secretaries who keep it all running. They also take in strays—people who push their hosting generosity and stay for months. Visiting the farm feels like living in a sitcom with characters coming and going. The fire in the kitchen hearth is always lit in cold weather. The kitchen counter seats twelve on high saddle-shaped barstools. The bar is stocked with single malts and Patrón tequila, and drinks are generously poured. They have five dogs (three on purpose, two that happened to be left there), numerous cats, birds in cages. Not surprisingly, there is always a pet commotion happening, some crisis where one is either sick, missing, or thieving food from the table.

Jack is a roaring type of New Yorker, Bronx born, a large presence: he's tall, loud, uninhibited, and flagrantly libertine, whose oft-repeated line is, "I'm a heterosexual nymphomaniac." To which Eve says, "Oh, honey, we know you are." I know her first marriage at twenty-two was to a closeted gay man, so maybe this time around she doesn't want any ambiguity. But I also know that couples always have a deal going on: what one puts up with, what one gets, what one ignores, where the boundaries are, and when they're permitted to shift. Jack's a wild ride, but Eve is exactly where she wants to be.

Jack has a soft side, too: he does all the cooking and entertaining. Like an Italian grandmother, he will make sure you're well-fed. He makes soups and roast chicken, puts out pasta salads and sandwiches, cooks up eggs and pancakes. Sylvie sums it up by saying, "Despite his alpha maleness, he has a maternal quality to him because he lost his mother at a young age. He expresses it mostly by feeding you and yelling at the horses."

We stop at Borgarnes to fuel up. The other Jeepful of women we are traveling with are wandering around the N1, too, hunting snacks. I don't know any of them and was only briefly introduced to them outside the hotel. When I find Sylvie between the candy counter and ice cream stand, she doesn't seem too happy the other car is with us.

"You know Eve. Everyone she bumps into at the Great Barrington co-op she says, 'oh come to Iceland with us.' I keep telling her that we need to limit it to five people. *Five.* Helga doesn't run a farm stay bed and breakfast. That's not her business. Her business is the horses. She doesn't open her farm up to anyone but us."

Sylvie gives me a quick overview of who's who: There's Viv, who is a friend of a friend. "She seems to be having a hard time with her sons. Oh, you know how sons can be, don't you? I certainly do with my two sons."

I do. My son has two more years of high school and I try not to let his behavior get to me, but our relationship has taken an odd turn and I can't seem to find him. Part of me is relieved. He was a colicky baby I could never put down, a shy kid who would never drop my hand when I walked him into a birthday party. So the separation is healthy and I approve of his independence, but it is also extreme. He's developed an apathy toward everything except his guitar and friend group.

"And then there is eighteen-year-old Melody, who likes to be called Mel—she sometimes keeps her horse at Eve's barn," Sylvie says. "And there's Mel's mother."

Mel's mother is dressed in big heavy cloaks that drag to the ground, covering her Birkenstock sandals that she wears with socks. My first take is that her clothes are a statement of religious modesty. And sure enough, when they sit down to a bowl of soup at the cafe, she grips Mel's hand, bows her head, and whispers a prayer that ends with "In Jesus's name we pray."

Sylvie says, "I don't know where Eve finds these people."

"Remember Dora last year?"

"Oh Dora. Eve was furious when she found out Dora was secretly drinking and mixing it with Klonopin the whole trip."

"No wonder she spent so much time in her room."

"We're lucky she didn't overdose in her bedroom." Sylvie loudly takes in air. "How would we have explained that to Helga?"

I notice Viv zipping around the aisles of the N1. She's a fast walker, doing laps around me and Sylvie. She doesn't seem depressed, she seems caffeinated. She buys yogurt drinks, chips, chocolate covered raisins, donuts. She eats quickly, nibbling like a rabbit, stopping briefly to tell us, "I have low blood sugar. I need to eat every hour."

While driving between Borgarnes and Hvammstangi, we pass a desert of brown sand hills and lava fields, but very few horses or green fields to brighten the mood. We're inland—away from any mesmerizing fjords. There are no towns to speak of and only a few farms off in the hills. A cold fierce wind shakes our Jeep, and snow flurries momentarily appear.

"What's the story with Mel's mother?" Sylvie prods Eve to divulge, as soon as Eve is alone with us. I'm sensing that Mel's mother was a last-minute addition.

Eve says, "I think she's religious. She was looking for a church to attend in Reykjavík this morning before we left."

"Yep, she was saying grace over the fish soup in the cafeteria."

"She's a born-again Christian or something like that. At least she won't be popping pills and drinking alone in her room," Eve says.

"Oh, okay," Sylvie says, but it's clearly not okay. "I grew up in Catholic schools and the nuns told me my red hair spelled trouble." Sylvie conflates all religious affiliation with her Catholic school upbringing.

"Mel is very sweet but she never gets always from her family. I thought it would be good for Mel to come with us to Iceland, as an act of independence, but then her mother booked a trip, too."

"In other words," Sylvie says, "you didn't invite the mother."

"I think she misconstrued my invite to Mel. Or maybe she didn't trust us. Maybe she thinks we will be a bad influence."

Sylvie groans. "Oh, I see, so we're loose women. And I've got red hair."

"The mom doesn't ride, so she won't be with us out on the trail. And, Sylvie, Mel needs this. Let's give everyone a chance."

"You know me, I give everyone a chance," Sylvie says.

It's difficult for people who consider themselves secular liberals to accept the other, the religious conservative in this case, Christians. It's the great divide: we get riled up about it before we vote, and we socially self-segregate for fear of offending and being offended. It's funny how Mel's mother and her quiet prayer over food is hair-triggering and associative for some of us: we fear being judged, while at the same time, we judge her. I know how this feels on both sides.

I tend to forget my own history with a religious sect. It is personal archeology I keep deeply buried within, an inconvenient story, inconsistent with who I am, and who I became, so I put the memories in little trash bins marked: no room for this, spam, junk, delete, delete, delete. If asked, I gloss over the details, as "my crazy first marriage" at 23. If I have to dig deeper, I toss it out lightly as "my brief, ill-begotten, impulsive first marriage." If pressed, I might admit he was religious, or if I'm feeling honest, I might add that he was a religious fanatic. Dig deeper, though, and my story falls apart: I was young, I was lost, and I was looking for something to save me.

So I know too well how this story would be socially unacceptable in my usual circles where revelations of misspent youth are somewhat rare to begin with, and definitely do not center on fundamentalist religious reformations.

It is liberating, therefore, to be traveling with Eve and Sylvie. I trust them with stuff I don't normally tell people at home (and Britt has her earphones in).

"So here's a story . . . it's about my first marriage," I begin.

Tern, Tern, Tern

Viv knocks on my door. "Do you want to go for a walk with me?" Something about the way she asks, hesitantly, as if afraid I'll say no, and the way I am lying on my bunk bed in a desultory mood half reading a book I'm not that interested in, reminds me of my college days. It's like the unexpected request from the girl down the hall who wants to make friends with you. And Viv is like the girl down the hall I would never have noticed in college, like an upstate or Southern girl who wears bright colors and full makeup while my favorite color is charcoal gray and the extent of my makeup a tinted lip balm. Viv is from Maryland originally, and she never goes out of the house without her "face on." It takes an hour for her to put on full makeup and blow out her hair in the morning to got out and ride a horse on sheep trails in northern Iceland.

"Sure, I'm not sleeping anyway." I have chosen the smallest, darkest bedroom in the house this year. It was Dora's room last year, and the walls are paneled wood, a rarity in Iceland where wood has been scarce since the settlement days. It fits one bunk bed and a bedside table. It has only one window that's covered with a dark plaid curtain to keep the sunlight out. I still can't sleep. Viv is a welcome distraction.

"This light is charging me with energy. But everyone in my room is asleep and snoring," she says.

Viv's in the big bunk room where the teenage girls slept last year, along with Eve and Sylvie. The mother and daughter team are in the room I slept in last year.

Viv is dressed for the Arctic: parka, hat, ski gloves, lined rain pants. I refuse to bring my parka to Iceland at the end of June. I bring a fleece and a few sweaters. But outside, the wind is fierce—it cuts through my sweater and fleece—but Viv is walking so fast, that to keep up I need to trot beside her. This warms me up, but my eyes are tearing from the wind. Even my ears are filling with it, and everything she says bounces around in the air and then straggles into my ears with a few seconds delay.

Viv talks about one of her sons who is dropping out of college for the third time or maybe it's the third college. She got him help and they told her that he has ADD or, maybe she says OCD. I'm nodding eagerly to tell her I'm listening, though I'm not exactly hearing everything. But I'm interested in her mother-son relationship, as it might mirror mine.

Viv stops to point out the sheep and their lambs. I take down the electric fencing and Viv steps in after me and puts it back up. We get in the pasture with all the sheep. If horses stir up the wild heart in us, sheep provide the antidote, a tame, quiet maternal protectiveness. I want to coddle these precious little lambs to my chest. But the mother ewes castigate them for going near us, and they run away.

"We're not going to hurt them," Viv says to the mothers.

Rejected by the sheep, we head for the horses in the pasture. The wind lessens. We walk into a field of young horses. They come right up to us to see what we are. Young horses in Iceland are naturally curious and friendly.

"Think of it, they're just let loose in large herds all year round. When they see a human, they're like, 'Oh you're not a part of my herd, who are you?'" Viv has a lot of conversations in animal talk, I am soon to find out.

Viv is a science writer, specifically on large animal issues. She owns two Icelandic horses and was one of the first people to own them in the States.

The importing of these horses started in the late 1980s, due to the interest of one woman in New Jersey. Viv knew her, and bought her own horses a few years later. She went from being a dressage rider on big horses—warmbloods and Thoroughbreds—to Icelandics. She was a true convert. "Once I got my Icelandics, I never looked back," she says.

She tells me Icelandics don't get diabetes or become insulin resistant, like so many horses in the States. "They're outdoors here all the time and their forage suits them. In the States, the forage is too rich, there's too much timothy which is great for dairy cows, but not for horses. So, they become prone to diabetes. But here, they don't get fat; they hardly have any health problems."

"Everything's better in Iceland. Even for the horses," I say.

"Everything's better in Iceland. Look at all this light."

It's easily past midnight. The sun casts long, attenuated shadows, at least ten feet in front of us. I don't know when I last noticed my shadow. What adult pays attention to it? But it's hard not to notice it here when it's so clearly joined us for our walk, preceding us at a slight rightward angle.

Viv tells me that winter is hard for her because she has seasonal affective disorder—she even sets up light boxes in her house. Darkness, the idea of darkness, scares her.

"But here, the sunlight never ends. I wish I could store it up for the winter," she says.

"It's day all night, like a version of immortality," I say. "If it never gets dark, if night never comes, if there's no end to the sun in the sky, then you never die."

We hike down to the lake and collect the iron-colored rocks. They are light, smooth, hollow-feeling, like a case of empty metal. Helga told us they are supposed to bring good luck. We pocket a few that seem special to us, hoping these talismans bring good fortune, which to us simply means good health and no harm to our children.

There are goose nests along the shore of the lake that we are careful not to disturb. Their nests are obvious: easy-to-see depressions along the banks of the river made of dried reeds and feathers. Some nests have a clutch of four or five white, speckled eggs. But in others, the chicks have hatched into fragile fluff, beautiful wisps waiting to be fed.

But when we walk through the tall grass on the way back, we don't see the nests of the Arctic tern, the *kría* (plural *kríur*). They are too well hidden, but we know they are there by the immediate assault on us from the adult kríur. They start calling out to each other, warning the chicks that we are intruders. They aggressively do everything to drive us away. They flock and swoop down in front of us with a deafening caw, yelling at us. They dive bomb our heads and peck at our hats to protect the eggs they've laid in the grass. We walk gingerly to avoid stepping on them, while waving our hands over our heads to shoo the kríur away.

"We understand, don't worry, mamas," Viv says to the birds. "We don't want to hurt your babies."

We cut out quickly from the grass where their nests are hidden in the pitted ground, and come out on the dirt road. But they follow us, sending out alarms, crying out a call to arms to their fellow kríur in the surrounding area. They gang up on us, come at us from all directions, about thirty of them circling and dive-bombing us. They are the motherhood of revenge. I remove my hat and wave it above my head to keep them away. Still they follow us like they are never going to forget we almost stepped on their chicks. They will not stop attacking us. As I fend them off with my hat twirling around my head, I feel them swoop so close that my hair lifts. I think one has pecked me. Viv and I start running down the road and they follow us.

We must be a thousand feet from their nests before they finally start to lose interest. The few dozen attackers have dwindled to only a couple of birds who still manage to do a remarkable job of harassing us. And even when those two finally stop hovering and bombarding us, they continue to yell at us from afar.

"Wow, wow, wow" is all Viv can say. "That was scary."

"I felt like Tippi Hedren in *The Birds*."

"And your forehead is bleeding," Viv tells me.

The Herd

Out of the saddle, we have developed a herd mentality. As with most herds, the oldest is usually the alpha mare, which in our case would be Sylvie, who leads the extracurricular activities: swimming at the pool in town, going to the Blue Cafe, driving to the *vínbúðin* (liquor store, literally wine booth). She may be a mess of insecurity in the saddle, but when her feet are firmly on the ground and she gets the urge to visit, say, the Sea Ice Museum, she is quick and decisive. She's out the door in a hurry with Eve. "You snooze you lose," she says, and some of us do get left behind, which is secretly what she wants. She wants to cull our population to five.

As a herd, we graze, literally and figuratively, in the guesthouse. There is a constant need to refuel, a mindless munching, like the horses in the fields. We repeatedly hang our heads in the refrigerator, looking for treats. On the kitchen table, Helga leaves us nibbles—a bowl of dried fruit, nuts, banana chips, and chocolate-covered raisins that she replenishes daily.

Except at college, I have never lived with a group of women. The balance is delicate, especially on the first day or two. There are prickly moments, minor skirmishes about how the coffee is made or how the dishes are dried. If we were mares, we would kick out at each other to establish our turf, and then forget about it and go back to grazing.

When I make calls home this year, it is still from the old rotary wall phone in the gray box. I dial in a series of numbers from a phone card. I stretch the cord halfway up the stairs to the spooky part of the house for some privacy. It is the same kind of phone I grew up with, a kitchen wall phone, and we had to stretch the cord down the basement stairs to speak to our friends without being overheard.

"How are the other women on the trip?" my husband asks. He knows this is a sticky issue with me from last year when I told him about Dora.

"They're fine." And then I add: "There's this mother and daughter duo, and the mom's really religious," I whisper into the phone to him.

"What? Why are you whispering?"

It feels awkward talking to my husband from Iceland; he's doesn't know the place or the women, and he doesn't get the nuances. I can't talk any louder or the person I'm talking about in the other room will hear me, which makes me realize I'm using the woman as an anecdote and that's not fair to her. She is generally of good cheer. She takes long walks by herself when we ride, and comes back with muddy wet socks and sandals. She didn't pack boots. When she says grace over meals, it is whispered on the down low, so as not to make us feel awkward, as if she is used to being heavily judged for her religious beliefs. Funny how that "judge not, lest you be judge" works.

"Nothing, never mind, I can't say it now."

"So you're not having a good time? You don't like the women you're traveling with?"

"No, I'm not saying that. I'm just reporting on the new people this year."

My trips to Iceland are not about looking for a rousing good time, they're more about having a respite, a sabbatical, a chance to focus on a life outside of my usual life, rather than taking care of people at home and at work. But I keep this to myself, because the life I need respite from includes him.

"How are things there?"

"The dog threw up," he says. "And I had to clean up her vomit before going to work this morning. Honestly, I feel like giving her away."

The "dog throwing up" is code for "you left me alone." He loves this dog, our rambunctious, lovable Airedale; he would never give her away. But the dog, unwittingly eating crap off the sidewalk and regurgitating it up in the kitchen, has become a hostage and bargaining chip in our marriage because of my trip. I ask about the kids. "They're fine, out with friends. They miss you."

"When are you coming home?"

It's a rhetorical question; he knows when I'm coming home. That question is meant to rankle me, to make me feel guilty about leaving him to clean up the dog's throw-up.

And then he has to get off, because he's going to dinner at a friend's house (the social bee, he schedules almost a complete week of dinner plans with our friends when I am gone).

When I get off the phone, I hear Eve on her Blackberry talking to her husband. It sounds like they're discussing business, "Uh-huh, uh-huh, uh-huh," like he's giving her orders and she's taking them down. But they are more used to traveling without each other, at least he is. He goes to Asia and London all the time without her.

Finally, I hear her say, "Okay, honey," in her cheerful way. "I miss you," she sings out. She walks into the kitchen after she hangs up and looks momentarily displaced. "He wants me to get on my laptop and get some work done. I told him there's no Internet."

Both of our husbands' calls bring us temporarily home, distracting us from where we are. We want to be free of responsibilities for a week, not to think about the dog and the house and dinner and business, but to be fully here.

Sylvie, because she is older and has been married longer, appears to have it figured out. Drinking tea in the kitchen, she overheard both our conversations. "I'm over that," she brags. "Being the wifey . . . I'm so over that. I did that for too many years. I'm happy my husband lives in a different state."

The expression harried people say, "There are not enough hours in the day," is rendered moot here. There are still only twenty-four hours, but they are all sunlit. You have enough time to do everything: ride for several hours in the morning and afternoon, take lessons from Helga, lounge with books and journals, go into town, watch Disa train the horses and take notes.

And our breakfasts . . . they are leisurely affairs. The morning ride doesn't start until 10:00, so we sit around for a few hours at the kitchen table. First with coffee and muesli, then with cheese and bread and jam, then we bring out the yogurts and AB milk. Before we change into riding gear and head to the barn, Sylvie leads us through hip-opening yoga stretches.

It is not so for the Icelanders. For Disa, Helga, and Gunnar, or anyone running a farm, the endless summer sunlight translates into long days of work, often from seven A.M. to two A.M. They save sleeping for the long months of polar darkness.

Out on the trail, there are six of us, plus Disa leading and Helga bringing up the rear.

One day I am on a horse named Gnott. She isn't the prettiest mare: her bay coloring is flecked with an orangey brown, her mane is short and frizzy instead of the typical flowing thick hair of most Icelandics. She doesn't even have pretty eyes, and hardly any eyelashes. She doesn't fit the glamorous image I have of a horse I would ride. And I can't say it but I want to be riding Viv's horse, Freya. I rode her yesterday and started to fall in love with her. She was a tölting machine. I was hoping to ride Freya for the second day in a row. But I got myself entangled in a bit of saddle skullduggery.

52

The saddles from Helga's barn are old, well-worn, good-enough saddles. Even though Icelandics are ridden mostly for long trekking and herding, it is much, much different from a Western saddle, which is a couch in comparison. Old Icelandic saddles are rarely softened with quilting and knee rolls. They have the basic structure of an English saddle, yet they are even flatter and sparer. When you're not used to riding all day, the friction from shifting your "sitz bones" back and forth between tölt and trot for many hours can cause saddle sores. Eve packs A&D ointment for this reason.

But I saw one saddle in the tack room that was new and quilt-padded with cushy knee rolls. Instead of meeting Disa and everyone in the barn, I chose to go to the tack room first, in a diabolically sneaky move to grab that saddle. I came out feeling victorious with the coveted saddle, but I spent too much time in the barn. When I rejoined the rest, I heard Disa say, "Viv, why don't you ride Freya today." I couldn't object. You feel pressure to be magnanimous. We all ride different horses throughout the week so that we get to sample them. You can't get possessive. It's like practicing polyamory, you ride one for a couple days and then switch. Go ahead, fall in love, but be prepared to share.

Viv is riding alongside me and asks, "How's your horse?" Ever since Viv and I have been taking nightly walks, she's been looking out for me, making sure I know what I'm doing on the trail.

"She's okay," I say, "but it's bumpy, I can' t get her into a smooth gait."

Viv takes a critical look at my horse. "She looks stiff in the shoulder. The saddle doesn't look like it fits that horse."

"I didn't know saddles came in sizes."

"You've never owned a horse. That one, see, doesn't lay flat enough on the horse's shoulders. It's too big. Let me tell Disa, she may want you to change."

Disa takes one look at saddle and horse and says, "That saddle is for Gunnar's horse. He is a much wider horse than Gnott. I don't know how you got that saddle. We didn't put that saddle out." It's always a mistake not to fess up to something so harmless, but I make the mistake and remain mum.

She looks up and down the line and decides that I have to change with Eve. We all stop, and Eve and I get off, undo the saddles and switch. I am left with a harder than usual saddle, and Eve says, "Oooh, this saddle is so comfortable."

Back riding, Viv says, "Now how's the riding?"

The saddle has made no difference to my horse's gaits. "I still am having a bumpy ride."

Viv sums up the problem quickly. "You're slumping in your saddle. Try sitting up a little." She's right. I tend to sit like a sack of potatoes when I am not concentrating on my riding. I sit up and find the center of my seat.

"And your reins are too long. She has a shorter neck, a small head."

I take Viv's advice and it helps. Viv knows so much; I know so little. I don't know if I will ever be able to look at a horse and say, "The saddle doesn't fit, or she's stiff in the shoulders," the way Viv can. I hope someday to get to the point when I can feel the horse is heavy in front, but horse knowledge takes years to acquire, and I took three decades off.

"How do you like Freya?" I ask Viv.

"She's great. This is a great horse."

"Yeah, I know." I am miserable not riding Freya today.

When the trail narrows and we are forced to go single file, my horse cuts off other horses to get to the front. "Sorry, sorry," I apologize to horses and riders. Sylvie growls at me, "Keep your horse away from mine. They don't get along."

"I thought my horse *did* get along with yours."

"Nope. Your horse gets along with Jarpur."

The horses have their friend groups, too, which Helga told us about in the beginning of the week. "Freya, Gnott, and Jarpur get along very well. They herd together. But Stulka doesn't like Jarpur and Jarpur kicks Orn, and Gnott doesn't like Orn riding up on her tail. And watch out for Perla, she's young and doesn't know her manners." As riders, we must keep all these relationships straight as we try to maintain control.

Meanwhile, Perla, who Mel is riding, is right on my tail and my mare kicks back. The bucking movement jolts me momentarily. Perla whinnies and pulls her head up short, jolting Mel, though she also stays seated. Mel is an assured rider. She's impenetrably quiet and calm, another resolute horse girl.

"Get control of your horse," Sylvie yells at me.

My mare tacks suddenly right to avoid a deep divot and cuts in front of Eve's horse. "Sorry, I didn't know she was gonna do that." This ride is turning into one long apology tour for my horse and, as everyone knows, for me.

"Glad I'm not on your horse," Sylvie says.

A Thin Place

After the miles of lupine fields, the long black sands of an estuary, and the sandy dunes, we arrive on the edge of Lake Hóp, a large tidal lagoon that empties into the Greenland Sea. Disa says, "We're going to rest here for a while before we cross the lake."

It is a wide lake; the other side is within view but at a distance. Maybe I wasn't listening that well back at the farm when they told us what we were going to do, but I'm looking at this body of water wondering how it's all going to work. We've got on our Wellies, we prepared that much, but I've never crossed anything more than knee-deep on horseback.

"We're crossing that?" Sylvie asks. She is on a different horse today, after insisting that Thoka tried to dump her yesterday. Helga put her on Stulka, a fifteen-year-old mare who has never been bred.

Helga says, "Yes, Queenie, we're crossing that."

"What if I don't want to?" Sylvie says.

"You can stay on this side and wait for us to come back," Disa says. "Or . . ." She opens her coat and gives us her dazzling smile with her twinkling wink. Her inside pockets are stuffed with small plastic bottles of booze. ". . . You have a choice: Cognac or Brennivín."

"I'll take the Rémy Martin," Sylvie says, and swigs it like a cowgirl. "This country is going to turn me into a lush."

Disa offers both the Cognac and Brennivín to whoever wants it. The takers are me, Sylvie, and Eve. I know alcohol is only a temporary fix, but the wind has picked up and is blowing off the cold lake, and a couple of sips warm me up and take my jitters away.

The horses graze on sparse, scurry dune grass that does not look edible, but they are used to grazing on almost anything. Horses that live near the ocean will eat seaweed to survive if that's all there is. After we let the horses rest and graze, we check their girths before remounting.

Girth tightening is a safety precaution I take seriously. I've heard of many riding disasters caused by a loose girth and saddle slipping under the horse and the rider slipping with it, which frightens the horse, causing it to bolt. Horses bloat a little when you originally tack up, and when riding them their stomachs tighten from the exercise which will loosen the girth, and the weight of the rider can push the saddle back, which will loosen the girth even more.

And after they've been grazing, their stomachs bloat again. I tighten the girth a few notches on Gnott and ask Disa to check it for me. She is still miffed about the earlier saddle mix-up, wondering aloud how that could have happened. She lifts up Gnott's saddle and resettles it more forward since it has slipped back some, and then she finds ample slack in the girth and cinches up the strap a few more notches. It alarms me there was so much room in the girth. I would be under the belly of the horse, dragged in the water with my head under, without her help.

As a precaution, Disa and Helga go around and check the girth on every horse before we remount. Then we wait for them to remount and the horses are edgy, prancing in place, so that we have to turn them in small circles. There is an undercurrent of explosive freedom in them as we wait. Horses give each other energy, and you can't help but feel it spreading from one horse to another in anticipation of the crossing.

"What if I fall in?" Sylvie asks. She feels what I feel. The Cognac has worn off and any temporary courage has faded.

"It's very important not to look down at the water," Disa says. "If you look down, you get dizzy and lose your balance. Just look straight ahead all the time and follow behind me single file."

Helga adds: "And knot your reins and keep them up on your horse's neck. You don't want the horse to get tangled up in them. The horse needs its head to move freely to swim."

"Swim? You didn't tell me we were swimming," Sylvie says.

Eve's laughter rings out across the lake. "Oh, Sylvie, didn't you know?" Here in Iceland, Eve is confident in the saddle, willing to take a chance with every horse and every ride, an attitude I never see when she is home, where she rarely rides and when she does, she never looks relaxed.

We start off trotting in the shallows that are only a few inches deep. It's difficult to keep my feet in my stirrups while in a trot. I do my best to keep a half seat and lighten my weight on the horse's back. But I don't ride enough in general to have those thigh muscles you need to grip the saddle without squeezing the horse's flanks and I lose my stirrups often.

I get behind Disa and focus strictly on her thick golden braids as if my balance depends upon it (it does). But then Eve passes me. I don't look down, I try not to look down, I look down ever so briefly, and I don't fall off. I go back to Disa's braids, and I look at the shoreline far off in the distance. Viv passes me, as does Mel and Britt. Even Sylvie passes me, cantering slowly, comfortably, with a beatific smile. So I bring my horse into canter because everyone now is doing it and it is easier than trotting, less jolting, and I'm less likely to lose my stirrups. So much is said about the Icelandics' special gait, the tölt, that I forget my favorite gait is the canter. It's what sold me on Icelandic horses to begin with: It's easy to ask for canter and it's easy to sit to. It brings a three-beat mantra to the ride: I'm cantering, cantering, cantering.

For the next ten or twenty minutes—I can't tell how much time passes—this slow canter in the lake puts me in a dream state: the cold water splashing like metallic beads of light against the horses' steaming breath, as we are all cantering the shallows. The other side of the lake doesn't get much closer—it feels as if we are permanently in the middle of the lake, which is fine with me, more than fine, it's where I want to be. I don't ever want this ride to stop. It's time out of mind.

As we get out of the shallows and into the deeper water the horses naturally slow down as the water comes up to their chests. I knot my reins and push them forward on my mare's withers so she can stretch out her neck. Taking a cue from the other riders, I pull up the stirrups and cross them over the front of the saddle. So that there is no drag, I hitch my legs up so that my feet rest on the back of the saddle. I lean forward and grab my horse's mane for something to hold on to, and my face nestles in her horsehair. My breathing and my mare's breathing are matched. She plunges into the deep water, submerging everything but the saddle, her withers, and her head.

The coldness of the water is irrelevant; I barely notice. My horse feels like she's swimming in slow motion; she's underneath me working hard but the gait is unrecognizable and we're floating together and drifting with the current. She's carrying me on her back, as if she is a kind of hybrid marine centaur. I think of the Celtic belief of a thin liminal place where the door between this world and another is cracked open for only a moment, and this feels like that place for me, or the closest I will ever get to that place. I have fallen into a crack of watery light, and for one icy moment I have been allowed a glimpse into the transparency of the other world. I think, *When I die this is how I want to enter the other world, on the back of a horse that is swimming in a cold lake.* And I will cross over into myth.

When we reach the other side of the lake, finally and all too soon, what greets us is a sharp climb up a short hill full of rocks. The horses in front of me begin to run up this 45-degree angled incline in a reactive herd panic. I hear Disa, amidst all the thunder of hooves and water and rocks, yell out, "Lean all the way forward," so I flatten myself on my mare's withers, hold tight to her mane, and give her all the knotted rein she needs.

She miraculously delivers me in a hurry to the top of the hill, and then she stops. Just stops. Her job done. My life depended on her completely and she is looking for nothing back from me. She was breathing hard in the water, harder up the hill, but now she is breathing calmly and looking to graze.

Disa calls out, "Everybody good?"

Eve yells, "Woo, we're good!"

Viv says, "That was wild. A little too wild."

Sylvie says, "What did we just do? I can't believe we did that!"

Helga says, "Well, you did. I knew you could, too."

My heart is pounding so fast I can feel it in my throat. This is usually my body's reaction to fear. But it's not fear, it's pure exhilaration.

I slide off my horse and land on shaky legs. I loosen my horse's girth and undo her noseband so she can eat all the grass she wants. I want to give her oats, riches, gold for that ride. But she is content with scurry grass.

When I was young, my dentist used to give me laughing gas (nitrous oxide) when I needed cavities filled, which basically turned me into a stoned little nine-year-old. I had a scary loss of self in that dentist chair: Who am I? Where am I? I calmed myself down by repeating my name, my grade and teacher's name, my school's name, my mother, father, and brothers' names. It is a similar sense after crossing Lake Hóp—a momentary loss of self, though not at all scary: Where am I? Who am I? Somewhere up North. Somewhere in Iceland. With this group of women I both know and don't know. With horses. That dream of horses.

We are all sitting separately on the hill, ruminating, eating the sandwiches we packed for ourselves in plastic bags. The sandwich I made is lamb salami, cheese, and sliced cucumber, with peppered, flavored cream cheese on sweet brown bread. The Cognac is passed around. A light wind blows off the lake, Helga and Disa talk quietly in Icelandic, kittiwakes call, the horses puff out and snort with contentment. All too soon there are the small murmurings of movement, the getting up and gathering of things as we get ready to be on our way.

Sylvie asks, "How do we get back?"

She realizes what I have just realized. We're on a spit of grassy land, surrounded by water.

Disa points to the lake we just crossed. "The same way we came."

2006

The Wind in Those Places

My father has been in a nursing home for five years, after suffering a major stroke. My mother visits him twice daily, eating lunch and often dinner with him in the home's dining room. When I visit my mother, which is almost every Sunday, she insists I go to the nursing home with her. It dictates a reluctant pattern to my weekend: an hour-long drive up to my mom's condo, an hour-long visit at the nursing home, an hour alone with my mother, an hour-long drive home. It's four hours out of my forty-eight-hour precious weekend.

My mother is loyal to my father, as befits her generation. When he was eighty, before he had his stroke, he served her with divorce papers. She told me about it then, but I didn't push for details and she didn't offer. I knew it hurt her terribly, but she trudged on, shaking her head, called him a "crazy man," and refused to sign them. He accused her of all sorts of collusion with all sorts of people. But looking back on that paranoid episode it was probably the arteriosclerosis talking, although given his history, it was hard to tell his regular craziness from thickening-of-his-arteries craziness. My grandmother, his mother, had it, too, and a few months before the stroke that killed her, she used to walk the two miles from her apartment to our house and prostrate herself on our front lawn, "Crucify me, go ahead, you're killing me, like Jesus." (She was a hardened Polish Catholic, first-generation, from a world we knew nothing about.) We'd look out from behind the living room curtains and laugh at her and hope the neighbors weren't watching. "You would laugh at Jesus," she'd say and shake her fist at us.

One warm day in May, I push my father's wheelchair out to the sunny spot where I often take him. He was once an athletic man with a natural musculature that few people are lucky enough to be born with; his body was cut like a rock. He played basketball when he was young and in college; boxing when he was in the Army Air Corps; tennis for the rest of his mobile life.

His left side is paralyzed, and he can't walk at all. His right hand shakes, but he can use it to feed himself. Even though all his food comes mashed, including beef, and his water and coffee is thickened with starch powder, he hasn't lost his appetite. He gets heavier and heavier and his body becomes a different kind of rock. It takes two aides to move him off the bed into a wheelchair or to the bathroom. He takes out his anger, his helpless immobility, on the aides, and verbally abuses them. My mother tells them, "That's not like him, he never spoke ill of women."

And it's true, my father had courtly manners when it came to women. Growing up poor with a single mother in New York City, he made it to Villanova on a scholarship. There, they groomed him to be a chivalrous young Catholic man. Their mission was "to take the peasant out of the slum-dwelling Pollack" (his words, not mine). There were weekly teas with white-gloved young women from Rosemont College. He was taught to stand when a woman came into the room. To pull out a chair for a lady. And, on the street, to walk on the outside of a woman to protect her from traffic. My father did this until he could no longer stand on his own.

I know he is miserable in a wheelchair in a nursing home, but his helplessness has selfishly provided me with an opportunity to know him better. His guard is down now, so he's more honest about the past. Before his stroke he only told me his selected war stories, cherry-picking a few combat details and bragging about his beloved B17. After his stroke, he fills in the blanks, sometimes unknowingly. Once, when he had a fever from pneumonia, he looked at me and started weeping. "I'm sorry for losing your husband, I'm sorry we couldn't save him." I started crying. "Dad, my husband's fine, he's home with the kids." It unnerved me so, like it was some kind of prophecy. But he kept shaking his head and wiping his eyes and repeating his apologies to the widow of a ball turret gunner that had died in 1944.

Though I initially resented all these forced filial visits to the nursing home, I no longer regret them. I know more about his missions, blowing up munition factories and train transports. I know what the odds were of his coming out alive: 25 percent of the planes on each mission never came back. I know that flak hit his plane and it went down in flames and the ball turret gunner died, but the plane landed in allied territory. That his job as a radio operator doubled as a side gunner during battle. He once told me that under fire, courage is spontaneous, it's nothing glorious, but more like a knee-jerk reaction. I know that his bomber squad gave cover to the ground troops on D-Day. And I also know that he blames his stroke, nearly sixty years later, on his second to last mission. Though he has been an atheist his whole adult life, he thinks God is punishing him for what he did in the war, specifically for being part of the firebombing of Dresden.

When I tell him that I'm going back to Iceland soon, I'm hoping it will shake loose some memories and I'll learn more. I am not so much of a peacenik that I don't find his war years the most interesting and important part of his life. I don't want to forget what he did. But it's not just the personal imprint those years left on my father and, in turn, on our family. It's also the way that war, that he knew firsthand, altered every inch of the world and the repercussions are the political power plays that still operate today.

Iceland became a strategically located island, stuck up there in the northern sea with German U-boats swarming around it. Though Iceland claimed to remain a neutral country, there was a worry that they would side with the Germans. In 1938, in W.H. Auden's *Letters from Iceland*, he writes frequently of bumping into Hermann Göring's brother and cohort, who were touring the country in search of the pure Teutonic roots. Fearing Nazi sympathies and Hitler taking hold, the British invaded the country in 1940 and set up the Allied occupation. The US, Canadian, and British forces built Iceland's airfields, giving the country a jump on modern aviation before they pulled out.

"You used to stop in Iceland, didn't you?" I ask my father, urging him to retell me.

He nods his head. "We used to stop to refuel. We had to stop in Newfoundland, Greenland, Iceland before making it to the base in England."

"What do you remember?"

"We froze. There was no heat in the planes. It could get to forty below. We had lined suits that were supposed to be electrically heated but they never worked well. So we froze in the air and then we landed and we froze on the ground."

A fundamental difference between our generations: What was a frozen hell to him is desolate beauty to me. What he wants to forget, I feel called to return to. What was his hardship is my comfort. He stopped in those places for survival: to refuel to make sure he made it home. I look out on those same horizons and see adventure, a place to comfortably get lost for a little while, to get away from my real life. And sitting with him, I realize that I also go so that I can forget about him and his life's suffering for a while, and forget that my mother is at the nurse's station trying to calm down one of the aides because he called her a "fat ass."

"I can't understand it . . . why you go there," he says. His foggy blue eyes look off into the tall maples that surround the nursing home. May is soft and green and gentle in Connecticut. But he doesn't see that: he is looking at his memories of those frozen places.

"The wind, the wind in those places," he says, shaking his head. "It could rip you apart."

And that, for me, is the defining weather characteristic of Iceland: Wind. It is the whistling background, the white noise machine in my ear the entire time I am there. It gets into my ears so much that it becomes an almost silent, yet constantly audible, partner to my inner narration.

Even in the summer, the wind often has a brisk Arctic bite to it. Fresh off the ice caps of Greenland and Iceland, it smells as clean and pure as snow. Most of Iceland is treeless, so the wind isn't filtered through or slowed by shaking leaves. It has no buffers. There has been an all-out government effort to plant trees in Iceland to avoid erosion, so driving around you do see fledgling pockets of brave saplings. But the common joke is: "If you get lost in the forests of Iceland, just stand up." It is hard for the trees to grow tall, particularly in the north of Iceland; the relentless wind stunts their growth and the trunks are bent with what looks like arbor scoliosis.

Up at Helga's farm, there is often a roaring wind, like an ocean wave that never breaks. When we are out on the trail riding and the already brisk wind picks up a notch, it brings an added dash of adventure to the ride. The horses, already peppy, pep up more. The wind gets their blood up, too. It's all we can do to keep them calm. When we get to the sea with the din of the ocean waves added to the growling wind, we often dismount. The horses get too wild to ride.

I have witnessed a few sunny and still days in Iceland without wind, and it disorients me. It's like the music has stopped, and I miss it. I see other people slow down, too. Icelandic women lay out in the sun, impromptu, taking off their shirts to lie down in the grass with their bras on. You can hear a conversation ten feet away. The sun bears down full strength. I need sunscreen. I need a brimmed hat to keep the heat off my face. It just doesn't feel right.

When I'm trying to sleep in my guesthouse bedroom and it's two in the morning, the wind throws itself against the window like a pushy, shrieking banshee: "Let me in."

So I do. I crack open the window and the full storm of fresh Arctic air whirls in with the keeping-you-from-sleep sunlight. The wind fills up my eardrums with its reckless chatter. It wipes me clean. It puts me right again. It helps me breathe. It makes my life seem large and the world larger.

The wind, the wind in those places.

———

A week before I am about to leave for Iceland, my father gets an infection. They take him to the hospital and the infection spreads to his kidneys; his kidneys start to fail and then his gallbladder is inflamed. They can't seem to subdue the infection. My mother says, "This may be it."

I cancel my trip to Iceland. I drive an hour every day to see him in intensive care and to eat lunch or dinner with my mother. This vigil goes on for two weeks—we are waiting for my father to die. When one of my brothers comes to visit, he says, "Nonsense, he's not going to die." And he yells at my father to wake up, "What are you doing, Dad, open your eyes!" And my father drowsily nods his head in mute confirmation. "See, he's fine," my brother says.

I marvel at the emotional gender gaps in my family. My mother and I are ready and willing (too eager perhaps) to weep at my father's side; I'm writing the funeral notes in my head and tearing up at the imagined recital of my public words for my father. My brother's response is to raise his voice and to shake my father awake. "Stop your crying, he's not going anywhere," he says with utter assurance.

And it turns out he's right. On what would be the third day of my Iceland trip, he pulls through. His fever and infection are gone.

When my father is cleared and back in the nursing home, my mother says that we should go to Scotland. "I'll pay," she says, knowing I would probably never spend my money traveling with my mother. I take her up on it because I don't know how much longer she'll be around, or how close she is to winding up in a nursing home, but mostly I want to go to see my daughter—she will be with a dance troupe at the Edinburgh Fringe Festival. My daughter feels no anxiety about traveling at age twelve without us. She likes to talk; unlike my son who has developed the art of dropping consonants and collapsing them into a vowel sound mashup, she enunciates clearly. She instinctively knows how to navigate and make herself at home anywhere.

But the trip to Scotland with my mother it not what I hoped for. At eighty-five, she has a hard time walking. She is easily winded, her hips ache, and we always need to find someplace for her to rest—and no one gives up their seat for the elderly any more, not even in Edinburgh.

Spending day after day with her for a week, I notice she is easily addled, confusing elevators for doors, chicken for fish—she picks up a salt shaker and looks at it as if it were a Rubik's cube. She is focused primarily on meals. We must stop and eat between meals, too. And she is losing her keen observations about people and places. She has little to say, except, when her granddaughter is on stage, "Is it just me, or is she not commanding all of the attention?" But then I notice she has her eye on the wrong dancer. I am not sure what she is getting out of this trip. My big regret is that I waited too long to travel with her—five, ten, twenty years too late. And it makes me reaffirm my commitment to travel every year to Iceland with Sylvie and Eve. Though I am still in my forties, there will be a day, even though it seems so many years away, when it will be too late, we will be too old.

BOOK II
THE TÖLT

———∞∞∞———

A natural, lateral gait, unique to the Icelandic breed. It is similar to a running walk, a very smooth, four-beat gait, which can be quite fast. Done well, it allows the rider an almost bounce-free ride at up to 20 mph.

2007

‒∞∞∞‒

A Reykjavík Night

I t's one A.M. on June 17. I'm in the Hotel Klopp in a double room on the second floor. I'm waiting for my roommate, a friend of Eve's who lives in the Berkshires.

I'm sleepless, restless, full of unrepentant independence. I try reading but get up frequently to look out on the street.

Reykjavík is overcast, so the diffused nighttime sunlight pushes an opaque twilight through the clouds. It is Iceland's National Day of Independence, their July 4th, and people are coming out of bars, drunk and singing. Two men walk down the street, unsteady on their feet, passing a bottle between them. They carry fishing poles and head toward the piers. Three women wobble toward the hotel, wearing disarrayed versions of the national costume: a long navy skirt, plaid apron, double-buttoned vest, puffy sleeved shirt, and the signature hat—a gold-banded black tail-cap.

My roommate shows up at two A.M. Trying not to wake me, she tiptoes in and then drags her heavy suitcase after her and it bangs into the wall. "It's okay, you can make noise, I'm not sleeping."

"Hi, roomie, I'm Lisa."

I turn on the light, not that it's dark in the room. Lisa is a middle-aged woman in a tight windbreaker, big in the way a lot of middle-aged women are, only around the middle. I have noticed that a lot of us—me, Eve, Sylvie, Viv, and now Lisa, are of the same body type. We all have skinny legs, we are heavier on the top than on the bottom, and we are thick around the middle. It makes me wonder if our ancestors all met in Neolithic times and scouted out cold weather and horses together on the Eurasian steppes before heading to Northern Europe.

After we introduce ourselves, Lisa is on a roll, nonstop talking about her flight, how she knows Eve. No awkward silences with Lisa. She tells me she and her husband met in their early twenties as skydivers, and that the two of them run the Skydiving club of New England.

"Wow," is the only response I can offer up, as someone who is afraid of heights and has recurrent nightmares about falling from second-story windows.

She tells me that she recently gave up skydiving because of her health. But she won't give up riding—she has a Thoroughbred cross—and she loves steeplechasing.

"Wow," is all I can say again, as someone who stopped jumping horses after one try with Charlie. He was lazy and arthritic on one side and I wasn't putting much effort into it, when he stumbled and knocked down the rail. The riding instructor came over and began to smack Charlie in the face with her crop to wake him up. She apologized later in the stables when I was putting salve on his neck and tried to explain: "I didn't want you to get hurt," she said, "because he was being lazy." I left the stable after that and felt awful for leaving Charlie behind. I can never forgive myself for not stopping her. And I cannot get over him, my old-man horse, how he tarried, how I wept for him.

Lisa goes out to have a cigarette, but first tells me she is going to give up smoking before her grandchild is born. "I've got five months to go." She stands outside on the sidewalk directly below my open window and the smoke wafts up. I don't mind the smell of smoke. In fact, I'm a non-smoker who likes the smell of cigarettes. My son is a smoker, and I hate that—that he has been tarring his lungs since fifteen. I brought him up on organic baby food, cage-free eggs, non-nitrate hot dogs. I had the pregnant Madonna complex and drank nothing stronger than weak green tea when he was in utero, so he wouldn't lose a point or two off his IQ. Somehow this all paved the way for his current habits of sucking in pollutants and intoxicants like candy.

So it's a forgivable offense, if late at night, when the smell of cigarette smoke from the patio curls into my bedroom window, I find it a comforting trigger. It means he's home and he's safe. I can go to sleep. Funny how kids wind up training you.

Lisa announces she's back by opening the door and coughing. She has a smoker's cough, a smoker's voice, a smoker's raspy laugh. She says a phrase in Italian, and when I give her a blank stare, she translates something she says is from an opera. She tells me that she went to an Italian boarding school in the southern Alps and became fluent in Italian. She ran away from the boarding school at seventeen with a boyfriend. She joined a hippie-type caravan and traveled around India on the roof of a train. The craziest thing she ever did was spend all night sleeping on a park bench in Tehran, before the revolution. She has two kids, but only one that she talks about—her pregnant daughter, who is brilliant and getting a PhD in computational linguistics.

Then she gives me the rundown on her medical history. She's had five abdominal surgeries in the past twenty months. It's not the surgeries that bother her, it's the fact that they are all the result of the first surgery and the surgical sponge the doctor left behind. "One botched surgery and four more to correct the botched one." She brings up a lawsuit she's thinking of pursuing, but then she goes on about how much she hates lawyers. But she hates surgeons more. A conundrum.

She's tough, opinionated, a risk-taker—a modern Beryl Markham, and I find myself liking her, though she's making me feel like my life is too staid, that I'm not wild enough. I'm not.

Comfortable now that we've spent a full ten minutes together, she lifts up her shirt and shows me the scars from the abdominal surgeries. And then other scars from other surgeries. Scars from her caesareans. Context is everything, and I feel inferior and wimpy that I have nothing comparable to show her: just a small horizontal line on my neck where my over-exuberant doctor, feeling a small lump, removed half of my perfectly fine thyroid. Other than that, a couple of playground scars. She's tough Robert Shaw and I'm weaselly Richard Dreyfuss in *Jaws*.

She is a one-woman show and I'm the only one in the audience. Except for my minor scars, I have revealed nothing about myself. And she has asked nothing. Not even the basics like, do I own a horse? Or is this my first time in Iceland? Or how do I know Eve? She doesn't even ask the secondary basics: do I have a husband or an ex lurking in the background? Do I have any children? Where am I from? I wait for these questions, but they are not forthcoming. And I am not in a rush to reveal anything about myself. I would rather listen to other peoples' stories anyway; I find relief from the fatigue of the narration constantly playing in my head. Some travelers are tell-all types; all I need to do is nod and agree and they spill their entire, scarred selves.

At four in the morning, as Lisa comes in from her last smoke of the night, I'm ready to take my sleeping pill. Lisa looks in her makeup bag, "I'm taking a diazepam."

"Oh God, me, too."

She loves the idea we are synchronizing the popping of our sleeping pills. "Down the hatch, roomie." Her smoker's laugh is the last thing I hear that night.

Mothers and Daughters

The skyline of Reykjavík—those two nouns I would never have put together a few years ago—is filling up with scaffolding and dangling construction beams. And we've taken notice:

"That bank building wasn't there last year."

"Nor were all these high-rises."

"Who's going to fill all these buildings?

"It's hardly like Iceland is a hot spot."

"I know. It's a teeny tiny country. We all love it, but I can't imagine that many others see what we see here. It's not like it's gonna have a huge population boom."

"It looks like they're building for big doings, though."

"But what for?"

"Reykjavík's a town, a town the size of New Haven, it's hardly a city."

72

There are six of us stuffed again into one van: Viv, now seventeen-year-old Britt, Sylvie, Eve, Lisa, and me. Suitcases at our feet, bags in our laps. The snacking has begun, with Viv taking out tea biscuits the minute we pulled away from Hotel Klopp. Lisa unwraps a package of assorted licorice, having fallen sway to Iceland's curious licorice fetish. Licorice is a national craze, and it's made in all different flavors like chocolate, white chocolate, marzipan, and pepper. I'm not a fan.

Per usual, Sylvie does most of the talking. She tells us that she has sold her house in Otis, bought property in Monterey, and is building a new house right down the road from Eve's farm.

Eve loves the idea of being closer to Sylvie. "I can't wait till you move in. You can just walk over every day."

"You know what though . . . my husband wants to move in with me once we get the new house built. So I'm hoping it takes a few years to build my new one. Ha! I'm a terrible wife. But I'm used to living alone now and I like it. And he wants to come around again. I don't know if I'm happy about that."

Eve and Jack took a yoga cruise to Mexico, but she didn't like it that much. "It was fine, it was fine, but the vibe was all wrong."

Sylvie clears her throat and remains quiet. But I know Sylvie, she has more to say about this.

In Borgarnes, we stop at a bakery. I sit at the table with Sylvie, while Eve, Viv, and the others are still in line. The bakery has long windows and though it's overcast and rainy, it feels bright with subdued light. The tide is low, so the mudflats stretch far out. People are digging for mussels, and if I have my directions right, we are directly across the fjord from where we asked for directions in 2004, from the family digging for mussels.

"Lisa has such interesting stories," I tell Sylvie.

"Yes, she does have interesting stories. She's done a lot of things. But she now lives in the shadow of her mother, who is eighty and retired but was a famous academic in ancient texts and world mythologies. Kind of a female Joseph Campbell type, you know the 'follow your bliss' guy. She leads these monthly salons at her house. She has quite a following. Eve goes to them."

"She didn't mention her mother last night."

"That's good. Eve invited her so she could break away from her mother, who's brilliant, don't get me wrong, but Lisa could stand to get out from underneath all that brilliance. So, that's good, you listen to her stories. You're good for her, you haven't heard them."

"She's tougher than we all are."

"You'd be surprised."

It's clear now that this is another "save the daughter from the mother" intervention on Eve's part. Overbearing mothers is a theme that Eve is sensitive to. I wonder about her relationship with her own mother. She has told me that Jack's children (and now grandchildren) from his first marriage are all the children she needs, and I suspect she didn't have children by choice.

My daughter is fourteen and I want her to come with me to Iceland. I don't want to wait until it's too late, like I did with the trip to Scotland with my mother. I want to be able to ride with her before I get too old. I want to gallop to the Greenland Sea with her. I want to impart my motherly wisdom and let her experience the wild freedom that only horses can give. But it's a fantasy of mine she doesn't share.

Before I left, I made her listen to Rickie Lee Jones, which always leaves me bubbling up with maternal mawkishness:

> "That's the way it's gonna be little darling, we'll be riding on the horses, yeah,
> Way up in the sky, little darling, and if you fall I'll pick you up, I'll pick you up."

I put it on her iPod and watched her listen with earbuds, looking closely at her face for any little reactive movement. "Don't you like it? Don't you love it?"

"Aww, it's sweet, Mom."

"Doesn't it make you want to ride with me? Some year won't you come with me?"

"Er, Iceland? Horses? Yeah, no thanks, Mom. Paris, yes. Take me to Paris."

Not all girls love horses, even ones who share my DNA. My daughter only likes them at a distance, preferable in digital pixels, or if in real life, from afar, out in the fields through a car window. She's a consummate urbanite. Even

Connecticut is too empty for her liking. She's not a fan of big animals, or animals in general. She likes our dog, but she often pushes her away because of her rank stinkiness. My daughter instinctively focuses on human relationships, reading social and emotional cues in a way I never could at her age.

I took her up to Eve's this past year. She went into the stables with me and hesitantly petted the horses' velvety muzzles. But when they snorted out the barn dust she jumped back, like they were going to run over her. Obliging me, she got on Snild, a gentle mare for beginners. Sylvie and Eve led Snild around on a lead rope and gave my daughter lots of encouragement. But she was interested in only two things: chatting with them and looking longingly at the gate, hoping to go back to the barn. When they gave her the reins to take over on her own, she took one loop around the arena and was done. "That's enough." She dismounted in a hurry, eager to get to have lunch and conversation with me and my horsey friends.

I'm not really sure what draws people, females in particular, to horses. Horse ownership is estimated to be 80 percent female in the United States. My daughter is unlike me in many ways. She has no desire to throw herself on the back of a horse and gallop to lands end. She has always been a garrulous girl, emotionally stalwart, an extrovert who manages people well, traits she gets from her father. They say it is the daughter's relationship with her father that sets her confidence level. I buy that. But more than that, I think horse love is for the lonely girls at heart. That's the club we once all belonged to, whatever our adult life may appear to be built upon. Whatever I or Eve or Sylvie or Viv have become, we started out quietly unsociable, spending too much time alone in our imaginative horse world. The only risk we wanted to take was with horses. The horse took us both away from and into the world.

All the Queen's Men

This year we have men (men!) riding with us. It's all very exciting, as one of the men, Olafur (Oli) is also our resident chef. He is a friend of Helga's and a zoologist by day, but he's off during the summer, and his hobby is cooking. I'm not sure what the arrangement is, but Helga has delegated to him the cooking for our group. Within an hour or two of getting back from our rides, he comes over from Helga's kitchen with Icelandic pancakes, which are thin, rolled-up crepes filled with strawberry jam and whipped cream. Or he brings in an enormous platter of soft, dark, velvety red wood–smoked salmon piled inches deep that melts as soon as it hits my gluttonous little tongue. It's served with *rúgbrauð*, a dense, sweet and steamed rye bread, and crème fraîche. For dinner, he makes baked sea trout with onion sauce, pilaf and salad. Or roast leg of lamb with potatoes galette. Or a mushroom barley soup with fresh baked potato bread and salad with Danish blue cheese. For dessert, he brings us skyr cake, like cheese cake but made from fresh cream and skyr and topped with blueberries, or Happy Marriage Cake, which is like a fruit buckle. Did I mention I love him? We all want to marry him. He is very big and very bald, very smart and kind, but alas, he is married.

His wife, Gita, presents herself as a serious woman: confident, soft-spoken, reserved. I fear we offend her sensibilities, raucous American women that we are. Especially after we've had a few beers at the end of the day, Sylvie's voice goes into higher, louder decibels and her laugh turns into a parrot's screech. And we join in because her laughter makes us laugh. Gita arches her eyebrows, looks at Oli with concern, and scoots out of the kitchen. She and Oli stay upstairs in the scary part of the house. But they are Icelanders and are used to living with ghosts.

And then there is the other male, seventeen-year-old Gudni, from the neighboring farm. The tradition in Iceland is to send the kids who grow up in towns and cities to their grandparents' farm for the summer where they help out with the farm chores, learn the old ways of self-sufficiency, and kinship. (And I spent all that money sending my son to a Quaker farm camp, where he learned how to whittle wood, forage for mushrooms, and behead a chicken.)

On the first day, Gudni brought over a couple of horses for us—some basic trekking and sheepherding horses that are good for novice riders. He took an immediate interest in Britt when he saw her, and since then goes out riding with us every day, ostensibly in case we need help with his horses. If Brittany has noticed this, she doesn't let on. Coy Britt. But the rest of us have noticed.

"Brittany is so lovely," Eve says, "who wouldn't be attracted to her? And he is one cutie of a boy."

"Not just cute, but Brad Pitt in the making cute."

"Is Britt really oblivious to his attention?"

"Boy, if I were that age . . ." Sylvie says.

"You never pass up an opportunity like that."

Out on the trail on our way back from the long trek to the Greenland Sea, Gudni rides beside Britt, attempting conversation. It looks like she's not interested, almost as if she isn't answering. It's driving us crazy.

"Why doesn't she get on with him?"

"Maybe his English isn't that good," Viv says.

"It doesn't have to be. These things don't require a lot of conversation," Sylvie says.

"How could she turn him down?"

Eve says, "Maybe it's because she has a boyfriend at home."

"So?" Sylvie says.

"It doesn't have to be more than a summer fling," I add. "A week fling. A four-day fling. We're already on our third day." I am invested in this romance as well and worry about the calendar running out on her.

"Life doesn't always give you these opportunities. Did I tell you I was married at nineteen?" Sylvie says.

"A few times," I tell her.

I ride near Lisa for a while and she says, "I don't get these horses. I don't understand them. I've tried for three days to see what you all see in these horses, and I have to tell you, I love big horses. I don't get Icelandics. It's a bumpy ride." She is posting to a piggy trot—a half trot, half tölt.

When people don't like Icelandic horses, I take it personally, as if they've insulted my kids. I dismiss them for life, they are forever to remain unforgiven. I don't want to be in the position of having to defend what I love. And a lot of "big horse" people dismiss Icelandics as cute little ponies. Or they confuse them with Shetlands. Or worse, they say things like, "Why don't you get yourself a *real* horse." In my more generous moments, I can see how they are misunderstood: Icelandics aren't shaved, trimmed, or blanketed. Since they are left out in the elements, their winter coat can be shaggy from October until June. The breed has a double coat that evolved for extra insulation: the outer layer is long, coarse, and thick to keep out the rain, wind, and snow; the inner layer is short and soft for warmth. Then there is the hair that grows on their chins, quite abundantly, and sometimes three to four inches long. So it is possible that if you happened upon a herd of Icelandics in the field during these months, you might think you've found a primitive breed, almost like the Przewalski horse, the wild and original horse of the central Asian steppes. If they stand next to a Frisian, or a horse like Lisa's Thoroughbred Cross that stands at seventeen hands, they look diminutive. Like an entirely different species.

But appearances are deceiving in humans and in horses. Once you take this small, shaggy, friendly horse out on the trail, it transforms into a high spirited, swift and indefatigable horse.

Lisa complains to me: "It's almost like there's not enough horse here. When I'm in the saddle of my Cross, I have all this real estate. I can sense what my horse is going to do before he does it. But here . . ." She lifts up her reins helplessly. "I can't read this horse. It just wants to go. I have no say in its movements."

"You should talk to Viv or Helga about how to sit so that you can get the horse into a tölt," I say, and I ride in front of her.

My horse has muscled his way up to the front so that I'm near Brittany. Gudni asks her if she'd like to canter and she demurs. That not's like her, she always wants to canter. I feel compelled, I can't hold back, I get closer to her and do that kind of shout whisper, "Go, Britt, get on with him, go canter!"

I am sure Britt has overheard us before talking about her and Gudni in the house and on the trail; we have, in our manner, not been subtle. Now, with my direct assault, she can't stand the pressure, and takes off in a canter probably more to get away from me than to canter with Gudni. But she goes swiftly, without warning, as if her horse had heeded my advice rather than her, and Gudni follows and he's trying to catch up and the two of them race back to the farm, their horses' hooves making clouds of dust, and it's a boy on a horse chasing after a girl on a horse.

Eve is pleased. "Look at that girl go!"

The Kingdom of Horse

T he kids beat us back to the barn and Britt has already unsaddled her horse and is leading it into the pasture. Gudni is by her side with his horse.

Sylvie asks, "What do you think of our little Romeo?"

"That was so romantic," Eve says. "The two of them, galloping off into the sunset."

Only there's no real sunset in June and I'm watching them from the barn door and Britt is shaking her head no and waving him off. She is in the making of a missed opportunity. "Looks like he's taking his horse and going home."

"That's a shame."

"She has a boyfriend at home, a 'boyfriend,'" Sylvie says with air quotes. "You know, a 'football player.' That's her life at home."

"But we're here, and she could have a young Icelandic hottie, no?"

"You don't have to tell me, being married at nineteen. I wouldn't pass this up at her age, knowing what I know now."

Poor Britt, she is with a group of forty-, fifty-, sixty-year-old women who can't help think about their own missed chances, and think they can persuade Britt to seize her own opportunity by seizing Gudni. But she stands firm against our pressure.

"Britt's not like that," Eve says. "Some people are, and some people aren't." The topic seems to make her sad. She is not talking about Britt and Gudni anymore, but something that happened between her and Jack. There was an argument before they left. I can only guess what it was about. A look passes between Sylvie and Eve.

"You know what, Sylvie? It's fine. I have to let it go. He apologized, said he got swept up in the moment, which is what we're all supposed to be practicing—being mindful and in the present. And I'm over it. I'm really over it. I have to let it go."

"Buddha says it's all about letting go," Sylvie says.

"Yep, I'm throwing it out to the universe. It's out there. It was a brief moment in time and it's gone. I can't hold shit like that in my heart. Being mad, angry, resentful, it kills your soul."

I admire Eve for this, she forgives people she loves, and she works hard to keep her soul healthy. A lot of us don't even try. We pollute it with impunity.

We get stuck in our reactive ruts and replay our hurt over and over again. Eve has a big heart and a generous soul and her love of Jack overrides whatever has ignited her resentment.

"Pema Chödrön says anger only lasts a minute and a half, just ninety seconds," Sylvie says. "The rest is what we do with it."

"I'm done with it. I don't want to dwell on it anymore. Not here. Especially not here. I'm in Iceland."

Not only are we in Iceland, but we're in the barn, which is like entering a sanctuary. And grooming a horse is a ritual of love and devotion. We can be a loud group when we're going full blast—we can scare the birds out of their nests. But in the barn, once we start the grooming process, we are unusually quiet. It's meditative.

We move leisurely, pensively. We give the horses treats as we groom them, so they'll stand for the pampering we need to indulge them in. If we see a nick in their skin, we put salve on it. We pick their hooves, then sweep up the pickings. We use a curry brush first to get the mud off; then we use a regular stiff brush to get off dirt and dust; then a soft brush on the face; then we use a comb to get out the knots in their manes and tails. Eve brought a hair product this year (for the horses, not us) called Cowboy Magic, and it makes their manes shiny and smooth. We spray and comb, spray and comb. Helga calls our fussing "the horse spa."

I don't want to leave my horse even after being on her all day—she took me to the other side of the lake. All of us stay in the barn and spend an inordinate amount of time making them tidy. There may be cultural differences between how Americans and Icelanders groom their horses. We're aware that we are overdoing it. I have seen Icelanders just swipe their hand over their horse's back to dust off the dirt and throw on a saddle. They don't even pick the hooves. In fact, we've brought most of these brushes with us, new from the States. Icelanders rarely bother with this much grooming, unless they're in a competition. They are, of course, no less devoted.

After the horses are groomed to sparkle and gleam, we let them out. The minute we lead them out to the paddock they drop and roll in the dirt and mud. A soft, steady rain has driven us back into the shelter of the doorway. Even without the horses in the barn, we keep our voices low, almost whispering to each other. There is a quiet stillness to an empty barn that is like the quiet stillness of an empty church; you just naturally lower your voice when you enter. Rows of empty stalls are like rows of empty pews, patiently waiting for the horses, waiting for the parishioners. The barn is orderly like a church, too. Everything in its proper place: halters and bridles hung up on brackets, saddles on their wall-mounted racks, floors swept, stalls shoveled out and raked. Like boat owners, horse owners can't be messy or there are consequences.

Helga built a new barn this year, complete with an indoor arena. She built a kitchen in the barn, too, which is a luxury. The coffee pot is heavily used. Packages of candy, chocolate covered cookies, and kleinur are on the counter for the taking. A bottle of brandy is near the sink, in case you want to spike your coffee after a long, cold day on the trail. On the walls are pictures of riders and horses, one of Helga when she is about twelve, in traditional Icelandic clothing, standing proudly with her first horse.

Above the kitchen table, there is a poster of a two-day-old colt. The face of a colt can look like so many different animals. This one looks like a llama, soft white face, black nose. Above its face in script is a quote in Icelandic: "*því að þitt er ríkið, mátturinn og dýrðin að eilífu. Amen.*" I once asked Helga what the words meant. She had a hard time explaining it at first. She said it was a prayer, "You know, the last line of that prayer." Then she finally came up with the English term: The Lord's prayer.

"For thine is the kingdom, the power and the glory forever. Amen."

The Day Lisa Found Her Tölt

I t's the opposite once we're back in the house: we are loud, ear-screeching loud. We hang out in the kitchen, putting our feet up on chairs, drinking beer before dinner. This is our favorite time for retelling the derring-do tales of the day.

Oli has dropped off a large plate of wood-smoked salmon, which makes a nice accompaniment to the darker, stronger beer we have this year, Kaldi. I eat and drink in short, repetitive motions—salmon crudo, beer, salmon crudo, beer, salmon crudo, beer—like a polar bear who has made it to college.

Helga comes in and says, "Okay, guys, I have an announcement to make." After riding horses all day and drinking beer upon return, we act like disorderly medieval knights back in the castle keep. I clap my hand on the beer bottle, wedding band clinking on the glass, to bring silence to the room.

When she finally has our attention, Helga starts off faux formal. "I feel bound to inform you, that the Queen's horse, Stulka, is pregnant. I'm sorry to have to break the news to you, Sylvie."

"She got knocked up?" Sylvie squeals.

"Yes, she was a seventeen-year-old virgin, quite old for a mare, but she was never meant to be a broodmare. We think she knocked down the fence and got into our neighbor's pasture. We're pretty sure we know who the father is."

"Well that horny little hussy," Sylvie says. "Knocking down the fence to get some sex. What kind of a horse did you put me on?"

We clap our beer bottles and Eve stomps her feet. "She's a geriatric hussy."

Helga laughs, too. She has such fondness for Sylvie's silliness. After she composes herself, she says, "Even though it wasn't planned, we are going to let her keep it. And you can still ride Stulka this week, Queenie."

Stulka has been Sylvie's horse ever since she cantered across Lake Hóp on her. She feels safe with Stulka. And we want her to feel safe. No one rides Stulka except Sylvie.

"I can't ride a pregnant mare!"

"You can, but if you don't want to, you can always go back to Thoka."

Sylvie mulls this over. "Thoka, the harridan. She pushes me around."

Lisa walks in, still in her riding clothes. After our ride, she walked down the road to find reception to call home. Her face is now red and wet. "Can I just tell everyone something?"

"You're pregnant!" Sylvie shouts out, which brings on the stomping of the feet, the clapping on the beer bottles. Not in on the joke, Lisa waits for everyone to calm down.

"No. I'm fifty-four years old and that was the best day of my life."

We stop laughing; she's serious.

"I cannot believe that I rode to the Greenland Sea. I can't believe how great the tölt is once you find the gait. I can't believe I'm here. I just want to thank you all for inviting me this year." She tears up and starts to cry.

Eve is overjoyed. Mission accomplished. One person admitting she was saved by horses in Iceland. "Oh, Lisa, that's so wonderful. That's what you're here for. That's what we're all here for. See, the universe opened up for you. It's Iceland. It's magic."

The rest of us stand around and offer meek congratulations. In movies, this is where we're supposed to have a group hug. But that's not us. We're happy for her—she gets Iceland and she gets Icelandic horses now—so many people don't. We're happy to have a convert. But we're more in the mood for that other movie, the one with the knights in the mead hall. We've got beer in us—why not slam down some tankards and raise a rowdy cheer? We've got a new tale to tell—the day Lisa found her tölt.

The Saga of the Bulls

It's our last trek of the trip. And like skiing—where saying out loud that you're going to take just one more run is sure to result in a nasty fall and a broken something—I feel anxious about taking the last trek of the trip. You want to try to fool the gods of fate. You don't want them to know you've had a good, safe week, or maybe, just for fun, they'll knock you off your skis, or off your horse. It's not that, as in Eve-speak, bringing negative thoughts attracts negativity. It's that you've gotten cocky because you've made it this far, and fate doesn't like cocky.

We spend the morning riding over to Hunastaddir, a farm about ten kilometers away. The trek itself isn't difficult, but there are a few small tributaries leading to larger rivers that we need to cross, and my horse resists going over them.

"You need to look forward, think forward, and he will follow you forward," Disa tells me cheerfully, as if sheer mental telepathy will work with horses.

I try it: I look forward, think forward, do not give my horse a choice. I even plant a Disa-like smile on my face. But he's not feeling it. He starts turning around as if heading back to the barn. He bucks out a little, just a little, but enough to make me ask for help again. Disa sees he is recalcitrant and though she is ponying two horses on her side, she gets off and rearranges the halters and ropes so that she is ponying a third horse, my horse. I feel like a kid at a birthday party being led across a few muddy puddles.

I no longer have a problem with water after that first crossing, but my horse seems antsy; in fact, all the horses seem highly sensitive.

Eve's horse shies from a boulder, rapidly cross-stepping into a field to avoid it. Eve takes it lightly. "Aren't boulders supposed to be trolls? Maybe he thought it was a troll. Maybe *it is* a troll."

Soon after, Brittany's horse breaks from the group and canters up an embankment. Britt finally gets control of her horse, but she's scared and starts to tear up. "Why'd he do that?"

"Circle him back and let him know he belongs in the herd," Helga says.

This unnerves Sylvie. "If Britt can't handle her horse, what chance do I have?" Not wanting to ride the pregnant Stulka, she's back on Thoka, and keeps a steady stream of conversation with her: "Shh, shh, slow, don't look at that bad horse Britt's on."

And I have to admit, Sylvie's not wrong: Thoka is ornery and does whatever she likes. She's the old alpha mare in the pack with that fuck-off attitude.

Once we finally get to the gates of the Hunastaddir farm, we breathe a sigh of relief. Gunnar, Helga's husband, with perfect timing, pulls up in his truck and unloads coolers of sandwiches and beer, two thermoses, and bags of donuts and cookies. The sandwiches are smoked lamb or sliced egg. The beer is Gull. One thermos has coffee, one has hot chocolate. It's a trail-ride feast.

Gunnar has the dog Gauper with him, so he can run back with us. I marvel at these dogs' stamina. My dog would faint. Icelanders treat their dogs the way they treat their horses—only the good ones, the tough ones, the smart ones, get to survive. It's natural selection, with a good dose of human intervention.

I'm on my third sandwich because I simply cannot resist smoked lamb and butter sandwiches. But I need to save room for Icelandic donuts, so I sneak Gauper parts of my sandwich and he stays by my side for the rest of the lunch. I lay back on the grass and look at the sky. It's overcast where we are, but there's sun over the lake.

I notice Viv buzzing around, checking out this horse and that, asking Gunnar lots of questions. He is very reserved, handsome and rangy like a classic cowboy, and he holds us all at a bemused distance. Viv receives only one-word answers and shrugs from him, but the curious mind of Viv cannot be stifled by taciturn men. The questions fire away until she goes back to tending her horse and looking pensive.

As our lunch hour wiles away, I feel apprehensive about getting back in the saddle. My horse is a handful and we started off our relationship on the wrong note with him throwing a fit about a little puddle of water. I almost wish I was on bossy little Thoka. But everyone is saddling up and so do I. Disa passes the ceremonial flask of Remy Martin before heading out. Sylvie says, "I really need this today."

When we all get to the gate and we're ready to pass through, Viv says, "Okay, stop!" which is really hard at this point. The horses are raring to go home the minute we turn in that direction. And to slow the momentum is not easy. Viv's "Stop" makes Sylvie groan. "What? Make it quick."

We have to turn our horses in circles, as we listen to Viv tell us: "I don't have a good feeling about this trip, I had a great ride so far, and I don't want it ruined. I'll go back in the truck with Gunnar."

Viv says aloud what we have all been subconsciously thinking—that there's a bad moon rising. But how could she do that, give language to what we all fear? It's like she's taken off her skis and walked down the hill, surely damning one of us to a broken leg.

Helga takes it in stride and tells her to take off the saddle and bridle so her horse will run home with us. That's the other thing about heading home: often one or two of the pack horses go freely home on their own, which makes the horses being ridden get extra frisky, seeing their herd members loose and galloping unencumbered alongside them.

The minute we go through the gate, the horses are straining at the bit—you have to ride a horse to get the meaning of this cliché. They keep jerking their heads forward, pulling the rein hard so that it slips out of your hand. If they have longer rein, you have less control, they go faster. Once on the path, they cluster together, outracing each other in a very fast tölt. When Viv's loose horse gallops beside us, it's all we can do to keep ours from galloping, too.

Eve giggles. "Whoa, they are feisty today; look at my guy go." Her horse is a sweet-faced five-year-old gelding. "Sylvie, how are you doing?"

"I'm in no mood to talk."

I can't talk, either. My horse is pushy, strong. The one who didn't like a puddle of water earlier now splashes through streams with aplomb. The ride basically feels like a semi-restrained bolt with Disa and Helga riding alongside everyone, saying, "Don't let your horse do that; shorten your reins; keep your leg off him or he thinks you want to go faster. You are the boss, remember that."

We come to a gate and we have to stop. Disa gets off her horse to open it. This briefly gives us a break and time to collect ourselves, to check our girths, and adjust our stirrups. Back in the saddle, I look down a small hill we're about to ride down and notice something up ahead of us on the trail.

"What's that black thing down there? A rock?" I ask.

Eve and Sylvie don't see it. The gate closes behind us and we're on our way again. If at times in the guesthouse we act like medieval knights in a mead hall, out on the trail we're sometimes more like Monty Python knights, clopping along clueless and chatty.

"What is that thing?"

"It's a rock, looks like a big black lava rock."

"Like a boulder?"

"I don't see what you're talking about."

"That rock up there."

"There's more than one."

"And one of them just moved," Sylvie says.

"No, they're rocks."

"I'm telling you one moved."

"It looks kind of like a bull from here."

"Bulls. There are several."

"Bulls! That's a good sign! The stock market will go up," Eve says.

"I see a bunch of black rocks," Lisa says, pulling up from behind us in line.

"They're not rocks, they're bulls!"

"The Dow Jones is going up, up, up!"

While we are laughing at Eve's enthusiasm and optimism, I'm also wondering how much she and Jack have invested in the stock market, that it's on her mind while we're riding in Iceland. It's not like I've given any thought to my stock-invested retirement fund while in Iceland.

Disa and Helga look appropriately worried, however, and are volleying back and forth rapidly in Icelandic. They tell us to stop and stay where we are. They ride down to scout out the scene. Gauper, who previously had been adding to the confusion, barking and getting under our horses' hooves, follows them.

Six bulls are in the path, lowing, mooing, looking aggressive, and coming toward us. Disa gallops up to them, yelling at them, in an effort to scare them off. But they don't scare. They become even angrier. They are moving in a herd toward Disa, and her horse shies out from underneath her and runs off, leaving her scrambling to get up, facing angry bulls. Gauper is barking like mad, joining in the general chaos, and the bulls are advancing on them both.

Disa's horse runs up to Helga, who dismounts and holds both horses, and moves down toward Disa. She yells back at us to dismount and hold on to our horses, though we had already instinctively dismounted the minute we saw Disa thrown from her horse. If those two were off their horses, we certainly had no business still sitting in our saddles.

Eve says, "I'm going to see if I can go help." She walks her horse down the hill, shouting, "Helga, Helga, is there something I can do?" as if she's volunteering at a Berkshire fund-raiser, like perhaps she'll get the job of hanging the party bunting. But as soon as she gets within shouting range her horse panics and breaks free from her.

It can be bad news when a horse in full bridle and saddle takes off, especially when they're spooked like this and in flight mode. Unless Eve thought fast enough to unhook one of the reins, the reins are completely loose and could get tangled in her horse's hooves. And if that were to happen, it's wouldn't be like in the United States, where they would do water therapy for a horse with a broken leg. It's the end of horse in Iceland. Luckily, Eve's horse runs to us and we grab the reins.

Disa and Gauper are facing off with the bulls. Helga is behind them twenty feet, and Eve behind her another twenty feet. Eve yells back to us that there's a cow having a calf in the field and that's what the bulls are protecting. "I wonder if we could help deliver the calf?" Eve asks, perhaps not correctly prioritizing the potential crises.

Sylvie asks, "What does she want to do?"

"Deliver the little baby calf."

"Are you out of your mind?" Sylvie yells to her.

"I've seen it done with foals on my farm when they get stuck."

Sylvie says to us, "She's out of her mind."

"Come back," we tell her. "Just come back."

In the standoff between Disa and the bulls, Disa holds her ground. She yells at the bulls, she even growls. She finally gets three to turn back and the others stop advancing. Disa backs up to Helga and they both begin backing up the hill toward us, and all looks peaceful. But the dog enters the fray again, that built-in herding instinct taking over. Gauper runs out in the field to the bulls, barking and nipping at their heels, trying to herd them. The bulls low and paw the ground, and then they charge Gauper. He suddenly realizes that he's not going to win this one, and runs back toward Disa and Helga, bringing the entire pack of charging bulls with him.

Disa doesn't run. She takes a stand. Makes herself big. Really big, the way you're supposed to when you see a black bear. She stretches out her arms wide, she stomps the ground and growls at them; she yells at them and bellows like nothing I've ever heard before. Her bigness gets bigger. Her voice fills the valley. Her whole body, voice, and mind are telling the bulls, "Don't even think about it." And they stop. They stand still looking at her. She gets them to reconsider. They don't want to deal with her—she looks crazy and scary. They turn and trot back to the calf being born.

Helga and Disa run up the hill. "Okay, let's go, everyone get on. Quick, quick." We swing out wide from the path so we don't have to pass the bulls. We cross the streams farther up the tributary where they are much deeper. We let our horses go fast: tölt, trot, canter. We no longer have the luxury of worrying about the speed and gaits. And we don't slow down until we are safely within sight of the black stone church of Thingeyrar.

In the Vinland sagas, Eric the Red's daughter, Freydis, takes her own ships and sails to her brother Leif's outpost in Vinland, what is now Newfoundland. She is a renegade badass in the Sagas, born from one of her father's Irish slaves. Unlike Hallgerd, Freydis is capable of wielding her own axe when she can't talk the men into killing for her. Over in Vinland, the Norse have had a few encounters with the local tribes, trading with them, curious and peaceful at first. But as so often happens in the history of cultures meeting each other, misunderstandings occur and it doesn't go well. The natives realize they greatly outnumber the Norse and gather up their forces to attack. The Norsemen realize the odds are not in their favor and retreat. Freydis admonishes her fellow Norsemen to stand and fight, but they ignore her and run for their long boats. The Saga points out that Freydis can't keep up with them in retreat because she is pregnant and "moved somewhat slowly," and the natives catch up to her. She stumbles upon a slain crewman, takes the sword off him, and turns to face the native tribe by herself. Freeing one of her breasts from her cloak, she smacks the sword on her naked chest and bellows. They stop in their tracks. They reconsider attacking her. They don't want to deal with her. She looks crazy and scary. They get in their skin boats and row away.

Next Year, Iceland

Honey I bought two horses, I'm so excited," Eve tells Jack on her Blackberry. "We need to wire the money to Helga."

"He's not going to say 'no' to her these days," Sylvie whispers to me. "She could buy Helga's entire herd and he'd go along with it."

Sylvie has made her own purchase, Stulka's baby when it's born. She's planning on paying Helga to train it for four or five years, and then ship it to the Berkshires. "One summer when the horse is ready, I'll come here alone and train with Helga," she says. I do the math. Sylvie will be seventy-four when the horse is ready. "My horse, Hátið, will be old by then and ready to retire," she says. But Sylvie won't be. When most people that age would be moving or thinking about entering a senior living community, Sylvie will be starting on a brand-new horse.

It's relatively cheap to buy horses in Iceland, especially for first-rate recreational horses, as opposed to competition horses. Eve is paying $7,000 for Arngrimur (she calls him Arnie), who is a large farm horse that is used for annual round-ups of sheep, and $10,000 for Yrdlingur (she calls him Earl), a higher level five-year-old trained by Helga and the Holar interns over the winter.

Shipping a horse to the States is not terribly expensive, either, about $2,000, and another thousand for vet bills and quarantine.

"When are you going to buy one?" Eve asks me.

"Someday."

Buying or owning a horse is not financially feasible for me. I might be able to squeeze out the initial payment, but boarding a horse, vet bills, and training, can average $20,000 a year in my area. At this stage of my life, any extras go to the kids, to their summer camps, piano and ballet lessons, but mostly to the ever-looming college tuition that will put us deep in debt. These are the costs of bringing up children in the Northeast.

These are not the concerns of the women I travel with. Some have plenty of money or, like Sylvie, they no longer have to support their kids, or, like Viv, they can keep their horses on their own property.

But this part of the trip pains me, when they buy horses to ship home. When we stop at the tack shop in Reykjavík, Astund, which is like Prada to us (even the sales rack can bring on sticker shock), they spend hundreds (Eve, thousands) of dollars on riding gear and clothes. They chat about the Icelandic trainers who are coming to the States to judge the sanctioned shows, about the Turkey Tölt weekend, the Easter Hop, the Memorial Day Parade, and all the other reindeer games they play in. This is a world I cannot be a part of without my own horse.

But when they talk about next year, going back to Iceland, I jump in. Eve begins with, "Helga says next year, we can ride to Kornsá, the inland valley. We can also do the trail all the way to Blönduós."

"Next year" is all I have to hear—my favorite two words. It is my only desire, that we keep this going. They can buy horses and ship them home and ride every day in forested New England, but the riding there is nothing like the riding in Iceland, where the landscape is vast and cleared and you can see and ride for miles upon miles. And riding Icelandics at home really doesn't compare to swimming across Lake Hóp on the back of your horse. I may briefly envy the horse buying I can't partake in, but what's most important to me is riding in Iceland, staying in Thingeyrar, and being part of this group.

"Let's do that. Kornsá. Blönduós. Count me in."

2008

Horsewomen of the World

Another year missed. Three days before I am meant to leave, I need a root canal. "But I'll be able to get on the flight to Iceland?" Of course, I'm reassured. But something goes awry after the initial surgery. I have pain the next day—two days before my flight—that can only be relieved with Vicodin and gin and tonics, which are not doctor recommended, but they sooth my fear of potentially having to miss my trip. The next day, it gets worse and in a slurry mood of pain and sedatives, I do what I had feared. I cancel. What follows is a week of surgery, abscesses, and aerobic and anaerobic infections that almost get the better of me. The endodontist tells me he's only seen it once before, the infection spreading up my jaw and through my face. But I'm lucky, I'm told, because the infection could have spread to my brain.

In what was day seven in Iceland, Eve emails me a picture of the group at their dinner party the night before they leave—Allie, Viv, Eve, Sylvie, her neighbor Margot, and two other people I don't know. In the picture, they have dressed up Oli as a king in a paper crown, a red robe, and a lupine scepter.

He is smiling, patiently, in the company of what I am sure is a group of loud, laughing women. The photo is from a Nokia phone, but it must have been taken by Helga—she's not in it—and they are all mid-laugh, heads back, yukking it up without me. The email reads: "Thinking of you. Hope you're feeling better."

I've gotten over my root canal, but I'm miserable from the ordeal. My daughter is on her way to Spain for language immersion; my son is up at his college for the summer, making up credits for classes he blew off during the year. My husband suggests we take a trip, maybe to an island. As long as I can find a place to ride horses, I don't care where, I tell him. We settle on Saint Martin, the French side. I have this idea that I am going to make this the Caribbean version of my Iceland trip. All I need is a horse and some trails and a beach. I pack my helmet and boots. I'm planning on riding every day, setting up a relationship with the stables so they know me for the next five days.

I find a stable in the hills not far from our hotel, and my husband drives me there and drops me off. "This will be fun for you." He has his kind of fun that I don't care for: scuba diving and snorkeling. And I have mine.

The woman who runs the place explains it is her family's farm and they have owned it for generations. She tells me that she is twenty-four and has never lived in France and doesn't have any interest in visiting there. She is darkly tanned as if she's testing her melanin absorption. She wears riding pants with flat sneakers, no helmet. She goes braless in a tiny halter top that exposes a lot of her chest, which is oddly and badly scarred with the wavy striations of burns. I wear my boots and riding pants, helmet, a light SPF sun shirt, a sturdy athletic bra, and cover my face in white zinc oxide.

I am the only one who signed up to ride at this hour, so it's a private tour. Once we head out I ask, "What kind of horses are these?" She tells me they are typical island horses. A little this, a little that.

She asks me how much riding experience I have. I tell her about the Icelandic horses I ride every year. She hasn't heard of them and doesn't seem impressed. I don't explain it any further. It is midday and about 95 degrees with no breeze from the ocean as we head into the hills. Away from the tourist beaches, the island has an impoverished hardscrabble terrain. We trek through scrub brush and sand, prickly bushes and gnarly mangrove roots. Insects whirr and tick around my head. Lizards flick in and out of the path.

My horse is white and tall, leggy and thin. I get him into a trot, but I'm too lazy to post to it. I try a half seat but bounce around in the saddle. I pull too hard on the reins, using them to reposition myself, which is wrong, bad riding, a disservice to the horse. When we head down to the beach, she asks if I want to canter and I say, yes, of course. She leads the way and my horse picks up the canter behind her, and we wind through a series of snaky turns on the path and low hanging bows of scratchy branches where I need to duck my head. I have a hard time finding my balance. I bounce hard in the seat. I *oomph* a lot. It is no fault of the horse that I can't find its rhythm. I have narrowed my scope of interest to one breed. While I can find the rhythm of the canter on Icelandics instinctively, it doesn't translate to other horses.

When we get to the shore, I am hoping to finally have a smooth go at it on the long beach. But it is the bay side with a narrow beach. We wade into the shallow, warm, blue-green Caribbean to cool off the horses. We only go as deep as their fetlocks. My guide asks me how I like my horse, and I tell her he's a fine horse. And, he is. With all my clumsy inattentive riding and miscues, he didn't think once of acting up or being pushy with me. Through it all, he was a horse with a generous heart, looking to please me. She nods, looks fondly at him, and tells me she likes him, too.

As we walk the horses along the bay, she lights a cigarette, and after lighting it, asks if I mind. Of course not, I tell her. Though she is decades younger than I am, I feel immature in comparison, and soft. Maybe it's the visual of her scarred chest and the swagger she shows in not hiding it, of making people confront the non-pretty. She strikes me as impenetrably strong, someone who had to grow up fast, a hard won freedom. I have an affinity for these tough horsewomen. They have as much machismo as the men in their culture. And they can be found in any outpost, carving out their place in the world with their beloved horses.

She asks again if I want to canter, but I'm ready to take it slow. The sun, the smoke, the heat has put me into a torpid daze. I am sweating from head to toe. Friends jokingly call me a penguin because I walk around in flip-flops and T-shirts in the winter, like a Québécois. The tropics simply immobilize me.

"Can we just walk? I like to walk," I request, echoing Sylvie on our first trip to Iceland.

—∞—

In January, Sylvie sends an email with the dates for our trip to Helga's. In her usual curt message, she writes, "You in?" as if she pays for her emails by the word.

I think of this as starting a charge. We are all in different states: Massachusetts, Connecticut, New Jersey, Georgia. I imagine all of us looking up from working on our computers, with our sights drifting northerly, sniffing the wind like polar bears, summer is a'coming in. Other emails then start to trickle in from the group. Viv attaches a few photos of the trip from last summer. Allie uploads an entire file of 600 photos to my Dropbox. I send out a link to an island for sale off the coast of Breiðafjörður. "Can we all chip in and buy this?" I write in the subject line. It sounds like a preposterous proposal, but I mean it and I'm hoping that someone will take me up on it.

Eve sends a video link attached with the message, "What an adventure!" I open it up. It's a short film of undulating broken ice, a place (not named) where Inuit men and women lower themselves down a treacherous ice chute to the bottom of a fissure during the low tide, risking their lives to collect pails of mussels, then climbing out by rope ladder before the tide comes rushing back in and sweeps them out to sea.

I get the message. We all get the message. The ice, the Arctic sea, the scary frigid turbulent water, the cry of the skuas, the endless white nights of the true North, Thule, Thingeyrar, Iceland.

I buy my tickets. "I'm in," I type back.

BOOK III
THE TROT (BROKK)

———— ❀❀❀ ————

A two-beat diagonal gait, faster than a walk. The horse lifts a hind leg and a front leg simultaneously, and in midstride has all four of its hooves suspended off the ground.

2009

‒‒ꝏ‒‒

The Situation

In 2009 tourists are getting more plentiful and Icelandair adds an extra flight that leaves at 2:10 P.M. I happily forgo the banging turbulence over the coast of Newfoundland of the midnight flight. Halfway through the day flight, I look out of my window and notice a few scattered icebergs. Then the few become many, white dots in a dark ocean, like stars in a night sky that amass into the larger ice shelf of the tip of Greenland. From 30,000 feet, it all looks like snow-covered mountains at first, but as we fly directly over, I can see the melted ice coursing through the valleys, dumping a cloudy, sludge-like green water into the Arctic Ocean.

My father would have appreciated the sight from the comfort of this plane. Or he would have shivered at the memory. My father died in January from congestive heart failure, and since his death, my mother has taken to dithering and forgetfulness fulltime. Either grief mimics dementia, or dementia sets in quickly when your spouse of sixty-six years dies. She now gets lost when driving, so I take her keys away. She has three checkbooks hidden in random places and hasn't brought down the balance in any of them. She has been the victim of credit card scams and exorbitant fees and her debt is multiplying, so I take over her finances. I hire a woman to come into her condo three days a week to take her shopping and to bathe her. I still see her only once a week, but her conversation is reduced to a few repetitive sentences: "What day is it?" or "Did I eat lunch?" or "Where do your brothers live?"

The tall, large man sitting next to me in the aisle seat is a Texan who naturally settles in to tell me a story, his life story, whether I want to hear it or not (turns out I do, I'm always open to the stories of traveling strangers). He's sixty-four, he says, and it's his first trip to Iceland. He tells me he is half-Icelandic, and I tell him he looks it. "Yeah? Really?" He has light-blue eyes and the kind of blonde hair that doesn't turn gray or silver, but rather turns into a lighter shade of yellow. It's hair color I've only seen in Iceland. He explains he's going to meet his extended Icelandic family for the first time. His father was stationed in Iceland during WWII when he met his mother. "Oh her family didn't like that—that my mother was pregnant, that he was in the American Army. She was the black sheep of her family. After she moved with my father to the US, they never talked to her again."

After his mother died, he wrote to his long-lost relatives in Iceland, and they were eager to meet him (being of a different generation and less judgmental). He researched the history of Iceland during the war and the Allied occupation. At one point, he tells me, there were 40,000 US troops in and around Reykjavík, and the native population was only 40,000. The Icelandic women who cavorted with these soldiers were cast out, considered prostitutes. Many were left pregnant by foreign servicemen, a condition euphemistically called *Ástandið*—the situation. "Luckily my father married his Icelandic girlfriend and brought her home to Texas, and she never looked back." He might be half-Icelandic, but he acts so big-hatted Texan that I wonder what his relatives in Hafnarfjörður will make of him.

"You never know what men do during war," my mother used to say. "You can't hold them to their vows or anything like that when they're going through a war." Two of her favorite expressions were "ignorance is bliss" and "what you don't know won't hurt you." These sentiments have sustained her. I've heard them my whole life, but lately she has been more specific. "Who knows what your father did in England when he was stationed there. I wouldn't be surprised if he had a girlfriend or if he had a child over there."

Who knows what he did. But if my mother has been holding on to lifelong secrets, I wish she'd been more forthright with me earlier in her life. Am I supposed to go searching for a possible half sibling based on my mother's shoddy memory? Her doctor told me her carotid arteries are 90 percent blocked. Who knows if it's not the arteriosclerosis talking?

What We Carry with Us

O ver the past year, Iceland's economy has tanked. Three bankers and three banks are being held responsible for the financial collapse. It sounds dire, but when we arrive in Reykjavík it doesn't look like the chaos that erupted in Argentina when their system collapsed. It's a nice, orderly, Nordic collapse: there are no runs on the banks, no one is standing in long lines to withdraw cash, cars aren't being lit on fire. People did demonstrate against government corruption back in January, notably on the same day that Obama was being sworn into office and we were having our Camelot moment.

On January 20, thousands of Icelanders gathered outside the Parliament building banging on pots and pans, pelting the politicians with eggs and fish. They called it the Kitchen Revolution. That's how you get things done in Iceland, demonstrate and clean out the fridge at the same time. And it worked: the prime minister was ousted and the bankers went to jail.

The financial disaster is, literally, altering the skyline: all construction in Reykjavík has stopped. Skeletal remains of office towers stand half-finished. The much ballyhooed opera house, Harpa, was started and put on hold.

This year there are seven of us and we've split up into two Jeeps. Me, Eve, Sylvie, and Viv in one car; Allie (Eve's former business partner from Atlanta), Britt, and a new person, Pippa, in the other.

Sylvie gives me the lowdown on Pippa, who is recovering from a blood cancer. Up until her bout with cancer she was a senior VP for a financial investment firm. She told Sylvie that the stress of that job caused the cancer, so she quit. I'm guessing she's the person that needs saving this trip.

"She's a friend of a really good friend of mine who asked me if Pippa could come to Iceland with us," Sylvie says.

"It's great she realized that the stress was killing her and that she quit. I hope she gets to heal here," Eve says.

So far, from the one day I've spent with Pippa, I'd say her healing program is heavily dependent on the strength of her credit card. When we stop at Astund, she easily drops $2,000 on riding apparel and gifts, and another $1,000 at the women's wool co-op in Borgarnes. She is single-handedly reviving the Icelandic economy.

There's another conversation going on in the front seat between Sylvie and Eve. They are talking in low tones as if they don't want anyone to hear, but I am a skilled eavesdropper, able to hold a conversation with one person and simultaneously listen to another conversation. Eve's farm is in financial trouble. The costs of running the barn are "untenable: the stable manager's salary, the vet bills, the electric bills." Sylvie says, "people who board their horses should pay." Eve makes excuses for the freeloaders: "They can't afford the cost of the board and I want to be able to give it to them."

It is not only the farm: Eve and Jack's business is in trouble, too. The recession has affected everything. Eve tells Sylvie, "It'll work out, it's gonna work out, you'll see. The universe will provide. And we've got these Chinese investors interested and Jack is over there now meeting with them."

As if on cue, Eve's phone rings and it is Jack. "Hi, honeeey," Eve sings out. "We're on our way to Sibba's uncle's farm in Snæfellsnes. Yeah, they're good. Yeah, it's beautiful, you know Iceland, it's like nowhere else."

Instead of listening in on the conversation, I take out my phone and make my "pill reminder" call to my mother. As we are passing Hvalfjörður and the sun is sparkling on the bay, I hear my mother put the phone down and get her pills. Then I hear them spilling on the floor. I tell her to leave them on the floor and call one of her condo neighbors and ask for her help. Then I call the pharmacy to call the neighbor to give out directions for my mother. After many phone calls between pharmacist and neighbor, and back to my mother, it is straightened out.

In the five years we've been coming here, we're depending more and more on our cell phones and laptops. It used to be we couldn't communicate with people from home that often, especially not from the car. But the "world is too much with us" and we are spending more time in Iceland connected to home and to work. That old feeling of escaping to Iceland is disappearing. We are carrying everything in our lives along with us.

When we get off our phones, Eve is more upbeat, and her voice is louder as she tells Sylvie that Jack is making good deals over in China. "It's the law of attraction; it will all work out."

Viv has been texting with her husband. She snaps her phone shut. "Well, it's worse than I thought. Jonathan is being deployed to Iraq sooner than expected." Her son joined the army after finishing college because he could not find a job. "We knew it was coming, but we didn't know it was coming that fast."

"Oh shit, Viv," I say.

"Yeah, oh shit," she says.

But then the conversation dies. Americans can talk about the war as a generic horror, or a political travesty, but at least in my pocket of the Northeast, they seem to have difficulty talking specifically about the men and women in the armed services. We are embarrassed that our country is in the war; that people like Viv's son, who we presume has other options in life, has joined nonetheless. Maybe, for our little group, the juxtaposition of green and peaceful Iceland with the desert of Iraq would just make any conversation seem trite and petty. And the universe does not provide equally for everyone. Or rather, it is limited, picky, and fickle about its provisions. I'm not sure why no one says any of the appropriate things, or what the appropriate things are to say. Maybe there's not much you can say to a mother whose son is about to head off to a hot and deadly desert war. Still, I am embarrassed that this entire carload of chatty women can't come up with anything supportive to say and that Viv is left with our uncomfortable silence.

Once we get up to Thingeyrar, Viv and I walk every night and she talks it out. "I feel like I got punched in the stomach. I can't breathe," she tells me. "What did I do wrong? I gave my kids a typical upper middle-class upbringing, and one joins the army and the other can't get his life together. Why couldn't I get the sons who go to MIT?"

We pick up and pocket the magic red rocks down by the lake, paying extra attention to the shape and the power they might impart. We avoid the Arctic tern nests so as not to unintentionally harm them. Her walking speed is brisker, her nervous energy inexhaustible. We go the full six kilometers to the Ring Road and back. I watch over her on these walks the way she watches over me out on the trail. We walk and walk and the midnight sun follows us. And she tells me, "I have to keep this place and this sunlight with me all winter. It's going to be a long winter."

Sylvie in Love

A funny thing happens on the way to Thingeyrar this year. Sylvie falls in love. She falls oh so hard and oh so briefly, in Snæfellsnes, where else, the mystical Jules Vernian center of the earth and, according to new age mythology, the center of a feminine energy vortex that causes supernatural phenomena. How appropriate.

In Borgarnes, we meet up with two of Eve's Icelandic friends, Sibba and Ljotur, and we follow behind their van as they lead us to the peninsula of Snæfellsnes. Sibba's uncle Ólof owns, what else, an enormous horse farm here. We drive west down the straight, two-lane road that cuts through the valley, acres of bright green farmland on either side, a lonely farmhouse or out building dotting the otherwise empty fields. To our left, the farmland ends at the ocean; to the right, the fields back up to tall cliffs etched with silvery waterfalls. Straight ahead, but miles and miles in the distance, is Snæfellsjökull, a purple-hued, snowcapped glacial mountain. We have never been to Snæfellsnes before, though it is not far off the Ring Road.

Viv says, "This place feels different."

Eve says, "Yeah, what is it about this place?"

"That mountain in the distance makes it look like Shangri-La."

"It casts a different light on everything," says Viv. "It's serene."

We meet Uncle Ólof in the driveway and we start with the introductions. All seven of us. Allie, who is friendly and forthright, begins by telling him her name and sticking out her hand to shake, so we all follow suit. But by the fifth person, we all wish it would stop, exhausted by the introductions and sure the polite Ólof wants to bolt. But he is Sibba's uncle, so he gives us a tour of his farm.

He is a tall, lean, elderly man with a handsome weathered face. He has courtly manners, like a rare and long-lost breed of gentleman. Naturally, his

English is perfect with that utterly charming Icelandic lilt. He has been an aeronautical engineer, a businessman, lived all over the world, including Connecticut, and in his retirement bought this farm.

We tromp all around his farm, following him single file over the rocky tussocks. But Sylvie, like an alpha mare, quickly pulls up front and has a conversation with Ólof that the rest of us can't hear, though we can hear she is making him laugh. He shows us his prized pregnant mares out in the fields and explains how he is building up his breeding stock. He owns eighty horses. Sylvie sticks close to his side. When he takes us into a barn full of shiny new tractors and farm equipment, Sylvie raises her eyebrows and whispers to us while he is getting on a tractor, "He likes big toys. He likes spending his money on big machines."

It is a typical summer day in Iceland: cloudy with intermittent rain, then head-splittingly bright and sunny for a minute; then a fog rolls in from the sea, enveloping us briefly before settling in around the snow at the top of Snæfellsjökull. When the fog lifts, we whisper to each other in astonishment, "Wow, oh wow, oh my, oh wow." I feel as if a spell has befallen us that makes us see only beauty—the sea is a glassy cobalt blue; the famed volcanic mountain is wreathed in wispy clouds; the farmland is a deep and verdant green. When Iceland is green in the summer, it is a rich, bright color-of-life green that your senses can barely take in. Your lungs expand as you breathe it in, full of extra oxygen.

It must be all this oxygen that gets to Sylvie. While the rest of us are being stirred by the mystical, seduced by nature, Sylvie is basically hooking up. After the walk, Ólof invites us all up to the second floor of the barn for coffee. It is a sign of a rich farm when there is not only a full-sized kitchen in the barn, but an apartment for the barn manager. The kitchen also has a picture window overlooking the indoor arena where we watch a trainer with her horse—it is a very nice farm indeed. While Ólof sets up the coffee maker, we watch as Sylvie works it.

She gushes on about the farm, "Oh the view, oh the horses, oh the tidal island." One minute they are discussing a silver dun horse Sylvie has taken a liking to, the next minute she asks, "Can we come back next year?"

This is forward of her, but I like what she's doing, and I always like those promising words, "next year."

"Of course," he says. It is hard to read if he is bewildered by her, amused, or just unfailingly polite. The coffee is poured and so is the heated fresh milk, a rich yellowy cream from the neighboring farm.

"Oh this milk is the best," Sylvie says. "Oh this coffee is divine." Sylvie drinks three cups of coffee and can't stop talking and flirting with him. She jumps up when the coffee part of the tour is over to help Ólof clean up, as if she has already moved in and is hosting our visit with him, and we are the ungainly guests who look politely at the family photos on the wall and the books on the coffee table.

As we go back out to look at his horses in the fields, Sylvie hangs over the fence and picks out the horse she wants to ride next year, a dappled silver mare.

"How about that one?" she asks.

"No, that horse is slow and old," Ólof explains.

"Then that's the horse for me!"

She catches him off guard with her honest humor, never one for false bravado, and he sincerely appears to be enjoying her company, preferring her company over ours. We are the stepchildren getting in the way.

He has more to tell us about the farm and points out a few horses he hopes will go to Landsmót next year. The dark bay is an 8.9 in tölt; the palomino a 9.0 in pace. We make noisy sounds of being impressed. He isn't just a farmer; he is a serious breeder. Landsmót is the biennial competition, the gold standard of horse shows, where the finest horses in the country are rated. Like Holar, it is for insiders of the Icelandic horse world, which we like to consider ourselves. Though back home a few more Icelandic horse farms have opened up, particularly out west, it is still a rare specialty interest horse breed. But out of all of us, only Eve has gone to Landsmót, and that was in the late nineties with Jack and one of the original horse importers. "There's lots of pageantry and singing," she told us, "you sit outside on the grass in the rain and whatever. You eat this dried haddock with butter and drink beer. You can't believe how good it tastes. It seems to go with the rain and the horse show."

Saying goodbye to Ólof, Sylvie trails behind and we wait for her in the car. When she gets in, she is humming, quite pleased with herself. "It's all arranged. We're coming back next year and spending two days before going to Helga's. He's going to provide the horses and we're riding out to the tidal island."

"How romantic," we tease her.

"Was I that obvious?"

"Sylvie, you were hot stuff!" Eve says.

"You're all invited, too. You can thank me now."

And it does seem like a great plan. Two days in Snæfellsnes, Uncle Ólof's farm, the ride to the same tidal island that is in one of the sagas.

Sylvie noisily does her intake of air. "He was soooo handsome, wasn't he?"

"He was."

"I don't know what came over me. It was the coffee talking. I must have had six cups."

"Three."

"Only three? But I had a double espresso at the roadside Kaffitar—my heart is racing." She's quiet for a few seconds.

"He has a wife, you know," she says cheerily.

"And you have a husband."

Sylvie thinks about this for a while. "You don't know me, I'm a terrible flirt. I make such trouble sometimes." She screeches, pleased with herself, and then falls silent, leaving us to wonder what trouble she made before that she is referring to.

When we reach Helga's, it is the first thing Sylvie talks about, while standing in the driveway, before we even bring our luggage into the guesthouse.

"Helga, we went to this Uncle Ólof's farm. He has eighty horses, over a thousand hectares, whatever that translates to. And he has a barn just for his tractors and other machines. He likes his big machines, you know, he's one of those men with their big toys . . . ha! And next year, we're going to ride there for two days before we come up here. There's this tidal island . . ."

Helga takes it all in with a wise, bemused look—Sylvie's enthusiasm for the man, his farm, and horses.

"It looks like you are a little in love with him, my friend," Helga says, slyly prodding her.

Sylvie lets out her parrot's screech. "Ha, you know me so well. I'm such a flirt."

"I guess you are."

"But he's married," Sylvie admits.

"Uh-huh, and so are you."

"I don't know what came over me. I was out of control, wasn't I?"

We chime in:

"You were smitten," I say.

"You were hot stuff, Sylvie," Eve says.

"Sheesh, she pushed us all out of the way so she could get close to him on the trail," Allie says.

Sylvie shakes her head. "You know what? There are all different kinds of love. Maybe this is one of those romantic friendships, okay? Let's call it that."

It could be Sylvie's caffeine level was near toxicity and that made her so forthright. And it could have been Ólof's handsomeness or his hectares of green valley and his oh so many horses. But I like to think it was a spell cast by mystical Snæfellsnes, a center of the feminine energy vortex, a source of supernatural phenomena. And that at a pivotal point in their dalliance, there was a moment of enchantment as the fog lifted and the sun broke through and the ice-covered mountain seemed to be smiling on us all.

Am I starting to believe in all this? The more time I spend in Iceland, the more I like to hold it as a place in my mind where reality and magic are conflated, and where worlds I don't know of, lives beyond empirical reach, are possible.

The Herd Changes, the Herd Charges

D isa isn't with us this year. She is living in Berlin with a rock musician. "Disa is in love," Helga tells us over dinner the first night. "And she left her horses here."

"Disa in love?" I can't imagine it. She always said she traveled so much, she would have to find a man like those little bottle of shampoos, that she could pack up in her suitcase.

"Yes, it happened finally. She was at a rock concert in Reykjavík and she was near the stage dancing . . . you know how she dances? It's hard not to notice Disa when she dances. She's a wild dancer and makes these big movements and the guitar player noticed her, and the rest is history, as they say. She moved to Germany with him."

Disa has been replaced by Frieda, a serious, petite German woman, only twenty-two years old, one of Helga's interns from Holar. When we first meet her in the barn, we ask her questions all at once, barraging her, as is our way. She gets flustered and takes a step back, looking to Helga for help. She later tells Helga she has too much work to do and can't join us for dinner.

And our first dinner is with Helga and Oli, who has cooked a welcoming feast: leg of lamb, boiled and buttered potatoes, salad, and peas. Oli calls it "the typical Sunday dinner" when he was growing up. Pippa helps herself to a stingy portion of only the salad and peas. Unlike many Americans who will proudly tell you right off that they are a vegetarian and vehemently express their complete distain for carnivores, the British Pippa waits to be asked. And then, all she says, is that she no longer desires any animal or animal product, that she's a vegan.

Pippa hasn't said much at all so far. She has that stereotypical British reserve that I generally only see in movies, and whether she is approving or disapproving, she gives you the same reaction: the merest of smiles, which dissolves in a few seconds. You have no idea what she's thinking. But being a typical BBC and Masterpiece Theatre devotee, tamping down my tendency toward Anglophilia isn't an option. And it doesn't help that Pippa looks straight out of one of the shows I like to watch—like she's the aunt of one of those beautiful, but bedeviled-by-love young heroines, who turns to her aunt for sage advice and is bustled away by a distracting tour of the continent to get over the perpetrating cad. She even has the received pronunciation thing going on. I think to hell with my usual tendency to be cautious with fast friendships. I am eager to befriend her. She will have lots of dry, witty perceptions of life to impart while we laugh over drinks or tea. I can't wait to say, "My friend, Pippa."

But so far, she's impenetrable. My conversations with her end abruptly in hard silences as soon as it's her turn to ask me what I do for a living, what I like to eat. Her quick little smiles evaporate as soon as they appear, and I'm left wondering if I imagined them. She is traveling with the wrong group if she wanted a week of silent retreat. I try to channel my inner Eve, and chalk this up to her recent bout of cancer and a meditative state of mind. Maybe she's just happy to be alive, happy to be in Iceland and she is finding her inner peace.

Mares give birth in the fields here, unaided, unsheltered, without a vet on call for medical intervention. Foals have to adapt to the environment, and horses have evolved so that foals stand within minutes of their birth. A foal is summed up immediately upon birth for its gait and size. And later a yearling will be evaluated again for defect, whether in conformation or attitude, or anything that compromises its usefulness. An Icelandic farmer has no compunction about weeding out the weaker horses. Horsemeat is still eaten in Iceland.

A set of adorable twins were born two weeks earlier on the farm. They are very small and Helga wonders out loud if they can serve as children's ponies. What she doesn't say out loud is that she is equally weighing the possibility of selling them to a butcher.

This is hard for our group to understand. Back home, we give every animal a chance. Dogs have $5,000 surgeries for hip dysplasia or $10,000 cancer treatments. There are retirement farms that take in lame, sick, too-old-to-ride horses with their list of prescribed medicines like someone in a nursing home. Most horse owners I know can't put their horses down and will spend all their savings so that their horse can hobble out the rest of their days in a field. But horse rescue sanctuaries in Iceland aren't a thing. Animal cruelty is considered despicable for sure, but saving hurt, damaged, or very old, unproductive horses is deemed crueler, and selfish.

At the same time, Icelanders are very protective of their horses. One of the benefits of banning entry of other horses for all these centuries is that they are disease-free. Horses don't need to be inoculated in Iceland because there are no equine diseases in the country. They have strict rules for visitors who ride while in Iceland. If you are visiting a horse farm, used leather boots, gloves, helmets, or saddles cannot be brought in. If you must bring them in, you need a vet's certification that they have been disinfected properly. Though lately I have noticed that this rule is lax, and it is basically the honor system for visitors. I am never checked at customs anymore.

After dinner, we walk out to the pastures with the mares and the foals. I have been told, we all have, that we should leave the foals alone to avoid imprinting the human touch on horses at so young an age.

It's hard to resist petting the foals with their brand new bodies on stilt legs. We scratch their ears, touch their little withers, then quickly pull our hands away as if guilty of horse coddling. We wander over to a less crowded pasture and Allie takes a bunch of pictures of us. She has us pose in a line, one way and then another. As we are posing and she is taking photos, we hear a growing thundering of hooves. A herd of young horses, maybe thirty three-to-four-year-olds, are galloping toward us.

"Is this a stampede?"

"I don't know."

We can't move; we stand transfixed as they gallop full speed toward us.

"Are they going to run us down?" I know, from my extensive reading of National Park pamphlets, never to run from bears, wolves, or moose. I'm a little less sure about a rambunctious herd of three-year-old horses.

Allie, always sensing a photo opportunity, focuses her camera on the horses.

They get closer and closer, gaining speed, and we keep asking each other, "Should we move?" But we don't. We stand frozen together, in awe, while Allie continues taking pictures.

The horses get about ten feet from us, and suddenly veer off right and left around us, like a school of fish. Then, having shown us what they can do, they circle back to us at a slower pace, curious about us. They move in between us and close up tight against us, so that we are squeezed in by their bodies. They nuzzle our jackets, nip at the pockets, snort in our faces, imprinting us into the herd.

Stallions and Mares, Oh My

Summer is mating season on the farm, and the horses, no surprise, do it au natural. No turkey-baster artificial insemination for these mares. And though the farmers may let them breed and birth naturally, they still choose the sire carefully. They bring a prize-winning stallion to each farm and fence him in with a herd of mares.

So one evening after we've put our horses out to pasture, a truck pulls up to Helga's and backs into the driveway. We can hear a horse kicking the sides of the wooden trailer. Gunnar and the other men unlatch the back of the truck and slowly go in and carefully bring out the stallion on a halter and lead rope. It looks like a dangerous job.

The black bay stallion comes out stomping his hooves, throwing his head around, nostrils flaring, neighing with a nervous wild energy. He is ragged looking, crazed and skinny like a coke-addled rock star, like Mick Jagger in his heyday, full of sexual swagger. Helga explains to us that he is a very highly ranked stallion who spends his summer touring farms. She has ninety mares, so the stallion gets a week with thirty mares each, and rotates with another thirty, and then another thirty. This is the stallion's life for the three months of his summer tour.

"Poor guy, strung out on too much sex," Sylvie says.

But Helga says, "Yes, but it's not an easy life for stallions. They spend their lives separated from other horses except for mating season. It's a very lonely life."

Eve says even on her small farm in the Berkshires, her stallion leads a desperate solitary life. "My Glitfaxi, he spends all day in his stall kicking at the walls. He spends his time outdoors alone in the pasture, except for the few times I let him mate with my mares. It's sad to watch. He's like a kept man confined to solitary with the occasional conjugal visit. Only the barn manager can ride him."

Sitting at the dinner table that night we have a perfectly framed view out the window at the unfolding mating scene. The stallion goes from one mare to the next, barely taking time to graze in between trysts.

"No wonder he's so skinny."

"Doesn't he get exhausted?"

"He's quite good at his job."

We're exhausted simply from watching all this rampant hormonal activity. Periodically we put our forks down to declare, "He's still at it."

When he isn't mating, he's watching over his harem. When Allie goes up to the fence to take pictures of the new foals, he is immediately suspicious. He quickly trots over to the fence and neighs threateningly in her face.

Allie comes back in. "Sheesh, not only is he horny, he's possessive. He's got thirty mares to keep him busy and he gets mad at me for taking a picture."

Viv says, "I was watching. He saw you from way over on the other side of the field. Stallions are super vigilant. You could see his head swivel almost the entire 360 degrees."

Helga comes over and leaves a dessert with us that Oli made: a still-warm marriage cake with berries that melt into the buttery crust and the ever-present bowl of fresh whipped cream. Eve takes a tiny piece of cake. Then another tiny piece, then another. She licks the back of her fork. I go back for a second slice, not tiny, and extra whipped cream, heaping. It's only the fourth day and I can't fit into the jeans I wore on the plane and I can't stop helping myself to seconds or thirds and an extra scoop after all that.

Now the stallion is closer to the fence, closer to our window, and he mounts another mare. But the cake has taken our interest away and by this point we're like ho-hum, horse sex, is that all this guy ever does? Pass the pot of tea, please.

Except that one horse, a pretty white mare, goes down after he is finished with her. "Is she hurt?" Eve rushes to the window and we crowd around her, staring out. "She's not getting up."

"We need to tell Helga," Viv says.

The stallion is hanging over the mare, sniffing her, nudging her gently with his nose. Suddenly, to us, this is an equine love story and we go all gushy, anthropomorphizing our horsey hero.

"Oh, will you look at that."

"I think we should tell Helga," Viv says.

"He's making sure she's alright."

"C'mon honey, get up," Eve says. "She's the love of his life."

"Yeah, the others were just procreational flings. Tell her, they meant nothing."

"Look, he's upset she's hurt."

He keeps nudging her, and the mare doesn't move. She is lifeless and we slowly realize the mare may have died during mating, which happens more often with natural mating than we like to think about. There is something called horse rape, when the mare isn't ready and her hormones haven't peaked, and the stallion forces himself on her.

"What's he doing now?" The stallion butts his head against her as if trying to bring her back to life.

"He's grieving," Eve says. "He's heartsick."

"We need to tell Helga," Viv says again, more forcefully this time.

The stallion stands over the mare, nudging her every so often—and then, sure she's dead, he struts up to another mare.

"Oh," Eve says, and then, "Oh, my."

We watch incredulously as he mindlessly, instinctively mounts the next closest mare while the dead white one is only a few feet away.

"Sheesh, how do you like that!" Allie says.

"Yep. It's a line up, girls—next!" Sylvie says.

"I'm telling Helga that there's something wrong with the mare." Eve runs over to Helga's house. She quickly returns and says, "Gunnar will take care of it."

In about ten minutes, we watch through the window as Gunnar drives his tractor out to the pasture and gets out to confirm that the mare is indeed dead. He then climbs back up and unceremoniously scoops her up into the front loader.

Except for Brittany and Pippa—who remains almost wordless throughout dinner, dessert, and window-watching stallion sex—all of us are in long-term marriages. And this scene gives us pause.

"I mean, that stallion didn't slow down for a second."

"Within the fifteen minutes it took Gunnar to take away that poor mare, he mounted three other mares."

"I often wonder how long it would take my husband to find someone new if I died."

We've all seen it before—the devoted husband who barely makes it out of his dear wife's memorial service before hitching up to someone new. Even in assisted living places, if a guy comes in still somewhat intact, he has a selection of women to choose from.

"I think Jack wouldn't wait long at all. He would be dating within a month."

"My husband can't stand to be alone," Allie admits.

We shake our heads in disappointed agreement, equinizing our husbands.

I am reminded how often my husband says, "I would die without you. My life would be over." I believe it every time he says it, but the odds are he would get on with his life rather quickly. Testosterone kicks up after divorce and, depending on age, after a wife's death. He would search for another mare, intentionally or not, or more likely one solo mare would sniff him out.

But on the other side, how many women unequivocally state that if they lost their husband, through divorce or death, they would never marry again? They might date, but they wouldn't marry. All of us who are married in this group have been married for a long time and, intentionally or not, we've played an acquiescing female role. Maybe for us equality in marriage happens later in life when you've seen enough versions of yourself, through enough decades, that you circle back to your original selfhood. Maybe our break away, our heading to Iceland as a group every year, is our reclamation of self outside of marriage, an optional test drive of what we would do if we were no longer married. This is how we would live without men.

Starting Horses

The three-year-old horse walks into the barn for the first time in his life. He is encouraged to go in from Frieda, who walks behind the horse and sweeps her arms upward in a large V as if funneling the air in a narrow path. He enters alone, unforced, though there is an older horse in front of him to put him at ease. He is neither calm nor anxious, but alert to the newness. He is hearing and feeling his shoeless hooves on the floor of the barn for the first time. His vision is narrowed from the wide expanse of open land, the only view he has ever known, to the long hallway of stalls in the stable.

Until recently, most Icelandic stables didn't have separate individual stalls. A few of the old farms still around have only a large space in the barn, a cave-like pit with dirt floors that horses get herded into if the weather is really bad. Otherwise, horses are left outside. Helga's barn is new and state-of-the-art because she is a trainer and breeder: the aisles are wide with two dozen stalls, larger than American standard size stalls and always a foot and a half deep, also an Icelandic standard, so that horses step down into them and up out of them. Often the horses aren't alone in these stalls, either; sometimes two or three horses are together in a stall. The idea is that they should always live like a herd.

Inside the barn, Frieda is still directing the young horse with her arm movements, without touching him. She waves her hands in such a way that she cuts him off from going right or left and he has no choice but to go into the stall where they have thrown in a fleck of hay. This kind of movement she makes is the first groundwork exercise. By making the horse move without touching him, she has begun to establish a relationship.

"This is Grettir," Frieda tells us.

Grettir's face is splashed white. A splashed white horse has blue eyes with the outer ring of the blue being a lighter blue, almost white. This is a common genetic trait in some Skagafjörður horses, so it's possible Grettir's sire was from the valley southeast of here. Blue eyes are not a hindrance to a horse's sight, and it doesn't make them any more susceptible to disease, but blue-eyed horses used to be called ghost horses. It was not a desired trait. That is not the case anymore—there is a growing population of horse buyers who like the look of the blue-eyed Skagafjörður horses and seek them out.

Frieda lets Grettir eat the hay for a few minutes, letting him acclimate to the stall; eating hay will relax him. Before he lifts his head up from the hay, Frieda slips into the stall and for another few minutes she lets him get used to having her in the stall with him, without making any demands on him.

Frieda's body movements mimic a horse in a herd. Her head is down, and she is not looking in Grettir's eyes. She is studiously nonconfrontational, trying to be emotionally neutral, setting up her presence without asking anything from the young horse yet. Humans are the predators, horses are the prey. If we want to enter their herd, we need to be less predatory.

Once Grettir looks up from his hay and notices Frieda, he is curious. He has an innate boldness that was evident from his first step into the barn, that "hello world" look. Frieda's position remains nonthreatening. She keeps her eyes down and her shoulders lowered, doing everything possible so that all her movements are nonaggressive. Trainers no longer "break" a horse, that old horrible way where out of ignorance or sheer cruelty they would beat a horse into submission—the idea being to break its spirit so that it feared humans. Now trainers "start" horses gently by mimicking herd behavior. Before establishing leadership with a horse, they establish trust, so that the horse willingly wants to please.

Finally, when Frieda feels the horse is comfortable, she reaches out to touch his flanks, where horse skin is the thickest. "There are two blind spots on a horse: between and above his eyes and his forehead and his tail. So, to put a horse at ease, you never want to start touching him in those places," Frieda says.

Once he accepts her touch on his flank, she moves her hand down his back. Then she pets him under his mane. She narrates what she is doing. "I'm getting him used to my hand. He's been loose in the mountains with his mother. I want to make sure his first contact with humans is pleasant." She slips him a treat.

She moves slowly to introduce him to the human touch, but frankly he acts like a circus pony. He takes to the touch as if he was born to be petted. It makes me wonder if carloads of tourists haven't been fawning over him in the fields, indulging him, establishing his first contact with humans without his trainer's knowledge. He is extraordinarily friendly. He's interested in us, too, thrusting his head forward so we can pet him, bypassing Frieda and nudging us, nibbling our coat buttons. We're not sure if it's okay to pet him, but his head is in our faces. One of us mistakenly goes to pet the space between his eyes, even though Frieda told us that's his blind spot. He's such a bold and friendly horse that even that move doesn't seem to faze him. We pet him and make cooing noises that I know, just know, we shouldn't be making. We can't help but remark on him with a chorus of "How cute, how friendly, how sweet is this guy!"

We make all kinds of generalizations about the Icelandic horse based on Grettir. "Look how smart he is. How willing to make contact with humans. How unafraid he is. This is why Icelandics are so special."

But Frieda knows better. "Each horse is completely different, even Icelandic horses. They aren't all this friendly at the start." She watches as he nuzzles our coats, going from me to Eve to Sylvie to Allie. "And perhaps he's a little too friendly. Sometimes they get pushy when they get too used to humans so quickly. Sometimes the quiet shy horse is easier to start than the friendly one. When they are this friendly, it can be hard to establish boundaries and gain respect."

Frieda introduces a lead rope she has made into a big loop. "I'm just going to see if he'll let me rub this rope on him." She runs it lightly over his back and you can see his skin twitching that same little shudder that would shoo a fly off his back. A horse's skin is one big hypersensitive epidermis canvas. He doesn't resist Frieda's touching his back or his underbelly or his tail, so she continues to rub the rope on him, letting it drop a little onto him to see if he shies from it when it comes at him unexpectedly. But he doesn't shy, and within no time Frieda slips the rope over his head and around his neck, while simultaneously slipping him a treat from her pocket. The giving of treats is consistent and instantaneous.

Within fifteen or twenty minutes she has taken a completely young, untrained horse and put a rope harness over his head. And he has been willing and curious the whole time. She stops, gives him more treats from her pocket, and takes off the rope halter. "That's enough for the first day," she says. "You give the horse fifteen minutes of attention a day. You want to keep him interested, keep him involved, so the next time you approach him, he wants to see you. And you have established the basis of trust."

I am falling in love with Grettir, and I do believe it's mutual. He's nibbling my buttons and jacket a lot more than he's nibbling the others' clothes. I think we're establishing a relationship. This is how love is across and over the stall gate. I like his blue eyes, his friendliness, his boldness. I am plotting out the possibility of buying him. I wonder where I can keep him in my area. How I can afford him. How I can make time for him.

Frieda opens the stall gate and Grettir walks out to join the others in the herd. "During the winter, the interns will start to really train him. This first summer is pretraining. We just get the horses used to us."

I ask Frieda when he will be up for sale.

"In two or three years. He needs two more years of training at least; they need to be five years plus before they're sold. It takes longer to train Icelandics because of the extra gaits. And I think the horse should really be six, if the rider is not very experienced. In the last year we try to make them bombproof. We try to desensitize them to external noises. We put them through a series of loud noises, popped balloons, people running at them screaming, loud sudden tractor engines, everything we can think of to make sure they remain calm in the face of the unknown."

In three years, he could be mine. I could have my very own horse that has been born and trained in this perfect horse world. I could bring home a little piece of Thingeyrar with me. But what kind of life could I give an imported Icelandic horse? A spot in a tight stall in an average American barn where I would pay almost the same monthly price as my mortgage, and where it would never be free to roam in the mountains? That is always the rub for me owning

ABOVE: The road to Thingeyrar. *Courtesy of A. Westphal.* LEFT: The first year, when we rode as a dozen. *From the author's collection.* BELOW: The black basalt church of Thingeyrarkirkja. *Courtesy of A. Westphal.*

ABOVE: Up close with the young horses. *Courtesy of B. Saadeh.* BELOW: Moldi (earth-colored) to the left; Thoka (misty-colored) to the right. *Courtesy of B. Saadeh.*

The barn is like a church, a sanctuary. *From the author's collection.*

ABOVE: The horses run. *Courtesy of A. Westphal.* BELOW: Mares and foals and the Vatnsdalsa. *From the author's collection.*

ABOVE: The view from the guest house. *From the author's collection.* BELOW: Snaefellsnes, the mystical Jules Vernian center of the earth. *Courtesy of A. Westphal.*

ABOVE: A very recent newborn with mare in Snaefellsnes. *Courtesy of A. Westphal.* BELOW: Blue-eyed boy, Snaefellsnes. *Courtesy of A. Westphal.*

The Nights of Magical Thinking. *From the author's collection.*

ABOVE: Lake Thingeyrar and the nesting grounds of Arctic terns. *Courtesy of A. Westphal.* BELOW: The Kingdom of Horse. *From the author's collection.*

ABOVE: Facing the Wild North. *Courtesy of A. Westphal.* BELOW: Volcanic black beach on the shores of Thingeyrasandur. *From the author's collection.*

Is this a stampede? *Courtesy of A. Westphal.*

ABOVE: They gallop toward us and get within ten feet, before suddenly veering off. *Courtesy of A. Westphal.* BELOW: They circle back to us at a slower pace, curious about us. *Courtesy of A. Westphal.*

New to the world. *From the author's collection.*

ABOVE: Taped-up boots for the ride through Lake Hop. *Courtesy of A. Westphal.* BELOW: At Illugastadir, now an eider sanctuary, looking toward the West Fjords. *From the author's collection.*

ABOVE: Riding through fields of lupine. *Courtesy of A. Westphal.* RIGHT: The little mare that could. *Courtesy of A. Westphal.*

ABOVE: Women on the verge of the Greenland Sea. *Courtesy of A. Westphal.* LEFT: Me and Sveppur at the Greenland Sea. *Courtesy of A. Westphal.*

ABOVE: The long trek home. *Courtesy of A. Westphal.* BELOW: The Golden Summerland of Thingeyrar. *Courtesy of A. Westphal.*

an Icelandic horse. It goes beyond the issues of cost and time commitment. It goes to the very heart and soul of an Icelandic horse, especially if I can't find it a home on a proper horse farm that knows how to treat the breed. Do I really want to remove this beautiful creature from its beautiful natural home, to risk exposing it to all of the diseases horses are subject to in New England? The Lyme, the Coggins, the Strangles, the sweet itch and other allergies. If, by chance, they eat an acorn or two among the millions that scatter on the ground every fall, it can cause kidney failure. And then there are everyday plants that one never thinks of as being poisonous: Eve's first Icelandic horse died in her field from eating red maple leaves. The environment is so hostile to them it hardly seems fair.

Years ago, I met a woman at Eve's farm who was temporarily boarding her newly imported Icelandic horse there. She was in her sixties and had been recently diagnosed with an autoimmune disease. She told me she had never owned a horse, but always wanted to. The horse she imported from Iceland was ten, which is old to be exported to the States. It was from a farm in the Skagafjörður region of Iceland. The horse's name was Gaska, which means playful and willing. When the horse was still boarded at Eve's, the barn manager let me ride her. The owner didn't have to know. Out on the trail for the first time in a New England autumn, everything was new to Gaska—the feel and the sound of leaves under her hooves, the large deciduous trees above, the odd moving wild turkeys in her path. She took in these new surroundings with a calm curiosity. She was a perfect horse: smart and intuitive with four smooth gaits. When Gaska left Eve's farm, the owner, who lived in Connecticut, kept her in a stable near me where she was the only Icelandic in the barn.

The woman's illness worsened, and she hardly rode Gaska. I reached out to her several times to ask, but she would not let me ride Gaska. Nor would she let me lease her from her. I asked many times. She waited all those years to own a horse and even though she couldn't ride her, she wasn't going to share her. Years later, I drove by the farm and stopped to see if Gaska was still there. She was. I was told the woman still owned her, though the horse hadn't been ridden in years. I found Gaska turned out in the paddock in the hot July sun. Her head was down, her back sagged; she looked bedraggled and dull. No energy, no spirit. The term for a horse like that is *turnip*. Lifeless, head stuck in the ground. No interest in other horses or people. It was a sad fate for an Icelandic horse that had been taken from the Skagafjörður valley for the fleeting pleasure of an American woman who wanted a horse.

2010

Annus Horribilis

Iceland is a mess in 2010. The financial meltdown in Iceland is all over the news, even in the States, where the media loves to point out that Iceland jailed the three bankers responsible for the crash, while in our country the bankers got raises. Then in May the volcanic eruption of Eyjafjallajökull halts European air traffic for weeks, curtailing tourism and causing more financial loss. T-shirts that shout: "Don't fuck with Iceland: we may not have cash but we have ash," run a brisk business. Oddly, bad news brings Iceland into global focus, and journalists and the travel industry take notice: What is this place, Iceland?

But the worst news of all, from my equine-centric view—an item that doesn't make international news—is that a horse flu has been brought into the country by a German trainer. Yes, they can track it down to the very person who caused it—though she doesn't go to jail.

And the unthinkable has happened. Horses never exposed to any equine viruses have now been exposed and it has left most of the horse population incapacitated. We don't know what we'll find when we get to Helga's.

By the time we land in Iceland, Eve and Sylvie are falling apart, too. Eve's farm is officially for sale. "We put it up last week," she says.

For the first time, Allie is driving instead of Eve. Allie is also talking on her cell phone, calling up each of her kids, asking them what they're doing today, and steering with two fingers on her left hand, while the other three fingers hold a licorice wand. We take a wrong turn out of Reykjavík, and we wind up near Mosfellbær. Allie keeps talking on the phone with one of her kids, "A game? Today? I thought that wasn't until Sunday?" as she manages to back up on an exit ramp, do a U-turn, keep the licorice balanced with her three fingers, and continue the conversation going at home. She is a can-do girl.

Finally, she hangs up, and I can breathe again and stop watching the road.

"Maybe it won't sell," Sylvie says to Eve about her farm.

"Or maybe someone will buy it and keep it as a horse farm and we can keep the therapy program afloat. I'm worried about the kids." Eve worked hard over the last year to get her farm certified for equine-assisted therapy. They have half a dozen kids, mostly with autism, enrolled already.

"Maybe we could *all* chip in and buy it and keep it as a horse farm. If we got four or five people. We could do that," I suggest.

As the idea quickly takes shape in my head, I plot it out. I can cut back to three days a week at work, leaving me with four days a week up at the farm. Like Sylvie when she first moved up there, I'd make the transition slowly from Connecticut to the Berkshires. My son graduated college in May and lives in Brooklyn; my daughter is in college. It is time for me to move on and be where I want to be—in the Berkshires. We could sell our house, find a cheap apartment to live in for the days of the week when my husband and I are working in New Haven. He could come up Friday night, leave early Monday morning. We could make it some kind of collective, cooperative horsey commune. It could be done; it could be fun. We could all own Eve's Icelandic horse farm together. We could keep the therapy program. We could make it work.

Sylvie jumps on board. "We could! We could all chip in and buy it." She's squeaking with delight at the idea. And it gets me going even more.

"We could set it up like one of those intentional group living places. There are a lot of communities where people do that. They share living expenses; but they have their own area to live in. There is plenty of room in that house. "

"This is a great idea. I love this idea," Sylvie says. "Margot could be one of the other people. She is a therapeutic trainer. She would be interested."

I offer up a number. "If I sold my house, I could come up with a couple hundred thousand." In the back of my mind is the nagging feeling about leaving my mother behind, not to mention relegating my husband to a small, shitty apartment five days a week because his livelihood is in New Haven, while I live the horsewoman's life up in the country.

"I might be able to come up with $100,000 out of my retirement fund," Sylvie says.

To Eve, that's chump change. With a few ominous words, she dashes all our spur-of-the-moment, admittedly in the infancy stage, change of life plans: "We owe the Chinese a lot of money. Millions." She makes it sound like some gang is going to kneecap them if they don't cough up the dough. "We need the money from the farm to pay off our debt."

Allie stays mum because she knows their business and knows the Chinese partners she is referring to.

Sylvie and I remain quiet, too. We can't come up with millions. We've never known millions. Pippa could, but she doesn't offer anything. Thankfully, too. I would not want to share a horse farm with her.

We are only five this year: Me, Eve, Sylvie, Allie, and Pippa. "Five is the perfect number of people," Sylvie says, cheerfully. "Let's not forget that. Five." But it doesn't feel perfect.

For one, I am missing Viv. She went to meet her son who is on furlough in Texas after eight months in Iraq. She emails me about what it's like to see him: they take him out to a restaurant and he will only sit at a table where he has full view of the room, meaning a corner spot where he can have his back to the wall. He's vigilant every time a person walks in, Viv writes, and every fork or knife that mistakenly drops on the floor makes him flinch.

And two, the idea of Pippa being my new best friend is not panning out. During the year, we all send each other emails, passing along pictures or articles about Iceland, cheerful reminders of summers past and promises of summers to come. She never once returned the friendly gesture, never once commented. More troubling is that she didn't say hello to me at the airport. I said, "Hi, Pippa!" and she ducked into her bag to look for something, like a third-rate spy. And, now in the car, she never answers me when I ask her a question. She pretends she doesn't hear. I have to repeat myself three times, only to finally get her reaction: that two-second upturn of her lips that I used to tell myself was a benevolent, if mysterious, smile, but which now looks an awful lot like a passing flick of impatience, or worse, intolerance.

I know she's only one-fifth of the company this year, but, unlike Sylvie, I'm wishing we had more people with us—the math is so much better. I'd rather have eight people, so that Pippa was only one-eighth of the company (and she could travel in a second car). I would take any of the oddballs Eve invited in the past to save their horse-deprived souls. But I remind myself that while Pippa has all the advantages of wealth, more so than anyone on these trips, she doesn't have the ace in the hole, health. She hasn't passed the five-year mark without cancer to label herself officially in remission. She may have more on her mind than social niceties and being my friend.

The other person missing is Britt. "She grew up," Sylvie says. "She's twenty and at U Mass. Holar is no longer on her horizon. And you know what Helga said about her? She said Brittany would never get into Holar. She's not tough enough. Those Holar girls are made of steel. Helga never forgot the time Britt got scared on her horse and started to cry. You can't cry at Holar when you get into trouble."

"She's a lovely girl," Eve sighs. "And I'm glad we had all those years here with her."

I ask them about Lisa, about Mel, and the others who traveled with us in years past. I ask if they have any interest in traveling with us again.

"You know Iceland," Sylvie says. "For some people it changes your life, for others it's just a trip."

Sylvie tells us her new house is finished and her husband has moved in. "It's working out. It turns out he was tired all the time and wouldn't do anything because he had a weak heart. They put in a pacemaker and he's a new person. He's building a man cave in the basement." But then she blurts out to Eve, "Where am I going to keep my horse when you sell your farm?"

Eve says, "Let's not go there. We only just put it on the market."

"Maybe it won't sell," Sylvie reminds her.

"I still like the idea of all of us chipping in," I say from the back seat, sulkily and not quite willing to let the topic die just yet. But no one, not even Sylvie, will take up the subject again.

Sylvie brings up an accident she and Eve had in the spring. "I was riding Snild and Eve was riding Glitfaxi out on the trail, and a mountain bike came up behind us, and it spooked the horses."

"Glitfaxi threw me immediately but Snild took off with Sylvie at a gallop."

"And then she threw me at top speed," Sylvie says, at high volume. "I cracked my titanium helmet. You know how hard that is to crack? I had a concussion for weeks. But it could have been a lot worse. The helmet saved my life. I'm very nervous about riding now."

"I'm always nervous about riding," I tell her. "I'm so nervous about it, I can't even talk about it, because I think if I talk about it, I'll talk myself out of riding or into falling. So, I don't ever bring it up."

It's like I've imparted some secret kernel of riding wisdom. Sylvie says, "Oh, I didn't know that. You have the same fears, you just don't say them out loud? That's so smart."

Eve exclaims: "You are so right! We should never talk about our falls, our fears, or accidents. That's brilliant!"

I have difficulty believing my mind-bending game of pretending bad things don't, can't, won't happen, has anything to do with intelligence. At best, it is delusional self-preservation.

"Let's do that! When it comes to our fears, let's just not go there. Let's never talk about our accidents. Let's not dwell on the bad." Eve is keen on this, but I thought I learned it from her—the negative attracts negative theory—and now she's acting like she's hearing it for the first time. She really is not quite herself.

Snæfellsnes Revisited

Outside of Reykjavík, the roads still have a white wispy layer of volcanic ash from the eruption of Eyjafjallajökull. As we drive over it, it rises and disappears like smoke from a massive smoldering campfire.

We are caravanning behind Sibba and Ljotur. We lost them as we went toward Mosfellsbær, but find them again at the bakery in Borgarnes.

As planned, we head to Uncle Ólof's farm. I'm hoping this will cheer up Sylvie. But last year's plan for riding his horses out to the tidal island of the sagas, of Sylvie on his slow silver dun mare, of the lushly green and miraculous meridian center of the universe is upended when we get there: Ólof's horses are in the middle of the flu epidemic.

And Sylvie isn't quite her usual loquacious self. In fact, she barely talks at all. A year has blinked by and changed everything. She hangs back, doesn't push in front to get close to Ólof. She is—dare I say it—shy, especially without the three cups of coffee that, just one year before, so effectively triggered her precocious flirting.

The rest of us have to fill in for the suddenly quiet Sylvie. And Ólof—as if knowing we teased her last year, perhaps hearing that her crush on him was our silly fun—tries valiantly to engage Sylvie. Since his horses are all sick and we can't ride, he drives us around in an enormous four-wheel-drive Escalade and gives us a more thorough tour of his farm than he did the year before. From one end of his enormous property to the other, the big wheels ford rivers and muddy valleys as we pass his horses recuperating in the fields. We make Sylvie sit up front with Ólof, but she still won't say much. Eve, Allie, and I, almost feeling bad for the lord of the manor, chat amiably, trying to make up for Sylvie's bewildering shyness. We get stuck in the mud a few times, a metaphor I'm sure, and Ólof has to rock the SUV back and forth to spin us out of the muck.

When we return from our drive, we are invited into his house, where his large extended family sits around the main room watching women's soccer on TV. No one looks up as our group, five women, not in our usual raucous mood but certainly audible, enter the house and stand in the kitchen. No one comes over to speak to us to see who we are, and I wonder again about the general standoffishness of Icelanders. Of course, their reticence likely has nothing to do with us—Ólof's wife, who was almost completely paralyzed the prior year from a stroke, is lying upstairs in her bedroom. No more teasing Sylvie about being a flirt. Instead, gamely, she painfully extracts the ages and names of Ólof's grandchildren, but we are otherwise forced to talk amongst ourselves, and after the minimal amount of polite time spent, we leave. There are no plans made for next year when the horses would be better.

Driving away from the farm, we ask Sylvie what's up, why was she so quiet? "Oh, he's married. He's a family man. And I'm married." She stresses, "I was just being silly last year. Anyway, the good news is that it doesn't matter, I'm over it. I'm post-men. You know what Buddha says, life is about letting go."

⸻

We follow Sibba and Ljotur to Stykkishólmur, an old, formerly Danish town on the Breiðafjörður. Like many Icelanders, they spend their summer vacations driving around the country in a small camper. They have both retired from Icelandair (she as a flight attendant, he as a mechanical engineer), and their camper van is, fittingly, packed as tight as a plane. We stop near the dock for a picnic and from the overhead cupboards they bring out our lunch: reindeer meat pâté, salmon smoked in sheep dung, gravlax, cheese and flatbread served with a homemade jam of local currants, and hothouse cucumbers and tomatoes. They give us plastic cups of tea with sugar cubes or Nescafé instant coffee with milk. It is utterly, indescribably delicious, like all the simple, unexpected, unpretentious meals that you somehow remember for the rest of your life.

We part company with Sibba and Ljotur on the eve of the summer solstice. Ljotur is full of jolly, midsummer mischief as he tells us about the Icelandic tradition on the longest day of the year, that the man of the house must run around his home, in this case a camper's van, naked, at midnight, and then roll in the dew of the grass. He omits what happens next, and Sibba is laughing and nodding agreeably with him. We have to be at Helga's by dinner, so we regrettably have to leave, missing his midnight naked run 'n roll.

⸻

The minute we turn off the Ring Road to Thingeyrar we become pensive. We're not even sure we will have horses to ride. Helga had emailed Eve and Sylvie that a lot of her horses were sick, but that some may be well by the time we arrive.

Helga greets us in the driveway. "And . . . how was Uncle Ólof's?" She has taken to using the title "uncle" facetiously.

And out it pours from us, all talking at once: we couldn't ride because of the horse flu, we drove around in his big Escalade instead. Sylvie becomes the most animated, as if she hadn't spent the entire time with him completely mute. She shows Helga a photo book of the farm that Ólof gave her, and spills her story to Helga, like Dorothy telling Auntie Em about Oz. "And he has eight stallions and 4,000 acres and owns the farm next door, too, another 1,200 acres. He has over 100 horses. He also has a river teeming with salmon!"

"Huh," Helga says. "So did sparks fly between Ólof and you?"

Sylvie brushes it off. "Oh, that was so last year. I'm off men. Didn't I tell you? I'm post-men."

I hope not. I appreciate Sylvie's love of love, one that denies it's ever too late in life for a summer crush, for a moment of pure whimsy and unlikely possibilities. Even if it is only an affair of the imagination (often the best kind). I like the fact that Sylvie doesn't capitulate to age, or practicality.

Herd Instinct

All is not well at Helga's farm. Most of the horses are sick with flu and can't stand up in their stalls. Thoka is in the throes of the worst of it. Lying in her stall, covered in her own muck, her white coat dirtied to a matted brown, she struggles for breath, wheezing and coughing. She looks to be near death, but Helga reassures us that the flu hasn't killed a single horse yet in Iceland. They get terribly sick, but they all seem to be surviving it.

We have to wait a couple days to ride until a few of the horses get better. We drive around a lot, but this makes me restless. Iceland to me is horses. I am almost regretting coming this year. It breaks my heart to see the horses so ill, and it's affecting the group, too. Riding gave us a common purpose. Our treks were our collective narrative, our team sport: something to revisit, retell, and exaggerate over a beer. Otherwise, we are a disparate group.

I think of Thingeyrar as Helga and Gunnar's farm, but they only have title to half of it—the other half is owned by the Icelandic ambassador to Japan. The two families share a two-story duplex. No matter how empty the countryside is, or how much room there is to build a bigger house, Icelanders prefer to live in small spaces. This 2,000-square-foot house, split evenly between the ambassador's family and Helga's family, is deemed more than sufficient.

This year, Helga has put in a hot pot midway between the guesthouse and her house. A hot pot is a hot tub without the jets. Because Iceland is volcanically active, it is quite easy to get natural, steamy mineral water by drilling geothermal boreholes in your backyard. Around the hot pot, they have built a wooden deck with towel hooks and chairs scattered around, though it's always too cold to sit around in a bathing suit and towel after getting out of the pot.

One day I join Pippa in the hot pot, and she doesn't immediately get out. This gives me hope that maybe she is finally acknowledging my presence. She stays for a little while and actually says a few entire sentences to me, just to me, directed to me. I am not invisible! "Iceland is one of those places where the geography influences everything, the culture, the people," she says. "I've only found a few places in the world like this. Iceland, India." I heartily agree with her, though I've never been to India. But I believe I am finally winning her over, why else would she talk to me? Then she gets out. Maybe she is really deep and it is a Buddha smile after all.

By the third day, a few of the horses that caught the flu early have recovered and are ready to go out on the trail. I'm raring to go. I don't care what horse I get, what saddle I use. I eagerly saddle up a horse that normally would qualify as "too much horse" for me. It's one of Disa's horses that she left behind when she got married. It's the horse she rode when she challenged the bulls.

Helga takes us on a trail we've never been on before. It is narrow, muddy, and rutted and runs close to the river. We are at a walk most of the time. The terrain, too muddy for tölting, sucks the hooves into the ground, so we trot.

Helga points out large mounds in the land and says that back in the Settlement Era this used to be a ship-building area. She tells us that the area is called Húnaflói, meaning "bear bay," because every so often an iceberg arrives from Greenland with a stranded polar bear floating on it.

"Bears," says Sylvie, "in Iceland?"

"Yes, every so often, but they're shot pretty quickly. We can't have them terrorizing our domesticated animals," Helga says.

"I wouldn't want to meet one of those," Eve says.

Except for the stray polar bear on the drifting ice floe, there are almost no wild mammals in Iceland. There is the arctic fox, and reindeer that roam in the east provinces, though those were imported two hundred years ago as a source of meat. No beavers, otters, coyotes, wolves, fox, brown bears, or black bears . . . nothing. Nothing that can unexpectedly spook the horse and unseat you.

We are down to a walk again. "Helga, I just gave my horse the leg yield, and she didn't move over," Sylvie says. She is riding the mare that took me across Lake Hóp. It's the easiest horse in the bunch, easier than her Stulka who is back at the barn, sick with the flu.

Frieda, who is helping Helga again this year and riding at the back of the line, explains to Sylvie that it's a farm horse. "This horse isn't trained in dressage, aware of every little aid, it's more of a work horse used to herd sheep."

We keep riding in the sucking mud along the riverbanks. Helga starts telling us another story that took place around this area. "It's a famous love and murder story that everyone in Iceland knows. There was this man, Natan, and he was like a very progressive man in his time and into herbal medicine and he was in love with a famous poet at the time, her name was Rosa . . ."

Eve interrupts, "Helga, my horse coughed, do you think it's okay?"

"Helga, Eve's horse coughed," Sylvie repeats, unhelpfully.

Frieda rides up beside Eve's horse, looks at her, and shrugs, "She's just snorting, blowing out dirt to clear her nostrils. She's okay."

Helga continues with the story, which seems important to her. "And Natan and Rosa have a daughter together, though Rosa is married to someone else."

This sounds like a typical Icelandic love story. The sagas are full of women who have children with many different men. In pre-Christian Iceland, when women divorced their husbands, which was not unusual or difficult, the shame was placed on the husband. And in modern Iceland, nearly 70 percent of children are born outside of marriage. Couples often have two children together before they consider getting married.

"When does this take place?" I ask.

"In 1828."

Eve interrupts, "Helga, my horse tripped. Do you think something's wrong?"

Eve is crooked in her saddle, pitched awkwardly forward, her shoulders rounded and hunched with all of her weight on her right hip. There is a saying: "Horses are a mirror." If you are nervous, they think they have something to fear. If you're unbalanced in the saddle, their walk is uneven and they trip.

Frieda again rides next to Eve and watches the horse for a while. "I think it's okay. You seem nervous though."

"I'm afraid my horse hasn't recuperated," Eve says.

"No, she is fine," Frieda says. "We would not put you on horses that aren't well. It would not be good for our horses." Though she is young and reserved, her German-accented, Icelandic-inflected English makes her sound authoritative and definitive. I am hoping it will put the matter to rest.

"I feel like they are still sick," Eve insists. Her obstinacy ruffles Frieda, who must feel as if her reputation as a horse trainer is being questioned. And unlike Disa, she doesn't bring a flask of cognac in her pocket to soothe us when we need it.

Frieda says something to Helga in Icelandic and they mumble back and forth.

"Maybe I'd rather not ride," Eve admits. "The horses tripping and coughing is not good. It's an omen. I think we should turn back."

Helga shrugs. "We can turn back, I guess. Does everyone want to turn back?"

Sylvie eagerly backs up Eve with a harrumph. "Fine with me, I've had enough!"

Allie says, "Sure, I'll do whatever anyone else wants to do." I was hoping she'd want to keep riding, but she is the ultimate sunny-faced conciliator.

And Pippa, as if picking up on and ready to counter my silent protest, throws in: "I think if one of us is uncomfortable and doesn't feel safe, then we should all support that and we should all turn back."

I am the only one who doesn't agree to this plan. This makes me the outlier who wants to go against the unsubstantiated omens and Eve's wishes, or worse, push sickly horses to their breaking point. I look longingly at the trail in front of us: the lupine fields, the dry areas, the muddy areas, the riverbanks that lead to the Greenland Sea. I do not want to turn back. What am I doing here if I can't ride? I wait all year for this trip. And because of the horse flu, it took us three days to get in the saddle; we only have another three days left before we leave.

But what do I do? They are my herd. I follow the herd back to the barn, going against my better judgment and strong desire to keep riding.

After unsaddling and letting the horses out in the pasture, Sylvie comes up to me. "Did you see how she was? So full of fear. I've never seen her like that on a ride here."

I agree with Sylvie—Eve, who had always been a fearless rider in Iceland, was scared for no reason. It's hard to believe this is the same woman who saw bulls in our path and took it as a sign of an uptick in the stock market. But it isn't only Eve that has lost her spirit; the rest of the group quickly gave up, too.

And it bothers me. This is our chance to let go of the world, to let go of the irritants of home, to let go of illnesses and complaints, money worries, and even, or especially, to let go of the petty grievances we have with each other, and all the larger numerous varied problems of the human condition. This is our time to ride fully, to kick up dust literally, to be with the horses, to think like the horses, to bring out the wild horse in us. Our only focus should be the rocks, the grass, the wind, the rain, the crossing. Our only concerns should be our seat, our balance, and the sound of our horse's footfall.

Frieda approaches me in the barn. "I am going out this afternoon to train some horses. Do you want to come with me?"

I am always pleasantly surprised when someone, especially someone as young as Frieda and someone I hardly know, gives me the courtesy of noticing. I was not as vocal with my needs as Sylvie and Eve were on the trail, but Frieda noticed and read me correctly. I did not want to turn around.

While the rest of the group leaves for Blönduós for another dose of coffee and cake at the Blue Cafe, I head to the barn. Frieda has me saddle up Loki to ride. Icelanders give a lot of thought to naming a young colt when they first see it in the field. Sometimes they are named for their personality: Kappi means brave; Galsi playful. Or they are named for their color: Skjoni is a pinto; Nos, a white spot on the nose. Or they are named after a bird, usually predatory: Orn means eagle, Krummi means raven.

And sometimes they are given a name from the sagas that are descriptive of their character: Loki is a Norse god, a trickster, a shapeshifter. I am wondering why he has been named this. He is big for an Icelandic, more the size of a Morgan, and is dark bay, almost black, with a large noble head. He is five, so not quite fully trained. "But he scored high on evaluations," Frieda says.

In other words, he's a potential powerhouse and is way out of my league. But I can't say no. I want to ride. I came to Iceland to ride, not to be stuck in the back seat of a car all day.

I would like to take my time grooming Loki. I would like to pick his feet clean and brush him and talk to him until I feel at ease with him. But Frieda is in a hurry to get out on the trail; she has lots of horses to train in a day and can't wait for me and my nervous fussing. So I saddle him up as quickly as I can, and have Frieda check the girth and the snaffle because I never trust myself when it comes to tack. For good reason, too: Frieda moves the saddle forward and tightens the girth and loosens the nose band a bit.

"He is very sensitive in the mouth, you know, because he is young. So be very light with your hands," she says. "And you must let him go fast in the beginning. If you hold him back when you first get on him, he gets nervous," Frieda says.

He gets nervous? Does that mean I should be nervous? Does "the horse is a mirror" work the other way around?

But I don't have time to overthink this. I am up and moving. I do what Frieda tells me to do: I keep my hands light and the reins loose so he stretches out his neck. I let him go fast over the deeply rutted tracks as we head away from the farm. His first gait is a trot, probably because his reins are loose, but it is a big loping trot, evenly strong from his hind and front, from side to side, and his back is supple and swingy. I don't need to post or find my half seat. It is comfortable enough to sit to. I see why this horse scored high in evaluations and why he will be a competition horse. There is a perceptible difference, a change of attitude, an inner hum to him. The competition horses are more sensitive, and because they are more finely attuned, you have to be very careful with your cues. They also tend to be better formed and better balanced, so they score higher on conformation. And Frieda is right—after I let Loki go at his own pace for about a mile, he gets his jitters out and is willing to listen to me.

When I want to bring him into a tölt, I keep my hands as quiet as possible but inch up on my reins so that he brings his head up, and I shift my weight back a notch (from the center of my sitz bones to the back), so his shoulders can move freely. His tölt is not perfect, it still has some trot to it, but it is the fastest tölt I've ever ridden.

After my afternoon with Loki, I spend my remaining afternoons with Frieda, riding out on the trails with her. I try to convince Eve to come with us, that there are horses for her to ride. They're not all sick. But she says she's fine not riding this year, she's okay just walking and driving around. It's all she needs. I disagree.

Lifestyle Envy

On our last evening, Helga takes us out for a drive, off-road, in a borrowed Jeep. "I know it's not the Escalade you girls are used to," she says, ribbing Sylvie.

Sylvie plays along and says, airily, "We'll live, I guess."

"I figure you know so much about Ólof's farm, I thought you need to really see more of this farm. I want to show you how big Thingeyrar is."

She drives us to the banks of the Hunavatn, where she tells us the best salmon in Iceland run. We follow the banks of the river to the bay's headland, an area we have never trekked to. Then she drives due east to another point we have never trekked to, where the beach has gray sand, windblown heather, and the remains of a washed-up seal. We have a clear view of the Hvítserkur landmark, a wave-eroded rock formation. Helga tells us that in Icelandic folklore, the rock used to be a troll, but it was caught by the sun trying to destroy the monastery of Thingeyrar (apparently a thing trolls do) and turned into stone.

"I don't know if you know this, but Thingeyrar was once the sight of a major monastery in early Iceland. It was a very famous learning center," Helga says. "Many of the sagas were written here."

Though I have a general grasp of Iceland's history, I have not done my homework on the Vatnsdalur valley, the part of Iceland I like to think of as my second home. Helga is filling in the vast blanks of my knowledge, continuing the lesson she started out on the trail the other day, imprinting in us the history of this place.

"They say there was a miracle that happened and that's why the monastery was built here, but, you know . . ." Helga doesn't give this explanation any weight. "They probably chose the area because of the fertile valleys and abundance of salmon.

"All this land, from this point here to the headland over there, is 8,000 acres." She raises her eyebrows at Sylvie. "Bigger than Ólof's, I believe."

"Oh, maybe just a little," Sylvie says, defending her man.

On the spit of land where the river and lake converge, we get out of the car. Helga points out that last summer she threw herself a big fiftieth birthday party here. Everyone came by horse. It was an eight-hour trek each way. Gunnar had driven out the day before and pitched a big tent, put down a temporary dance floor, and lugged out coolers of beer. He built a temporary paddock for the horses to stay in. They grilled salmon on the campfire. Everyone camped overnight under the large tent.

This, of all things, throws me into a state of despair. I thought I was at a point in my life where I was done with the wished-for alternative lifestyles (despite my recent flirtation with buying Eve's farm—that was within reason). I have done all the envying of friends and acquaintances, for their alma mater, their brilliant careers, their inherited money, or their lucrative earnings. I have made myself morose coveting the lifestyle of winemakers in Napa and writers in Cape Cod. But I know that these are petty externalities, that we've all got our own shit to deal with, and I wouldn't want to trade my shit for anyone else's.

So it alarms me to confess this: I want to be Helga. I want her looks, her horse skills, her uncomplicated identity. I want to live on an Icelandic horse farm. I want to have been born Icelandic, to speak the language and be a part of a culture where my ancestors have lived for a thousand years. I want the surety of my place in this world. I want my bones buried here, to dry up and break apart and forever be a part of this land. And I want to be able to throw myself a birthday party on this remote beach and provide a tent, a dance floor, and a paddock for my neighbors and friends who will take an eight-hour ride out to be with me, as easily as I throw myself a backyard cookout in Connecticut.

This remote spit of land on the tip of northern Iceland, where the river meets the bay that meets the Greenland Sea, windswept, barren, gray, tossed with sea foam and sea mammal detritus, has produced my worst case ever of lifestyle envy.

Sylvie has a running joke: "In my next life I want to come back as Helga." Fuck that. I want it now.

I am quiet and sullen as we drive back to the farm, realizing this life will never be mine. Helga pulls over before we get home and takes us into one of the fields of young horses, the two- and three-year-olds that have not yet begun their training. We are looking for Sylvie's horse, Sonneta, Stulka's filly, that Sylvie plans to ship back home. Sonneta is hard to find in the herd: she has a pretty face and a white blaze on her nose, but there are a lot of palominos in this herd. Helga unlatches the gate and we enter the pasture to get a better look. Once we are in their territory, the young horses rush toward us, curious and friendly, greeting us with head-on stares and soft guileless eyes.

About fifty horses crowd around us, closing in until we are completely engulfed by them, shoulder to shoulder, part of the herd. One of them nibbles the back of my jacket. I feel their velvety mossy noses on my neck. They have the grassy, grainy smell of horsehair in sunshine. Though I love the smell of all horses, I particularly love the smell of Icelandics. I put my face on their backs and sniff deeply. If I had high blood pressure or suffered from anxiety, this would be my medicine—the smell of horses. When I'm around horses all day, their earthy, musky oil rubs off on me, and I don't want to wash it off. It's my horse bath. I like to sniff it on myself as I go to sleep and wake up with that horse smell on my skin.

Helga shoos the horses a little bit to give us room. She points out which horses are beautiful to her: a tall and leggy chestnut, a dark dappled mare with a silver mane, and a dark bay gelding with a full mane and strong face. She tells us these horses already have buyers from the States. I am aware that Helga's horses from Thingeyrar are becoming well-known for their breeding and training and are routinely sold to North American clients. I look at these young horses, though, foaled in these fields and raised in these mountains, and imagine their destiny, shipped to the gentrified, groomed paddocks of Westchester County, hemmed in for the rest of their lives.

Finally, Helga points to a delicate palomino with a white star under her blonde mane, Sonneta.

"There she is," Sylvie squeaks out the sentence, in love with her two-year-old filly. "Here she is." She runs her hand through the mane, which is short and sparse, but will grow in thicker as she ages. She touches the blaze on her nose.

"Can Ólof give you that, my friend?" Helga asks.

Next Year, Iceland?

We always leave Thingeyrar at 8:00 in the morning. It's a five-hour drive to Keflavík and we like to give ourselves plenty of time before our evening flight to stop along the way. We say our goodbyes to Helga and drive away, but Eve is glum, Sylvie fretful, and I am unsettled.

"What if I can't come next year? What if Jack and I don't have an income? What if I can't afford to come next year?" Eve asks, before we even pass through the gate of the farm.

Sylvie says, "If you can't go, I can't go."

Allie says, "Luke is graduating high school next June, so I may not be able to go."

Pippa says, "Maybe I'll go to India next year instead."

If the domino that is Eve falls down, we all fall down.

It was a bad year in so many ways, but is this how we end? I'm not sure how "we" became a thing, but I don't want "us" to end. I feel it is unfinished, the experience with this group that has nothing to do with my life back home. I am the woman who rides horses in Iceland. I depend on us coming here each year. It's become part of who I am, and though I keep up ties with Eve, Sylvie, and Viv throughout the year, we exist primarily in Iceland, specifically in Thingeyrar. We have our own house, our own rituals, our own ghosts.

We have been a herd, a clique, a clan, with all the attendant problems. Sometimes I regrettably succumb to the social insecurities of my pre-teen self, wondering if am I part of the in group or if I am on the outs. Sylvie is the queen bee; Eve is the relentlessly upbeat cheerleader; Pippa is the girl who will always snub me; Allie is the can-do, dependable girl; Viv is the vulnerable one, who will always have my back and vice versa. Even the extras, Dora and Mel and Lisa, making their cameo appearances, add new blood, new stories to the group. But who am I to this herd? What do I bring to the group? These are the things I had worried about, but now the group itself is poised on the edge of an existential crisis. Will we exist after this year? Is our time together done?

Thingeyrar fades behind us as I plot out alternatives for my trip next year. There are several other outfitters, well-known people in the Icelandic horse world who lead riding tours now. It won't be the same. I won't be part of this group, but I've done it before, gone by myself, thrown myself in with strangers. I won't be at Thingeyrar, but I will be riding in Iceland.

It is six kilometers on a dirt road from Helga's farm to the Ring Road. We have to slow down and stop for a lamb in the road. "Mama, get your babies off the road," Eve says, but the lamb can't get back under the fence and the mama is bleating for it on the other side of the fence. Eve gets out and helps it reunite with its mother.

"Those sheep are from the farm that mistreats their dogs," Sylvie says.

"I don't like them because of that," Eve says.

"Oh, will you look at all the babies in the fields." Sylvie's talking about the foals, not the lambs. "All their skinny little legs!" she squeals. Allie slows down and takes out her camera.

When we pass the Steinnes farm, Eve says, "Remember when we stopped there and they brought out coffee and cookies for us?"

"Dora fell off her horse there. And it was standing still."

"Right, she just slipped off." Eve laughs. "Boy, I had no idea how drunk she was. Was I dumb."

"No, you always see the best in people," Allie says.

We are silent for thirty seconds.

"The boy who liked Britt was from that farm," I add.

"Our little Britt."

Another thirty seconds of silence and Sylvie asks, "How can we give this up?"

"How can we," Eve says, with no question in her voice.

Another kilometer of silence.

"I'd like to see the area where the volcano went off. Maybe we could spend a couple of days in the south before heading to Helga's next year," Eve says.

"We could come in a few days early and be at Helga's by solstice."

"There's no better place in the world than Thingeyrar when the sun stands still."

"Do you think we could ride to that place where Helga had her birthday party?" I ask.

Allie says, "I'd be up for that."

"It's a long ride, eight hours each way," Sylvie says. "I might skip that one."

Eve says, "But maybe we could do half the trip. We could ride out and Gunnar could pick us up in the truck and take us back. I'll send Helga an email when I get home about dates."

And that's that. It is settled. By the time we reach the end of the dirt road and swing onto the Ring Road, our plans for next year have been put in motion.

Shortly after we hit the pavement of the Ring Road, we pass the dry dirt mounds formed by a landslide during the last Ice Age. And a few miles down from that, we pass one of the roadside pull-offs with the green signs, which means that some significant historical event happened there. Allie slows down to read the sign: "Þrístapar."

She reaches into her bag and brings out a bag of pretzels. "Next year, we should stop there and see what it's all about."

BOOK IV
THE CANTER (STÖKKI)

———— ⚬⚬⚬ ————

A three-beat diagonal gait. Because the four hooves lift from and touch the ground in an odd-numbered sequence, two legs must simultaneously bear the weight of the horse.

2011

※

Ask for Canter

I could never get Charlie to canter. Every class I took, I would try it. I would trot and post and three quarters of the way through the class, the instructor would tell me to "ask for canter." You always ask when you are going around the corner of the arena, because the horse is already bending his head and neck and body. You shorten the inside rein, shorten and bend your inside leg while applying pressure, lean a tad forward, and, presto, the horse is supposed to canter. Only, Charlie wouldn't. Sometimes after the instructor got after him, he'd take a few steps in canter and the movement would throw me—I would bounce around in the saddle, and he'd stop or go back to a trot. I was frustrated with the whole gait. And canter was all I really wanted to do. In my fantasy of myself horseback riding—the same fantasy I've had since I was seven—I am never trotting and posting around an arena. I am cantering outside on a trail, or in a meadow, or, after I had been to Iceland, down sheep paths through the Arctic tundra.

One day when I was on Charlie, the instructor came close to me and said, "When he goes into a canter, you have to sit to it and encourage it from your seat." Then she hesitated slightly before saying, "You have to make the same movement as having sex, you know what I mean? It's like the same motion."

Then she added, "I'm sorry if that offends you."

I don't know what she took me for—did I look like an old time matron who would faint at the mention of sex? I tried to see myself from her point of view. She was ten years younger than me but did not look it. She was hard-bitten and scrawny, with premature lines around her tight mouth. She lived in a trailer on the farm property and drove an old truck. I was the married woman with a well-fed face, two kids, a Yale job, and a brand-new Camry. Wealth, status, it's all relative and often not what it appears.

I assured her I wasn't offended, and nodded knowingly like "I got this," and went off to prove I could "make the movement of sex" in the saddle. I trotted up to the corner of the arena, preparing for canter on the curve, and when Charlie did take a few steps in canter, I thrust my hips unnaturally and out of sync. The horse was noncompliant and slipped lazily into a slow walk, as if to emphasize my complete, almost arthritic lack of skill, and my inability to conjure up the sex movement in the saddle. The instructor looked disappointed.

It has never been that way for me with Icelandic horses. It seems so easy: I lean forward, give a little leg, give 'em rein, and they go. And it's easy to sit to. I don't have to make the movement of sex. The movement on an Icelandic comes to me naturally. Maybe it is the size of the horse, the smallness, the quickness, but the seat finds me, it fits me. For years I have had a Benjamin Disraeli quote taped to my computer: "A canter is the cure for all evil." When I sit at my desk at work and see that quote, I imagine myself cantering, not as a cure for evil, but as a cure for complacency.

I know lots of men make pervy jokes about why women like horses so much. But being in the saddle, and especially being good in the saddle, is not a substitute for sex or a sublimation, or god knows, a stimulation or simulation. It's just a movement, like sex is a movement, like dance is movement, but your partner happens to be a semi-wild, semi-domesticated beast, and you're trying to control it but you're also never completely in control. But it's not about sex. Not really. It's about freedom and speed. It's about losing yourself in something else. At its best, it's an I-Thou relationship. And maybe a little about sex.

All That Is Missing

This year we are only four. This year we are miserable. As forewarned, Allie had to, wanted to, attend her son's high school graduation. But unexpectedly, Eve backed out at the last minute. She called me to tell me the bad news only a week before we were to leave. I begged her to come with us. She said it cost too much. I countered and said we would all chip in and pay her way. She said, "I can't, I can't, I'm starting a new job," though Sylvie later confirmed she wasn't starting her new job for another month.

In year's past, Sylvie claimed there was a waiting list to go with us; that she had to turn down lots of people. She made a big deal of the A-list and the B-list, as if each year it was a carefully culled admissions process. This year, however, she can scare up no one else. It's not her fault: there are many other ways to travel here and many people going on their own. Even the novelty of being introduced at home as "the woman who rides horses in Iceland," has worn off. I will now often get this response: "I know people who do that." So, the "Sylvie group" as it was known in the Berkshires, isn't the only group or the only option. People are discovering Iceland. Though no one, at least no one I know of, has discovered Thingeyrar.

Viv and I fly in together from JFK; Sylvie and Pippa from Logan. There are no hellos when we see each other at the baggage area at Keflavík airport. Sylvie waves her hand at us and says, "We'll be out front."

Sylvie sticks close to Pippa, who busies herself with car rental business, a task Eve used to do.

Pippa gets in the driver's seat. "I can drive if you get tired," I tell Pippa. Viv says the same. Pippa says, "I'm quite fine driving."

Viv and I get in the back seat and we start in on what we think is a most amusing anecdote: about how I was moved to first class, while Viv asked to join me up there and they refused. We're talking over each other, finishing sentences for each other, as we usually do, but we realize we are talking to ourselves. Pippa ignores us completely. Sylvie says, "Huh," and looks at Pippa, the disapproving school principal who is about to tell us to keep quiet back there . . . or else.

As planned, we head straight to Hotel Ranga in the south. No stopping in Reykjavík. Pippa drives fast, and when I mention what the speed limit is, she tsks and says she knows. The tires squeal as she takes a curve too fast. She tsks again because I have been proved right.

This is normally the period when we catch up with each other and fill in the blanks of the past year, but Pippa does her best to discourage us from talking in the car. She doesn't want to know about our past year. Her frosty attitude has even shut up Sylvie, who is usually the one who facilitates the conversation. Viv pushes on anyway with harmless chatter. She points out the window and says, "Have you been noticed people are building these cairns all over the place now? Look at them all over the side of the road. It must be tourists building them. Because I imagine real cairns were put there for a reason. Maybe for travelers to know how deep the snow was? Or were they put there to mark trails?" This is Viv on a roll, asking questions and answering them herself. She does this when she's nervous in social situations.

On the flight over, under less social strain, Viv and I had a normal conversation with the usual give and take. She told me that her son Jonathan was coming home from Iraq in a month. And her other son, Eric, was having a hard time finding work. I told her about my son in Brooklyn, that he moved on from his first job out of college already, and except to ask for money, he rarely contacts us. We hashed out the pros and cons of supporting kids after college. "The truth is, I'm afraid he'll just give up looking for a job and move back home with us." Viv understood this. "We're enablers and we'd rather pay their rent than have them living with us," she said. "How did we get here?"

In the car, Viv is beginning to pick up the awkward silence in the front seat. She says to Pippa and Sylvie, by way of an excuse, "My son Jonathan is coming home from Iraq soon and I'm on pins and needles. So if I'm quacking more than usual, that's where I'm coming from."

In the rearview mirror, I catch Pippa rolling her eyes at Viv's confession. Sylvie simply says, softly, "Okay."

"I feel like holding my breath for a month," she says, quietly to me.

While she's holding her breath, I have to hold my tongue. Because I can't tell her what happened to my neighbor's son during the past year, who only had two weeks left in Afghanistan when he was blown up by an IED. I can't tell her about how we heard his mother scream from down the street with the army messenger at her door; how my husband went over and hugged her while she pummeled his back with her fists. I can't tell Viv about the funeral; how the town lined the streets as the procession passed; how the high school he had graduated from draped black bunting over the school name, and the students stood outside as the hearse passed; or how the Vietnam vets on motorcycles led the slow procession on the highway. This would give her no comfort. And I definitely cannot tell her how a horse stood at the gravesite with a pair of boots facing backward in the stirrups as a bugle played taps followed by a twenty-one-gun salute. I can't tell her that he was gone in one blast, one step in the wrong place before he was to return home.

This is what I am thinking as we speed along the highway in Reykjanes at one in the morning: Viv's son Jonathan making it out alive; my neighbor's son not. And sadly, but not in any way comparable, how my son's emotional distance feels like a loss that I cannot grasp.

Less importantly, and almost in relief, I wonder why Pippa is pissed and Sylvie is mute. The trip is off to a rocky start.

In our room that we share at Hotel Ranga, Viv tells me that she is missing Eve.

"I agree. We are missing something without her here," I say.

"There's more laughter with her. She has a lightheartedness that lifts us all up. It's not there without her."

"You weren't with us last year. She was only half here. She did brighten up the last day however."

"And Sylvie is not herself when Eve's not here. It's not the same without her."

Whatever is missing, whether it's Eve or not, we are falling back to our lesser selves and our churlish instincts. Sylvie is overrun with anxiety, giving short, curt responses. I am feeling neglected and ignored, and, yes, my worst trait, sulky. Viv is nervous about her social anxiety, thinking she is always doing and saying the wrong thing. And Pippa is schoolmarmish and manipulative.

But I'm in Iceland, I tell myself. I'm here again for another year. This is our continuing saga. I'm with my girl pack. Though we don't feel exactly like a pack. And it does not feel friend-ish. It feels end-ish.

I think of Sibba and Ljotur as Eve's friends, but they don't cancel their date with us, even though Eve isn't with us, even though we must be looking glum. If they miss Eve and her usual good tidings, they don't show it. Ljotur is his usual jolly self and Sibba his laughing companion, and they bring levity to what is turning into a tense trip.

They get to our hotel after dinner and take us to the volcano area, Eyjafjallajökull. Wisps of ash still rise and settle on the street, a year after the eruption, and for a long time we're on a road that cuts through miles of mudflats. Ljotur points to a black sandy beach, wide with columns of basalt cliffs. "People have died there. Just standing on the beach. A wave comes in and sweeps them out," he says, sweeping his hand through the air.

I think this is apocryphal, or I'm not hearing him right. But Sibba confirms this, "Yes, a model was on a shoot there last year, standing on the beach, and she was swept away."

Icelandic women say their affirmative, "Yeow," on the inhale, much like French women say their "Oui." So Sibba says her "yes" in English with the same intake. There are a couple of ways Sibba reminds me of a French woman. It is rare for an Icelandic woman to be petite, yet Sibba is only five-two, thin yet curvy, so even though she has a smiley elfin face that says Iceland, her body and the way she dresses says Paris. In town and around the Reykjavík area, she wears silk cropped pants, ballet flats, Hermes scarves, and cashmere sweaters. Having worked for Icelandair, she can fly to any city on the route for free, affording her the opportunity to take shopping trips to Paris and New York. Even when she is hiking with us, she wears the highly stylized, brightly colored, high-tech outdoor wear, Cintamani.

"People think Iceland is safe, and it is in the cities. But you can easily take a wrong step hiking, or get swept away by a wave. Our nature is dangerous," Ljotur says.

It is midnight when we reach a waterfall. It is not the first time this has happened to me in Iceland. I am a passive passenger being driven somewhere; I'm not expecting anything. I don't know exactly where I am, nor do I care. At midnight, the dusky twilight is cracked with sunlight that funnels like a spotlight on lush green hills and fields where sheep and horses graze. When we park the car and get out, we spread out, each on our own path. There are maybe thirty people, gentle-looking humans, milling about, talking quietly. The bird sounds are louder than the human voices—the cackling of fulmars and the drumming of snipes' tail feathers—their mating calls that sound like ghostly sheep bleating in the grasses. But louder still is the waterfall, deafening when I get close to it. Because of the low angle of the midnight sun, the mist is fanned out in a rainbow, as if it's no big deal—that's what summer midnight mists in Iceland do. I walk down a path that cuts behind the waterfall. I lose sight of everyone and everything else. I'm peacefully alone and temporarily lost here. I have no sense of self, or that nagging urge to nail myself down, describe myself—that is gone. I have only the enormity of a sense of place, the aching beauty of the universe, which is all consuming and fulfilling.

Gift Horse

Helga observes people the same way she observes horses. She does it instinctively. She stands back, watches who moves first in the herd, what the action is, aggressive or shy. She quickly summarizes the details, taking in any off-kilter physicality—a stiff hip from the car ride, a slight limp from a hip replacement, or a shuffle from a torn meniscus. She even tilts her head as we talk, taking in the tone of voice and volume.

She must be picking up all sorts of cues from us when we get out of the car. If we were a herd of mares, we would all have our ears back. We would all be standing with our heads turned from each other, ready to flick out our back hooves at the slightest attempt to crowd into our space.

Helga says, cautiously, in order not to rile up any emotion, "So, Eve couldn't make it." Even though Sylvie is her closest friend, she knows the value of Eve's good cheer in this herd. I can sense her disappointment with only the four of us and no Eve. She has no idea how disappointing this is to me. But if I can ride every day, it will make the trip worthwhile. I am here for the horses. All the other social and group dynamics are secondary. Or tertiary. I'm here for the horses, the sense of place, and, lastly, the company. Helga asks about Eve out of concern and we each say something different.

"She's starting a new job," I tell her, relaying the information, false or true, that Eve told me.

Viv says, "I think it was difficult financially for her this year."

"Maybe she'll join us next year," Pippa says, all smiles and kindness about Eve, though she has stayed mute and disinterested about her so far this trip.

Hearing Pippa use that phrase "next year" doesn't give me the same hope as it does when Eve and Sylvie say it. In fact, the "us" in that sentence gives me a slow-burning dread. Pippa is planning next year with us. I can barely make it through two days with her.

Sylvie finally puts the matter of Eve to rest: "I got an email from her and she's already regretting that she didn't come. But I'm telling you, what she can't say is that she doesn't want to leave Jack."

"Why is that?" Helga asks.

"He needs her. Especially now that they sold their farm. They lean on each other."

Pippa wants to change the subject. She is bristling with the anticipation of bringing forth all the gifts she bought for Helga. One of her suitcases is stuffed with Helga's gifts. Sylvie has brought horse supplies that are expensive to get in Iceland but cheap in the States. Viv and I have chipped in on some of these gifts, but they are relatively minor: halters and ropes, brushes and hoof picks—basic stuff. We hand them over in bags and Helga peeks in and says, "Thank you, my friends."

But Pippa has gift wrapped all of her presents and makes it ceremonial, so Helga has to untie the ribbons and bows and carefully remove the wrapping paper. And Pippa has a story about each gift that she bought for Helga, where and why she bought each scarf, sweater, bottle of bath oil for her. Pippa has bought horse supply presents, too, but fancy ones—braided reins and what looks like a horse headdress for Helga's prize-winning mare. Helga is surprised and grateful at first, but with each new gift, her thankfulness wears thin. "Oh, this is too much, you shouldn't have." And she means it.

When Pippa takes out the grand finale gift—a midnight-blue riding cloak made of cashmere and alpaca wool, Helga says, "Oh, this is really too much." But Pippa wants her to put on the cloak. "It's for those cold winter nights when you ride to your neighbor's house, and look, there's a hood, in case it snows." Helga puts it on reluctantly, touching it gently, recognizing its worth. Pippa tells her to pull up the hood, so for Pippa's sake, she covers her head with the hood. The color and the flow of the cloth gives it a royal look, like a queen's robe. Sylvie says, "You're like a goddess in that." Pippa is pleased, but Helga takes the cloak off quickly, thanking her for it, and putting it back in the box.

Viv and I back up into the kitchen to discuss. "Is Pippa doing that to make us feel bad?" Viv whispers. "I bought her two little rubber curry brushes."

"I only contributed a can of Cowboy Magic. It looks so cheap of me."

"She must have spent a thousand dollars on those presents."

"But it's so over the top. She's setting a standard I could never keep up with. Is she trying to buy Helga's friendship?"

"You can't buy Helga's friendship. She is not materialistic," Viv says.

This is Pippa's third year with us, and I know how she really wants to be here, but I also sense she wants to be here without us. In horse language, she wants to push us to the outer edges of the pasture; she wants to drive us into the mountains all winter and never herd us back down in the summer.

I once took an archeology course in college and the professor spent his summers on digs in Canada, studying the paleo tribes of the Maritime provinces. He was writing out the names of each tribal group on a blackboard and the time periods when they inhabited the area, and all the supplanting or usurping of one group after another, when he stopped for a second. He turned to us and said, sadly, but resolutely, "It's over turf, whether it's the good hunting grounds or fishing shores. All wars are turf wars. It's the history of humans. One group tries to replace the other."

This is the modern-day version of it: Pippa trying to either usurp us, replace us, or somehow get in tight with Helga so she can secure an invitation without us. But as far as we knew, Helga only opened her guesthouse in the summer for us, Sylvie's group.

Viv and I once composed a painstakingly careful email to Helga, asking if we could stay an extra two days at the end of our trip. She could pro-rate it, we would not bother her, we explained. We only wanted to walk and spend time in the sunshine. Helga's response was to not reply at all. She simply ignored the email and the follow-up email, which is the typical Icelander way of refusal. Helga didn't want to turn her farm into a horse-trekking B&B—or give any indication that the guesthouse was open for business. She was a professional trainer, not an inn hostess.

But maybe I am being too harsh on Pippa. Maybe staying alive another year and making it to Iceland another year is all that she is trying to do and we're not on her radar for good or ill. Her left leg is wrapped in compression bandages, a result of recent bone surgery she had over the winter and fear of edema that can be caused by air travel. She sits in an armchair and props up her leg on a kitchen chair. I don't know what the status of her remission is. She doesn't talk about it and we know not to inquire.

And Pippa is a good sport when it comes to riding. The first two days she rides the chestnut gelding, Orn, and my experience with Orn is that he is a bumpy ride with a piggy-tölt that's hard to break. I see her wincing in the saddle sometimes, but she never complains. Despite all my prior reservations about this woman, I do find myself admiring her stoicism. Despite her refusal to socialize with us or her questionable gift-giving motives, she is a true horsewoman.

After three days of riding, however, she is done, "regrettably so," she says. She looks like she's having trouble walking.

Sylvie also says she's done. "I don't have to ride, either. I'm gonna quit while I'm ahead."

Viv says, "I ride all the time at home, I come here to walk and to soak up the light for the rest of the year."

Viv tells me privately that she doesn't like to take risks anymore. Sometimes we go too fast for her on the trail. "The older I get, the more I fear breaking my bones," she says. "And the more I know, the more fearful I am."

All three women decide to bag the riding for the rest of the week. And again, I'm left with this question: if we're not here to ride, what are we here for? Pippa's brusqueness? Sylvie spends all her time on her iPad, even in the car, doing crossword puzzles and keeping up with Facebook friends. And Viv plugs into her Audible books in the car and in the house. She says she's happy spending the rest of the week walking in the sunlight. But I can meet up with Viv anytime back home to walk and talk. We don't have to fly to Iceland to do that.

I try hard to suppress my frustration, but it takes a lot of rearranging my regular life to get here. Each year there are financial strains that threaten even the possibility of the trip for me. Each year it gets more difficult and more expensive to arrange my mother's care when I'm gone. At work, our fiscal year ends the last day of June, and I worry that I might appear negligent by not being there.

With Eve's farm sold and her horses dispersed all over the country, I rarely get to ride in the Berkshires anymore. Although Sylvie anticipated importing Sonneta, Helga wrote her midyear that the filly had to be put down, something was wrong with the horse's pastern joints and she would never be rideable. Sylvie keeps two Icelandic horses at a barn twenty minutes down the road from her. One horse is twenty-two years old with a bad case of spavin and shouldn't be ridden. The other horse is a rescue, similarly old and shouldn't be ridden because he has a nasty habit of walking off trail and backing up into trees. Often they get ornery and lethargic because New England pastures are riddled with deer ticks and the horses carry a fluctuating amount of Lyme titers. Once the titers reach a certain high level—her horses tend to cow-kick at that point—they are prescribed a round of antibiotics.

When I see the two horses out in the pastures, which is only a small contained field surrounded by forest, I can't help but think how diminished they appear. They are overweight and dispirited. They bear little resemblance to the horses of Iceland and they are hardly a replacement for riding in Thingeyrar.

Frieda is willing to take me with her as she trains her horses on the trail. And she is willing to give me lessons in the arena. But it's not the same this year. Nothing is the same. I'm tense in the saddle. I can't loosen my hips and I pull at the reins too readily. I'm terrified of Loki, and I decline to ride any new horse. And when I go to saddle up the old, dependable Gnott, she skitters away, breaking free of her halter rope, and trots out of the barn, done with me.

Frieda says, "You don't seem here. You are not here with us, with me or the horses. You are not enjoying yourself. You are not you. And the horses, they sense that."

Horses are a mirror. You can't lie to a horse. They are mind readers. They pick up the nonverbal signs—that my body is rigid, my hands shaky, as I try to put on the saddle girth. They pick up tone of voice—my throat-constricting vibration that signals tension and fear. My trusty Gnott looks at me and runs. Horses can't save me if I am shut down.

On our last night at Thingeyrar, Helga sends us to Oli's in Holar. Oli has just returned from guest teaching at a university in Uganda, and invited us to dinner. This is the most exciting event of the week. We even dress up for it, meaning we put on our nicer sweaters, and the pants and the shoes we wear on the plane. Viv spends an hour putting on makeup and doing her hair. Sylvie comes out of her bedroom wearing lipstick and eye makeup, with her hair pinned up in mini clips, à la Helga. Pippa comes out of her room in one of her thousand-dollar Icelandic sweaters. I put on lipstick instead of ChapStick and blow out my hair.

Pippa insists on driving. Viv whispers over the gravel crunch of the driveway, "I don't know why she doesn't let us drive. She can't manage with a leg like that. She can barely walk."

Pippa drives fast and furious. It's supposed to take two hours, and we get there in an hour and fifteen minutes. I'm not sure if the heavy-footed driving is caused by her water-retentive leg or if she just wants to scare the shit out of us. Oli looks a little surprised to see us arriving ahead of schedule when he invites us in, and we already killed a half hour stopping at the historical museum in his town.

The Truth about Elves and Trolls

We're sitting in Oli's house on his orange leather sofa, a golden sun pouring in the window at eight in the evening. Oli sets out four shot glasses of amber-tinted aquavit—and Sylvie and I are the only ones who imbibe. We have two each and then Oli fills the glasses again, probably not realizing we're the only two drinking. A purple mountain glows outside the living room window, ringed in cloud wreaths, and the town sits, scooped out, shoveled out, at the bottom of the mountain. It's a Tolkien town. The historical museum we stopped at featured a traditional turf house, which looked much like Bilbo Baggins' dwelling. Coincidentally, on the coffee table, where our empty shot glasses sit, are the first and second books of the Lord of the Rings trilogy, one in English and another in Icelandic. This starts to add up to something, even in my slightly woozy mind.

I drink Viv's shot because she doesn't drink. Sylvie drinks Pippa's because she's driving, and she's already enough of a risk on the road. Oli pours us another two shots and I am in another state of mind, and it is one of sheer contentment. The world is stilled or at least slowed. I sink deeper into the sofa. I smile at Pippa and realize I have been overreacting, petty, even paranoid. I have been reading her wrong. She hasn't been rude to me, at least not purposely. I need to be more magnanimous toward her. I need to love people more, the way I love the aquavit. I cannot move or speak so I send out love vibes to everyone here with me. Why haven't I thought of this before? All you need is love. Love is all you need. Plus this beauty and peace that has descended like the mist around the mountain here at Oli's house in Holar.

I imagine that Viv and Pippa, who aren't drinking, must surely feel it, too. They glow in the sunlight. When I glance at Sylvie, her eyes are closed and her face bears that beatific smile. I get drowsy looking at her and sink deeper in the sofa. Sylvie might be napping, and I wonder if I could do that, too. The room is warm and I hear the metal din of pots and utensils, and Oli's voice asking us if we want some Icelandic caviar. "I love caviar," I tell him. And he brings out a small bowl of it with crackers. He refills our shot glasses and Sylvie, midway through downing it, holds it up and says, "What's this called again?"

"It's aquavit, or aquaveet. Water of life." That's about the limit of my Latin.

"Ah, water of life," she says, as if that rings a bell.

My mind is buzzing from this water of life; my body is inert and my tongue is stuck, but my heart, let me tell you, my heart is singing. Love vibes all around. With just a little help from the water of life, I'm channeling my inner Eve—positivity, openness. If she can't be here, I'll be here for her, or I'll be her here. Finally, Viv does her Viv thing: she finds Oli in the kitchen and asks him a lot of questions. Her questions, and his answers, are an overlay to my harp-like heart.

Oli's wife, Gita, comes home from Akureyri where she attended a conference on the fish economy of the Arctic States. She has new glasses, a sleek new asymmetrical hairstyle, and wears a business suit. She looks full of information and important doings. She names the other delegates at the meeting: Siberia, Lapland, Greenland, Finland, Norway, Alaska, Nunavut, and the Northwest Territories. It's like a map of my geographic desires. Thule is calling. Viv asks Gita a lot of questions, questions I wish I could ask, but she's doing a better job of it. Oli calls us to the dinner table. I float there. He puts out a meal of onion quiche, mushroom bisque, tomato salad, and rolls. He has performed his kitchen magic.

Pippa says it looks delicious and thanks him for making it all vegetarian.

"That's so nice, it's all vegetarian," I say, and pop a dinner roll in my mouth.

Viv likes the menu, too, and states thus.

"He made it for you, too!" I pass her the tomato salad, and the heavy dish wavers in the air until she unloads it from my hand just in the nick of time.

Oli opens a bottle of red wine, a bottle with a cork, no less. I rarely see wine in a bottle in Iceland; it's always from a box. He goes around pouring it into everyone's glass. I've lost count of how many shots of aquavit I had, so I must say "no," better say "no," I must politely refuse and say, "None for me, thanks." But he's hovering the bottle over my empty wine glass, and instead I say, "Yes, please, thank you!"

Gita talks about the Sami people's beliefs, and the topic turns to cultural interpretations of the supernatural. "My favorite topic," I say, and spoon mushroom soup into my mouth, or the approximate space around my lips—it takes a bit of practice after all the aquavit.

"Why is it your favorite topic?" I'm not sure who has asked that; I am busy with my bisque, and I can't look up or I'll miss my mouth again. I should be able to figure it out by deductive reasoning: was it in a British accent? An Icelandic accent? American? Too late, the evidence is gone.

I decide to address the table in general. "Because I've had a few encounters with the supernatural."

Sylvie seems to come alive. "Oh, you have?" she asks, as if she doesn't remember.

"I definitely heard the ghosts in the bedroom at Helga's guesthouse." I've had other encounters, but it seems showy to bring them up all at once.

Sylvie says, "That's right. Does everyone know the guesthouse is haunted? Not only did she"—pointing at me—"have an encounter, but Eve felt them caress her arm, and Allie woke up and saw a woman in old-fashioned clothes sitting on the end of her bed."

"I didn't know that about Eve and Allie." I shake my head and reach for the onion quiche.

Viv wants to know why we haven't ever told her about the ghosts, but I'm not fielding that question—creamy onion quiche is melting in my mouth.

Oli tells us that ghosts are common all over Iceland, and so are elves and trolls.

This might seem like a minor point in this discussion, but I think, or at least the aquavit thinks, that ghosts are more believable than elves and trolls, which are, obviously, more fanciful and the stuff of folktales. I don't even consider them in the same family as ghosts—who would? But I need to be polite and listen. I've also finished most of the onion quiche, which prompts Oli to jump up and say, "Don't worry, I've got another whole quiche in the kitchen."

Gita continues, clearly in cahoots with Oli, "Not that long ago, a road crew built their road to avoid a boulder. They went out of their way to build the road around it. They didn't want to disturb the troll who was lying in wait there and incur his wrath."

After all these years, I can never tell if Icelanders are pulling my leg when they tell stories of elves and trolls. By most standards, Iceland is the most practical of countries, but the sagas and myths are still lodged deep in the modern psyche. I give a lot of leeway to the supernatural, like ghosts and past lives, thin places and feminine vortexes, but trolls? They are basically belligerent rocks that talk. They don't make sense. At the moment, though, politeness and another helping of onion quiche stops me from asking Gita if she actually believes this stuff.

Oli and Gita continue matter-of-factly to explain the not-so-obvious.

"Trolls are giants. It's the Icelandic word for giant. Trolls can only move in the night. If the sun comes out and catches them, they turn into boulders."

"I thought they were boulders to begin with."

"No, they are giants to begin with. They are always making trouble. Mostly with their engineering feats. They start moving things around so that roads and houses can't be built."

"And what are the elves?"

"Elves are invisible people. They are the beautiful people."

"How do you know they're beautiful if they are invisible?" I ask.

"You know because there are times when people can see them. You can corner one at a crossroad, for instance, and if you do, it will offer you everything to let it pass. There's a story about an elf cornered by some guy and the elf offers him gold, silver, horses—anything to let him pass. But all the guy wants is sheep fat." Oli laughs at this.

"Oh, I see." I am nodding vigorously, but completely confused about the sheep fat. Why is that funny?

"Elves know the secret of the universe. If they tell it to you, you have to keep it quiet. Or else."

"Or else, what? They kill you?"

"Mishaps happen," Gita says, wistfully.

I'm going with this. If some people are foxhole Christians, I am an alcohol-fueled believer in the supernatural of Iceland. I can't believe I ever doubted the existence of elves and trolls. It is so obvious, especially from where I'm sitting in Holar, which feels more and more like the peaceable kingdom of Valinor.

"If an elf told me the secret to the universe I would never, ever tell a soul. I'm good with secrets, especially if it's from an elf." I feel as if I need to make that clear to the table. That I would be a good person for an elf to talk to and divulge secrets to if he or she felt so inclined.

And I am yearning to see one of those beautiful elves. I want to know the secret of the universe, but I'm also sitting back in my seat feeling pretty happy just knowing that there are elves out there that know the secret to the universe. And that there *is* a secret to the universe . . . because I have always suspected it.

Gita looks at Oli and says, "Icelanders love to tell stories. It's our gift."

Oli says, "Elves and trolls and such are the subconscious at work. These tales of the supernatural are a projection of dreams, or anxieties, that sort of stuff."

Well, that's a buzzkill. I want to believe in elves and trolls, not in my subconscious projections. I can feel myself sober up at the grim reality of life without magic. Luckily, Oli brings out dessert, his famous skyr cake topped with blueberries, to take away the dreariness of an elf-less world.

But then, later that night, as we are driving home on a mountain road, troll-like boulders are perched along the edge of a steep cliff to our right and to our left. We come to the crest of the road just as the blinding sun cuts at an angle that obliterates our vision, including Pippa's, who is driving. She takes her heavy foot off the gas for once. She says, worriedly, "I can't see the road. I can't see where I'm driving." If she steers to the right too much, we'll hit a boulder or head right off the cliff. Too much to the left, there could be oncoming traffic. She stops the car in what feels like the middle of the road.

"You can't stop in the middle of the road!" Sylvie panics.

Viv says, "What are we supposed to do?"

"Can anyone see anything?" I ask.

"NO!"

We are encased in the glare of the midnight sun, waiting for it to move just an inch on the horizon, to give us room to see. Time passes slowly waiting for the movement of the sun, especially when you think your life depends on it. But then a shadow passes low on the horizon, just long enough for Pippa to see the road, hit the gas, and drive us out of danger.

The shadow might have been a cloud. But in those few moments, when blinded like that, I'm ready to see anything: an elf at the crossroad or a troll who sets himself down and turns into a boulder to block out the sun. We need our myths.

Next Year, in Iceland?

Viv waits until we have separated from Sylvie and Pippa in Keflavík Airport. On the line for the flight back to JFK, she says, "Let me tell you, I never want to go to Iceland again if Pippa is with us."

I nod in agreement. "That was not a good trip."

"I felt like I was in middle school and the mean girl was being mean again."

"She was really rude to us."

"She ruined the trip for me."

"I agree. You're confirming everything I was feeling."

"And Eve wasn't there as a counterbalance. And Sylvie . . . Sylvie acquiesced to Pippa," Viv says.

"Sylvie's not the same in Iceland without Eve."

"The trip is not the same without Eve. I will never go without Eve again."

"I agree."

"I feel like I have to decompress from that trip that was supposed to help me decompress from my life. Double decompression."

Viv and I aren't sitting together on the return trip. But we go through the long lines of passport control together, and wait for our luggage together in

New York, still brooding about Pippa. We hug and say goodbye to each other as we get out of customs. We promise to get together soon.

I wait two hours for the Connecticut airport van to pick me up at the terminal. I'm the last on his list of pick-ups. The driver heads onto the expressway going way too fast and the van's windows are all open, giving the ride a rattled, reckless feel. I fear the tires will flatten on the next pothole if the driver hits it, and at this speed we'll jump into the next lane and collide with oncoming traffic. He passes everyone on the road, mostly on the right, then quickly cuts into the left lane. He even goes up on the shoulder of the Van Wick to pass another car.

I want to say something. I had wanted to say something to Pippa, but I didn't. I weigh the benefits of expressing my concern to the driver. Should I confront it or ignore it? Should I back down and acquiesce, like I did with Pippa, never confronting the bullying aspect of her aggressive driving or her general meanness to Viv? Because I did notice that while Pippa gave me the proverbial cold shoulder, she downright bristled at everything Viv said and did. And I didn't say anything. I didn't step in to point out how harsh it all was. I let Viv be bullied. And I will not be bullied now by the van driver.

"Excuse me," I shout up to the driver. I am seated in the middle of the van. It holds about twelve people but there are five passengers, me and four men. "Excuse me, excuse me, but could you slow down! I feel like you're going way too fast."

"You think this is fast, lady?" the driver snorts, challenging me.

"Yes."

"Well, it's not."

A passenger speaks up, and says, "Lady, this isn't fast. This is normal."

Another passenger, shakes his head, "He's right, lady, this is not fast."

First of all, what kind of driver argues with a passenger when she asks to slow down and, second of all, what kind of passengers stick their noses in our disagreement to agree with the driver? Third, what's all this "lady" crap? It's being used in the pejorative to put me in my place, make me look nagging and my request silly, like I'm a daft and prissy middle-aged woman. Don't they know I'm tough? That I ride fast horses in the wilds of northern Iceland? I am not afraid of speed; I am not afraid of recklessness. I just don't like it in rattling vehicles swerving down the Van Wick.

"He's going eighty."

"He's going sixty!" the first guy says.

"He's not going sixty, he's going faster than sixty!" I'm not going to back down, even if I'm not sure of the exact speed. I am not going to let these guys bully me into acquiescence. I am done with that.

Another guy feels the need to get into the fray, "I don't care how fast he's going, I need to get home. I wish he would drive faster."

The van driver says smugly, "See, lady, you're outnumbered," and speeds up.

These four men have ganged up on me. Confrontation is never as satisfying as you think it will be. In fact, it's messy and unrewarding and for the rest of the trip I'm reduced to glaring at them, boring my eyes through their brains, like I'm batshit crazy mad and they should not have messed with me. I wish I were an elf, or a troll, and had special powers. I want to blast them all away.

I am still tense and angry when the driver, who has seemed to have forgotten, or not even registered our confrontation, drops me off at my house. It's midnight, and my neighborhood is hot, humid, and noisy from the scratchy racket of crickets. Walking up the path to my house, I feel the weight of the constant overgrowth of summer in New England. Big, leafy, deciduous trees, Norway maples and old oaks, line my street. Hundred-year-old pines stand watch along the back border of my yard. Dogwoods, rhododendrons, hydrangea, and mountain laurels ring my lawn. The night sky is obscured by the heavy canopy of the shade forest. For the first time in over a week, the sky above me is dark. There is no wind. No Arctic bite in the air. And I am already longing to return to northern Iceland's cold vastness and endless summer light.

2012

But the Sheep Réttir

I have become the de facto expert on Iceland in my local social circle. I get calls and emails from people I don't know: "Hi, I am a friend of Tina's and she said you go to Iceland every year and I'm planning on going and was wondering if you had some advice." These inquiries come more frequently now as Iceland is becoming better known.

I've learned over the years not to come on too strong, not to gush. And if someone is on the fence about going, that is, if they have not bought airline tickets yet, I start with a disclaimer: "I love it, but it's not for everyone." I do this because I once told my neighbor it was the best place in the world and she should definitely go there and she must, *must* ride the horses and, and, and . . . she came back unconvinced. "Eh? I don't get it. It's a strange place," she said. "Cold and damp and I had a rough ride on a nasty horse in freezing rain." I said, "Yeah, that happens, you have to get through that part of it," but I could see she thought I had steered her wrong.

So I have learned to curtail my enthusiasm. I field the typical tourist questions. What is worth seeing? Everything. What can be skipped? Blue Lagoon.

I send long emails with helpful hints that can go on for pages. On a budget? Eat at the bakeries. Only have three days? Drive out to Snæfellsnes. I suss out whether they are animal people, and if so, I tell them to try out the horses on a short trek.

And then I get a call from Holly, a friend of a friend. She tells me she stopped over in Iceland for three days last October and she wants to go back and ride the horses. She added, "I heard you go there to ride the horses every year. I want to do that."

I quickly invite her over for a glass of wine.

Sitting in my backyard with Holly, I pour a newly opened cold white wine into our glasses. It's the beginning of June and one of those days you wait all year for: the sun is gentle at 5:30, the trees have all leaved, the ornamental bushes are blooming, my garden is growing. Rabbits hop. Chipmunks scurry. Hummingbirds dart in the trumpet vines. Goldfinches eat at the bird feeder. The world around us hums in a Beatrix Potter tranquility.

But Holly sits on the edge of the chair as if she is going to flit away. She's thin and sinewy, with no visible menopausal belly, a hard look to pull off at this stage of middle age. I get the feeling she isn't trying for that look, that she doesn't work for it, that it's a combination of genes and high energy, mostly nervous. She tells me she took early retirement this year from teaching special ed and has a pension and she loves the freedom of not working. I would love that, too, the freedom and a pension.

Holly switches to why she's come over. She has been taking riding lessons, she tells me, and she is *dying* to go back to Iceland to ride. Her emphasis, not mine. "I should have tried them when I was there. But I didn't see them until we got out of Reykjavík and there they were in the fields. And it's hard to explain, but I saw all those horses and an old, odd excitement came over me. I thought, *what is this about?*"

There should be a specific phrase to capture this feeling toward Icelandic horses. In Icelandic, *Gæðingur* literally means "dream horse," and refers to a horse that has great gait abilities, good temperament, willingness, charisma, strength, and expression. But there also should be a word that connotes that peculiar, particular, thunderstruck feeling that overwhelms some people when they first catch sight of Icelandic horses. Even pixelated versions, as mine was.

Holly is jumpy and ill at ease, and I worry that I make her nervous. But I overlook this because, after she reveals that we share this strange attraction to Icelandic horses, I'm ready for her to be my new best friend.

"I'm leaving for my Iceland trip in two weeks. Why don't I see if there is room for you to come with us?"

I have never asked to bring a friend along because I never had a friend from home who wanted to come. But Viv isn't coming this year. True to her word, when she heard Pippa was coming again, she bagged it and booked a tai chi trip to China instead. But Eve is going, and Sylvie, and amiable Allie. Pippa will not be able to commandeer this trip.

"Really? Because I'm spontaneous. I'd go," she says. "That would be my dream."

I can barely tamp down my excitement at finding someone like Holly. None, I repeat, none, of my friends at home are the least bit interested in horses or Icelandics. And I am trilling like a cricket at finding a new convert to join our group.

"Let's look at some ticket prices then." I get my laptop and she gets up to open the bottle of red that she brought. The white wine emptied quickly, and it vaguely registers in the back of my mind that I had only one glass.

We find the ticket prices are expensive this close to the date. They are running over a thousand. "Oooh, that's a lot. I'm on a limited budget."

"But we pay hardly anything to stay at Helga's."

Then she says, "What I really want to do is—I don't know what you think about this, if it's crazy—but I found out you can join these sheep roundups."

Now she has won over my heart. It's as if I am connecting with my long-lost soul sister.

"I can't believe you said that. I've always wanted to do the sheep roundup."

"I'll do it with you. I mean it. I'm a risk-taker."

It's called the *réttir*; it's a once-a-year Icelandic tradition of herding up the sheep that have been grazing in the mountains all summer and driving them down to the corrals where they are sorted out. It's long, hard days in the saddle, lots of galloping down hills and moving the sheep along while being pelted with wind and cold rain in early autumn. I have been dying to do this, but no one in the Sylvie group wants to do the réttir; they like it at Helga's in the comfort of the guesthouse, and can't make another trip back in the fall. I have never found anyone interested in the réttir, and here is Holly showing her chops, and whether she follows through or not, her eagerness is rare. She's one of the few women I've met who hasn't let life and age beat the wild heart out of them.

"There's also a horse roundup in the autumn." I feel obliged to mention that, because it is also on my wishlist. And because that would be more challenging, wilder. "It's the same idea; you round up the horses from the mountains in the fall and drive them down to the corrals to be sorted out by the farmers."

"I didn't know about the horse roundup. I would do that. I would definitely do that."

Holly is more like what our group used to be like in the early days, up for challenging rides. The Sylvie group has been very timid riding over the last two years.

Years earlier I had met Holly's husband when he sat across the table from me at a dinner party. He was an unconventional, bearded guy—bearded before it became popular—and so full of opinions about everything, I mistook him for a New Yorker. He was from the Midwest. He was a RISD graduate, a sculptor, who had to make a living doing carpentry. Holly wasn't there, but I knew through mutual friends that they had a difficult, contentious marriage. After a lot of drinking, he divulged the story of how they first met at a music festival. They were cooped up in a tent together because of the rain; the next weekend they got married at a courthouse, though they both were engaged to other people. After he had told this story, I realized I had heard it before. It had made the rounds in our acquaintance group because it was unusual.

It is not quite the origin story of me and my husband, but it bears some resemblance. A sense of impetuousness, of flight, of disregard for other committed relationships. I guess I should have been wary of hasty coupling, but I threw myself into it heedlessly. We made no sense to the outside observer. Nobody favored us as a couple, not family, not friends. And we didn't so much meet as smash together and hole up in bed for months, flush with the discovery of each other. We committed instantly, wordlessly to each other, as if no other path were possible. It happens sometimes—from pretty much the first look, we were a fait accompli.

I retreat from the laptop and looking up airfares with Holly and squeeze a rubber ball. I've diagnosed myself with carpal tunnel: my left, and sometimes my right, hand goes numb. My toes have also been having spasms where they stiffen and separate for a few minutes. I left a message for my doctor earlier in the day, and he manages to call back when Holly and I are discussing the finer points of which should we do first: the sheep or horse réttir?

For privacy, I take my cell phone into the house, leaving Holly alone with a bottle of red wine she has already half-finished. I am so full of good cheer when I start describing my symptoms to my doctor—because I've been busy making réttir plans with Holly, and who has time to be a hypochondriac about fingers and toes acting weird—that when he reads back the description of symptoms I left with his medical secretary, I reassure him, "I'm sure it's nothing but I thought I should run it by you."

I am watching Holly through my kitchen window as she finishes off the bottle, thinking, *my new best friend drinks a lot, I didn't even get a glass of that.*

My doctor asks how long and with what frequency I have been having these symptoms. I tell him the truth, but lightheartedly. I'm feeling stupid for calling him and complaining about my fingers and toes, and I've got the sheep réttir to plan. "Only for a few weeks and, yes, I guess it's getting worse." I hear him mutter, almost as if I'm not supposed to hear, "I hope it's not MS."

"What? What did you say?"

"I'm sorry I blurted that out. You're actually not the right age for it, you're too old for it so I'm not worried. It usually strikes people in their thirties, but we should check it out."

It hardly eases my worry. He patches me in to his scheduler to set up an appointment for the next day. That's unlike him. He's an overbooked doctor and he doesn't have you come in unless he's worried. The secretary tells me, "He wants you in here right away," and schedules me for the next day. Now I'm really scared.

I don't know what to do with Holly sitting outside. "That was my doctor. He wants to put me through some tests." She takes in what I'm saying, but I don't explain any more except to say, "I'm sure it's nothing."

But she reads me correctly, I want to be alone. Talk of the réttir or horses is ruined. My mind is full of dread.

In the next few days, I go through a series of scare-the-shit-out-of-me tests, and then wait a few days for results. My symptoms worsen. I can't go to work. I can barely lift my arms and in ten days I am supposed to go to Iceland.

All the tests come back normal. "None of the bad autoimmune issues," my doctor says. I am elated with the news, yet I can barely walk now and I am to leave for Iceland in five days. I wait a couple of days to get better, but instead it gets worse. I get my doctor on the phone. "What's wrong with me? I can't get off the couch." He sets me up with a neurologist for an appointment two days later. The neurologist can find nothing wrong with me in the initial examination. But he can't be sure unless I get an MRI. The first one available is on the day my flight leaves for Iceland. I have no choice but to cancel my trip.

I am asked if I want a tranquilizer for the MRI or if I just want to keep my eyes closed. I opt for closing my eyes and under the MRI dome, I try to concentrate on visions of Thingeyrar: the horses, the fields of lupine, the rivers and lakes. Through all the bangs and knocks of the imaging machine, I wonder if I will I ever get back there. What if the test shows up something dreadful and debilitating? What if I lose my facilities? Who will take care of my poor, sweet, demented mother? I toy with the idea that if this is our fate, I'll take her for a ride in the car and we will drive off a cliff, Thelma and Louise style, rather than the two of us being a burden to everyone. My mother, myself! We'll go out of this world together, how symbiotic. I am working myself up to tears, which is bad under the dome of an MRI. I must not cry, it will start a regrettable cascade of runny nose, short breath, and opening my eyes and confronting the claustrophobic dome.

The word *vik* means "bay." The *ing* ending means "a people." So the Vikings were the people who sailed into bays. But that was the term applied to them by others. They considered themselves Norse. Before Viking was a noun, it was a verb. To go "a Viking" was to go raiding; it was an activity, a choice of employment, let's say, like piracy. Some Norse, though, were looking for places to settle and bring their families. They were the emigrants. They came in different boats, called *knarrs*, which were cargo ships. But the other Norse who went "a Viking" did so in the dragon-headed prow long ships that had shallow drafts allowing them to row into inlets and bays and up the rivers to sack towns.

We were not Vikings, we were not settlers, we were not immigrants, but we were also not tourists. We were repeat visitors. And we turned it into a gerund, "going Iceland." Viv and I were talking on the phone one depressing winter evening, and she was telling me about her horse's illness, her one son's antics, and the withdrawal of troops in Iraq that didn't include her other son's unit. She and her husband were besieged with these issues, when she said to him, "I'm sorry, Bob, I can't take it anymore, I'm going Iceland on you." He knew she meant not just that she had bought her plane tickets for the coming summer. She meant it mentally, to keep sane. She was going to Iceland in the summer, but she was going there now as a state of mind. "When it gets dark here, my minds goes Iceland. I'm walking in the midnight sun."

It became Viv's and my refrain, a mental survival trick, for when we sought peace of mind, when we needed to emotionally check out. We never shared it with the others. It helped us withdraw from worldly or personal matters and gave us a mental destination. When life overwhelmed us at home, we went Iceland in our minds. For Viv, it was walking in the midnight sun by the Vatnsdalsá River. For me, it was being in the saddle heading out north to the sea.

Sometimes I would be cleaning up my mother after having messed herself, and I would think, *I gotta go Iceland.* But it didn't have to be during life's difficulties, it could be when life felt static and dull, when I was sitting in meetings at work and had nothing to add to the conversation. I'd remind myself I was more than this person at a meeting: I'd ride North. I'd go Iceland.

There's a picture of us that someone took in the early years: we are on the sand dunes near the Greenland Sea. We're giving our horses a rest, so that each of us has our horse loosely held with a long rein as we let them graze. We are in various stages of repose: I am next to my horse, my arms resting on the saddle, looking out at the sea. Helga has a stalk of grass in her mouth, studying the horses grazing. Sylvie is flat on her back, knees up, eyes probably closed. Eve is checking her horse's bit and rein. The sparse scruff grass on the dunes is flattened from the wind. You can't hear it, but you can fill in the background noise with Arctic birdsong, the gulls and the mating calls of snipe. In the early years when no one carried a cell phone to Iceland and no one knew where the hell we were, we were there, riding horses, resting horses, somewhere on the far northern shore, where the view of the world was so vast you could see the earth's curve. And that's where I went in my head, to that spot, when I was going Iceland.

The MRI is over and it is read then and there—and it shows nothing wrong. Nothing. No MS, no degenerative disease, no autoimmune problem. They shrug and tell me that it's probably viral, or a fish toxin, or a fly bite I got in the Caribbean. My symptoms retreat, ever so slowly, over the summer with a lot of recommended massage therapy and hot yoga.

Since there is nothing wrong with me, my husband is relieved he isn't going to lose me or have to spoon-feed me. He says, "I was really hoping you'd make it to Iceland, I know how much it means to you."

He now sees it as a part of who I am, and I know it's become something he likes about me. "That's my wife, she goes to Iceland to ride horses every summer."

He suggests a trip to Block Island where there are stables and I could ride on the beach. When I get better, I tell him. When I am fully recovered.

"And maybe Holly will go with me on the sheep réttir this fall." I catch a quick flinch from him, like, "let's not go that far."

As for Holly, I should know by now I am never good at making fast friends. I imagine I see too much that isn't really there. While I was going through all the numbness of limbs, all the testing, all the uncertainty, we kept in touch by email, but I downplayed my fears. I could not bear to put a chink in my physical armor—my strength and vitality were pivotal to seeing myself as tough, as someone who could ride horses in Iceland.

When fall came and I said to Holly that it's the time to go "a réttir-ing," she backed out. She said she couldn't spend the money, that they needed a new washer and dryer and that the cost of that alone was the price of the plane ticket. I get this, I do. I lived on the cheap for so many years. But things have eased up financially for us, enough so that money issues are no longer on our marital argument docket. But Holly was on a pension, and her husband was subject to seasonal work. So that freedom of retiring she talked about, of no longer having to show up somewhere, of making your own days, also meant that they were bound by the manacles of living on a restricted budget. And gradually, as if I represented some kind of lost opportunity, an adventure that passed her by, she stopped answering my emails and texts.

We Went Some Places

My mother is down to living in one room with five pieces of furniture: an armchair, bed, coffee table, credenza, and a dresser. When she's not in bed sleeping, she is sitting in her armchair, often sleeping there too. She eats her breakfast and her lunch in her armchair. She uses the seat in her walker as a table.

I moved her to an independent, assisted-living place in New Haven so I could see her more often, be able to drop in on her, shop for her. She barely talks now, and my relationship with my mother used to be all talk. We would talk about everything for hours, leaving off our conversation one day and picking it up three days later midstream, as if the days that passed were just dutiful interruptions of our conversation. Now she repeats the same questions out of habit: "How are the kids? How old are they now?" I tell her, and she acts surprised each time, as we repeat this question and answer at least half a dozen times during a visit. And that's a good visit. A bad visit is when she asks if she is married and how many kids she has. A really bad visit is when she asks if I'm her mother. And then there are those visits after she's been sick and feverish, when she hallucinates and thinks her husband, dead for many years, is living next door with the "kitchen lady."

The golf channel is on. It is the only channel she watches. She used to play golf, it was her only sport, though she doesn't remember that. She watches it blankly as I cut her nails and tweeze her facial whiskers. I brush her hair repeatedly, trying to tame the stubborn cowlick that sticks up like a straggled bird feather now that she spends all of her time either lying in bed or sitting in her chair. I buy her Ensure. I buy her Depends. I shower her if she smells too much in between the showers the aides give her. I dish out ice cream to put her in a better mood. I care for her like an old baby. Her memory has been failing for six years, as the disease shrinks her brain to one third her normal size. Dementia is like watching a mental illness slowly overtake someone's mind.

I am her anchor in this world. I don't tell her when I'm going away. I used to, but it caused her too much distress. For weeks before I would leave and weeks after my return, every time I saw her she would break down and cry, "You're back. I thought you were gone for good." It is easier to keep my travels a secret from her. But sometimes in her foggy mind, she has eerily prescient moments. "Are you going to Finland soon?" she'll ask me, only days after I booked my Iceland flight. Or on the very same day I booked a flight to Newfoundland, she asked me, "Why do I think you're going to Nova Scotia? Are you?" She isn't exactly spot-on about the location, but she nails the general area.

Once she was an avid reader, but now she is down to two books in her apartment: A Bible that an evangelical nurse's aide dropped off and a collection of the Best American poems that I brought her. She hasn't picked them up in years. On her coffee table that she bought in Hong Kong—glass top, mother of pearl inlay, hand-painted, carved dragon legs—she has twelve photo albums from her trips abroad. Though it was a big part of her life for many decades, she doesn't remember where she traveled anymore. And the photo albums don't help. They only seem to confuse her. If I point to a picture and say, "You're in Bangkok here," she'll say, "Was I really? Huh."

Throughout the 1970s and '80s, when my mother was in her fifties and sixties, she traveled with her two friends Rosemary and Edie. They went to Greece, Turkey, Hong Kong, Thailand, Egypt, Morocco, Tanzania, Brazil. They were not fainthearted travelers. For the time, their age, their social class, their gender—they were mavericks. I liked this trait in my mother, though I never had much interest in the funny stories she told when she came home—I was too eager to open my gifts. And if my daughter only half listens to my funny tales and gives only a cursory glance at the videos of horses on my iPhone, with me narrating, "And this is Loki tölting," I understand. It's Loki tölting, where are the presents?

I knew my mother's two friends well; I saw them often. Rosemary was the giddy, flighty one. Irish background. She was a spendthrift, which irked my mother's frugal mind. "She has a problem with money, that one." When Rosemary's husband left her for another woman, my mother said, "He probably found someone who doesn't spend money like water."

Edie was the dark, voluptuous one. The term used back then was "sexpot." Twice divorced. Jewish. She picked up men on vacation. "She has a problem with men, that one," my mother summed her up. It irked her Puritan mind.

Then Edie picked up a third husband on a Greek island. He became her third divorce. "She married him after knowing him for about a week. He married her to get a green card."

The three women met while they were getting their psych nursing degrees. Psych training was still heavily Freudian then, and they were prone to throwing out the terms like weapons. "That's so oedipal." Or, "She has no control over her Id." Or, "It's anal retentive of you to do that."

Each era has a belief system or two that influences our view of things. We stake everything on it and pity the poor antiquated people who came before us and didn't have the benefit of this enlightenment, this bright new wisdom. Welcome to a whole new theory of life, a new religion to replace the old order. And then it too is deconstructed and tossed, deemed worthless, or, worse, dangerously wrong.

In their Freudian exuberance, I believe my mother and her friends went too far and said some things—diagnosing each other—that they could not retract. The three of them had a falling out. According to my mother, Edie "never forgave me for saying that to her." I never found out what the "that" was because my mother regretted it, but also defended it as something Edie needed to hear. And with Rosemary, it was something Rosemary said to my mother. "She had no right saying that, she of all people." Again, I had no idea what "that" was about, either.

They made efforts to patch things up, but they were tepid and temporary alliances. My mother moved to Connecticut to be close to me, and Edie and Rosemary eventually retired elsewhere. The three of them never got together again.

But toward the end of my mother's cognitive-aware life, before the gaps in her memory gradually grew larger than the memories themselves, these were the women last on her mind. Not her sister-in-law, my aunt Anne, whom she lived near for close to thirty years; not her early friends in our neighborhood who she went through young motherhood with; not her later "condo" friends she met and golfed with in retirement.

It was Edie and Rosemary she asked about when we'd take walks around the duck pond in her condo village. The women she traveled with in her fifties were the women she talked most about, who figured in greatly as she was summing up her life, trying to make sense of all the years. "We had a lot of fun together. We went some places. I wonder where they are now?"

2013

—⊶⊷—

Welcome to Iceland

Arrival in Keflavík is always a dreary affair. Maybe it is because we arrive just before midnight, but it is eerily quiet for an airport, even though five flights have deplaned one right after the other, and there are new shops brightly lit and open for these arrivals. And even though the sun is on the horizon, peeking out now and then between the rain clouds, and it is the longest day of the year, the light is gray and dusky.

At the passport check, the uniformed men and women ask us the usual questions with poker-faced officiousness: How long are you staying? Business or vacation? Iceland, with a population of 320,000, is expecting a million visitors in 2013. But all this attention to their country seems to leave Icelanders apathetic. When Viv steps up to the passport booth, she tries to awaken them with a loud, "Hello!" Then they take an especially long time looking at her passport, flipping the pages back and forth. "It's like a book of Iceland, with one trip to China," she says. Their response is deadpan. It means nothing to them that we suffer from Icelandophilia.

What welcomes one to Iceland now are the billboards that line the airport corridors. They are friendly, pretty, and culturally informative. This year it's a campaign that includes Icelandic sayings. "As we say in Iceland: Everything that is nice is green." "As we say in Iceland: They who splash the skyr own it." At least the tourism industry is trying.

The geographical placement of the airport is not exactly welcoming, either. It is on the western tip of a rocky, brown, inhospitable part of the Reykjanes peninsula. Nothing but volcanic rocks, a lunar-like landscape on which our first astronauts practiced their eventual encounter with the moon. This is the first look at the country and it is not pretty. Certainly no green and pleasant land, no matter what the billboards say. Just hardscrabble lava turf and a scattering of rough grass. And rain. I have never landed in Keflavík without it raining.

So upon arrival my enthusiasm initially wanes: Um, why am I here again? Even after missing last year and vowing I would never miss the trip again, I arrive and I wonder: Why this otherwise forgotten island thrown up by volcanoes in the North Atlantic Ocean? Do I make too much of this place? Do I get carried away with enthusiasm and expectations that it can never live up to? Iceland—the country, the land, the horses, the people, or the people I travel with—owes me nothing. Horses misbehave, people can be irritating, and the weather is subarctic. Immediately upon my return, I am filled with such doubts.

I got into a conversation on the plane with the woman sitting next to me, who sheepishly admitted that she had been to Iceland three times already and people can't understand why she keeps going back. "Welcome to my world," I said, "This is my eighth trip."

Viv has come this year, warily so, at my urging. "Eve's going, Pippa's not," I told her in the middle of the winter. We bought our tickets in February. In April, we found out Pippa was going and bringing two others with her, a friend and the friend's fifteen-year-old daughter. I had to talk Viv out of backing out. "Why should we let her dictate our trip to Iceland? Why should she take Thingeyrar away from us?"

As we wait for luggage, I have to cheer up Viv. "Eve says they're getting their own car. Sylvie says they are doing their own trip." When Viv shakes her head, I say, "Let's make a pact, we won't let her get to us."

Viv shakes her head again. "I don't know, I don't know. I'll try."

"C'mon, we're in Iceland, let's leave all worries behind." But I know it's not that. Although we can leave our home lives behind us, if Pippa is snappish with us here, we'll be forced into a self-protective stance, and that is the opposite of everything we come here for.

It has been two years since we last saw Pippa and I know from Eve that she has had more medical issues. Last year she came with her own breathing apparatus and Eve said she stayed in her room the whole time. "She looked close to death. I thought she was going to stop breathing, I thought she was going to die on us. I'm not even sure why she came," Eve said.

I'll give Pippa the benefit of the doubt: She comes to Iceland for the same reasons, for the same validation, as I do. When I was going through my medical scare last year with its imminent threat of chronic ill health, everything in my mind became last wishes. If only I could get to Iceland again, if only I could ride again. This must be how Pippa feels, and she goes through medical scares and medical procedures more frequently than I do. She must think of this place as an antidote to her malfunctioning body.

Viv and I meet up with Eve, Sylvie, and Margot coming in on the Boston flight. It's Margot's first trip to Iceland after a five-year hiatus. She greets us most enthusiastically. "Hi guys!" Eve goes off to pick up our rental car and we wait and wait some more. We meander into the airport's food mart and buy yogurt and chocolate-covered cookies and pretzels. An hour or more later Eve comes back with a set of keys to an older model SUV. "Our luggage should fit in this."

Five of us are traveling in one car this year and we don't know how to pack light. We need our Wellies and riding boots, our helmets, chaps and riding pants, plus multiple jackets, fleece and rain, which require many suitcases and bags. We stuff, push, jam our bags in the back of the SUV and slam the hatch door shut. The latch catches and we cheer. Then, with the overflow luggage at our feet or on our laps, we head merrily to Reykjavík. And I mean merrily, too. All of us are talking at once in a voluble banter.

Eve explains about the snafu at the car rental place. The station wagon we reserved was too small but the people who reserved the SUV thought it was too big, so we switched. "It all worked out. See, the universe takes care of us."

Margot talks about her equine-assisted psychotherapy, and the influence of the positive psychologist Tal Ben-Shahar.

Viv talks about her tai chi trip to China last year, which segues into Sylvie talking about Iyengar yoga.

"Finding the perfect balance is nirvana," Sylvie says. "I think it's like Freud's 'oceanic oneness'—a religious energy, the sensation of being one with the universe. There were some good things about Freud, not many, but some."

I want to hear more about "oceanic oneness" but Margot, who is brimming with news, jumps in with: "Guys, can I tell you how this trip came about for me? I was sitting around with Sylvie and we're drinking beer . . ."

Sylvie says, "All good stories start with this line . . ."

"And she says, 'Why don't you come to Iceland with us this year?'"

Sylvie says, "Can you believe she hasn't been back in five years?"

"And so I finished my second beer . . ."

Sylvie intakes air: "That was strong beer, a stout . . . 9 percent . . ."

"And I went online and just impulsively bought my tickets . . . Oh, and this is the best part . . ."

Sylvie: "Yes! Tell them about that . . ."

"The next day my horoscope reads 'you will travel far and fall in love.' So, guys, listen up, I'm supposed to fall in love on this trip."

Eve squeals. "You're gonna fall in love with an Icelandic guy. Maybe he'll have horses!"

"That's what I was thinking."

"Wait, Margot," I say, "it might not be a guy you fall in love with. It could be a horse. We often fall in love with horses in Iceland. Look at Eve, she's bought five horses."

Margot thinks about this for a second. "I'm good with either. Preferably both. A horse and a guy."

This is a cheery thought for everyone. When Margot first moved to the Berkshires she was getting over a bad marriage and her ex was stalking her. He worked for the government and had high security clearance, so who was she going to report him to . . . the local police?

And like Sylvie and her crush on Ólof, this is how we do men in Iceland: it's all projection. Our imaginations quickly run to cheery visions of a mate and horses. We've got it all figured out in the next ten minutes: Margot's

Icelandic boyfriend, his farm, and his horses, the back and forth between Boston and Keflavík.

Viv jumps in with an astute calculation: that Margot will collect so many air mile points that every fifth trip would be free.

"That would be great, it would cut down on costs," Margot says. "I could keep my life in Massachusetts but come over once a month to be with my boyfriend, and then in the summer stay longer."

"You could do that, and we could visit Helga first and then you and your boyfriend's farm."

In our minds, it's a done deal and we are all very happy for Margot and her Icelandic boyfriend and having a new farm to visit. All we have to do now is find him, meet him, and get this thing going.

"I hope it's up north near Helga's," Margot says, somewhat wistfully, as if she'll miss us all if dumb luck would have it that her boyfriend's farm is in the south.

———

Farther down the road, Eve and I start debating, defending, the reasons for liking *Game of Thrones* so much. "I know it's horribly violent, and I hate that, but the story is riveting. I can't stop watching it," I say.

"It's such a great story. Jack and I are so wrapped up in it," Eve says.

The others are squirming. Viv says, "Not for me."

"It's filmed here. The Wall scenes at least, and others."

"In one scene you can tell it's in Iceland because they are all riding Icelandic horses and tölting," Eve points out. "It's not like they can import other horses."

Margot says, "Maybe I'll start with the book first."

Then we are on to people we all know. Brittany is getting a degree in social work. Lisa's mother has died, and Lisa has moved into her house. Eve brings up her sister, Maggie. "She's into roller derby. She's joined a team and they dress in sequined outfits and she competes regularly."

"Maggie must be sixty by now," I say.

"Something like that," Eve says, cagily, as if I might be doing some quick math—unlikely—to figure out her age.

Viv talks about the necessary ingredient of friendship. "It needs a measure of grace. You have to be able to recognize shortcomings and move on."

She might be aiming this at me for talking her into coming on this trip with Pippa. She is giving me, this trip, maybe even Pippa, a measure of grace.

Margot says, "Friendship is like energy attracting like energy."

Sylvie, apropos of nothing, declares: "I have hypomania. I do!"

The engine light is on and the brakes grind and squeak, but Eve assures us, "the car rental guy said that was normal." After a short pause during which we all stare with concern at the incomprehensible symbols on the dashboard, we pick up where we left off. Sibba will meet us at the bakery in Borgarnes tomorrow.

"Pass the gluten," Margot says, meaning the McVitie's and pretzels.

And then the dreary landscape, mile by mile, starts getting softer and greener. A farmhouse on the coast is illuminated by a burst of two A.M. sunshine.

Margot says emphatically, passionately, "I can't believe I'm here, you guys. This is so beautiful."

And it is.

I am with this group of women for another year in Iceland, and my heart is full of deep affection for them. Hurtling toward Reykjavík with lousy brakes and an intense camaraderie, there isn't anywhere else I'd rather be, or anyone else I'd rather be with.

Ridiculous Women

Pippa's car is already in the driveway when we pull up to Helga's at Thingeyrar. "Huh. She wasn't supposed to get here until dinnertime," Sylvie says.

Viv is tense. I am tense. And the idea that pulling up to Helga's makes us tense is all wrong. And Helga isn't there to greet us, either, to defuse the tension.

As we drag our stuff into the guesthouse, Sylvie sees her usual bedroom has luggage in it. Eve sees her usual bedroom has luggage in it. My little bedroom has luggage in it. That leaves one bedroom for the five of us.

"Excuse me," Sylvie says, walking into the kitchen where Pippa is drying a teacup. I am expecting to see a pale, wan, sickly Pippa from the way Eve described her visit last year, but she looks sturdy and healthy, even rosy colored.

"There are three of you and you've taken three bedrooms. There are five of us and you've left us only one bedroom," Sylvie says.

"But it's got two sets of bunk beds and one twin bed," Pippa says. "You can all fit in there."

"That doesn't work for us," Sylvie says. "I suggest you move out of one room."

Pippa throws the dishtowel down and walks out of the room in a huff. Yep, she's feeling her oats.

Karen, Pippa's friend, comes out looking confrontational. Everything about her is tight and small. She wears workout tights, a tank top, and a microfiber jacket designed to show every inch of her muscular skinny body. She's got short, light brown hair. She has a fifteen-year-old daughter, Madison, who follows not-so-closely behind her and looks nothing like her. She's five inches taller, heftier, with thick black hair and dark eyes.

"I don't understand," Karen says. "Why do we have to move bedrooms?" Viv, Margot, and I have never met Karen or her daughter, but this is no time for introductions.

"Because you don't each get your own bedroom," Sylvie says. "You have to share, like the rest of us."

Sylvie is in her cowboy stance, feet apart, hands on hips. She's using her teacher tone—*I'm losing my patience with you and I'm done explaining.*

Karen is in her barbell stance. Feet planted, knees bent, arms by her side, ready to lift a weight and throw it at somebody.

We've just pulled into town, our luggage is still in the stagecoach, and it's a face-off, a stand-off, high noon for cowboy Sylvie and barbell Barbie.

"Karen, why don't you share a room with your daughter?" Eve asks sweetly and we all look over at Madison, ready to coo maternally at the child.

"Are you crazy? I am not sharing a room with my daughter."

Margot audibly gasps at her response. But Madison's face has that blank bored-ness teenagers practice to perfection.

Sylvie says, "Okay, we're going to go outside and get our luggage. You three figure it out."

Outside, we huddle. Margot is shaking. "I hate conflict. I feel like throwing up. I'm not good with conflict. Maybe I'll get a hotel room down the street."

Eve says, "I just don't understand what is going on here. Why isn't she being reasonable?"

Sylvie blames herself. "I should not have invited her this year."

"But why is she angry at us?" Eve asks.

I remember that all wars are turf wars, she's fighting for her turf, and a sizable expansion of it. Sometimes it's a few bedrooms in a guesthouse, sometimes it's a country.

"Guys, I'm gonna get a hotel room. I don't mind. I really can't deal with this kind of stress."

"I should not have invited her," Sylvie repeats. "She's trying to push us out."

"I hate to say this, but Viv and I saw this coming."

Sylvie takes in air. "Did you?"

Viv says, "We sure did."

"You know, Pippa didn't want you two to come. She didn't want me to invite you. She doesn't like you two."

"She didn't want us to come? Specifically, me and Viv? I've been here since year one. Viv since year two."

Sylvie nods. "I should have known she was trouble from that alone. But I felt pressure from my friend who's friends with her."

Viv and I walk away together to discuss. "Wow," Viv says, "wow. I can't believe this."

"At least they now see Pippa as we see her."

Viv says, "Why would Pippa say that to Sylvie? Why would she mention that to us? This puts me right back to how I felt in middle school with the girl cliques."

Unfortunately, this is one of the moments when I wish age didn't seem so fluid. I am reminded of the day my girl pack dropped me. We went from sixth grade to eight grade tight as a knot, and then we all entered high school together. In the lunchroom, we commandeered the same long table every day. In a short time, we went from the girls who ran in the woods to the girls who ruled the cafeteria seating. One day it was Valerie who found herself on the outs—there was an "ew" every time her name was mentioned. And one day when she went to sit down, there was no chair for her. And one day it was me.

"This is taken, you can't sit here." I spent the next three years of high school on a social ice floe. Who are the Pippas of the world who decide these things?

—◦◦◦—

We move our stuff inside the house and leave it in the hallway. The five of us huddle in the big bedroom, waiting for one of them to move into a different bedroom. We repeat in a stage whisper what we said outside to each other: Margot feels sick from the conflict; Sylvie blames herself; Eve is ruffled by Pippa's anger; and Viv and I repeat "we saw it coming."

When we look up, Pippa is standing in our bedroom doorway. She waits awhile before saying anything. Eve smiles at her and says, "Hey," and I know she is hopeful that Pippa is going to apologize and be reasonable and the universe will come together and attend to these human disturbances. But Pippa draws in air and stands tall. In her most British Queen's English, her most matronly attitude, she dresses us down. "You are ridiculous women. Ridiculous women. I do not understand why you are making this fuss. I do not understand you at all!"

"Which bedroom are you vacating?" Sylvie unflinchingly drills home the important point.

Pippa walks away in disgust and we hear her bump her suitcases upstairs to the spooky bedrooms.

The Nights of Magical Thinking

When Viv and I take our midnight sunlit walk, we rehash the flare up and we get incensed about what Sylvie told us—that Pippa didn't want us invited.

"Us," I say, "the original travelers to Thingeyrar."

"I picked up that personality trait on the second trip she was with us."

"I picked it up the first time. She would not talk to me, and I really wanted to be her friend. I thought we would be good friends."

We are quiet for a while, lost in our own hurt thoughts, and then Viv asks, "Do you wonder why she singled us out to dislike?"

"Because she couldn't pick on Sylvie and Eve. They are her ticket here."

"So we're the easy pickings. Or were."

"It's turf," I say. "It's a fight over this beautiful place and who gets to share it."

"But what does it matter to her whether we're here or not? Why does she try to kick us off the land?"

"She doesn't want to share it."

On our walks with each other, Viv and I still talk about our lives in ways we don't ever talk about in front of the others. Her son Jonathan is back from Iraq in one piece and looking for work and her son Eric is still looking. "You know the prefrontal cortex is not fully developed in boys until the age of twenty-five or even later. That's the part that controls impulsivity, decision making, reason."

Ever since the news about this research came out, every parent I know with a wayward son is talking about it. "What are we to do? The synapses haven't connected yet!" I've said it myself. Boys make bad choices caused by lack of brain connectivity. They haven't learned to be risk-averse. That's why they willingly join frats and the army. But my son is closing in on twenty-five and Eric is twenty-six. Our boys are pushing the age limit of this theory.

I need these walks in the sunlight as much as Viv does. We pass the sheep and they safely graze; we pass the Steinnes farm where the horses notice us walking by and trot up to greet us. We walk down to the edges of the lake to pick up the magical red rocks. We have added another stop to our nightly walks, visiting the church on the property, Þingeyrakirkja. This beautiful little church, rebuilt in the 1800s on a monastery site from the 1100s, has become a popular tourist site. A few years ago, we watched as they built a visitor center, complete with a café and illustrations of the Vatnsdæla saga that was written here by monks 800 years ago. During the day, we watch the busses pull up and the people disembark at what we once thought of as our little, private church that only Helga held the keys to.

But at midnight, the church is empty. I feel like a pilgrim when I enter it, as if here in this sacred space some grand revelation will come to me. My eyes are drawn immediately to the midnight-blue ceiling with a thousand golden stars. Above the choir loft are ornately painted statuettes of the twelve disciples, brought to Iceland in the late Middle Ages. After sitting quietly awhile in separate pews with our own thoughts, Viv and I get up, put coins in the wooden box and light the votive candles. I know she's wishing what I'm wishing for. I indulge in magical thinking more in Iceland than at home—the red rocks along the river are good luck talismans, yes, they are. They are. Lighting the church votives in this hallowed space will protect my children from harm and angels will watch over them. Because at the root of parenthood there is an unspoken helplessness to how things will turn out for your kids. Maybe when you're a young mother you dream of grandeur for them, but as you get older and you watch the world and all its trouble, all you hope for is the absence of bad luck.

"What we are reduced to," Viv says, lighting another candle, "is to request you just stay alive, kids. Just stay alive until you grow up more and those synapses form."

That maturation process, it can kill you.

The Sisterhood of the Ridiculous Women

The flare up with Pippa weighs heavily on all of us. We don't like conflict. My husband likes to point out the difference between men and women when they fight: a woman's instinct for conflict avoidance, he says, causes deeper and longer lasting wounds. He claims that guys just deal with it head on. When a friend of his acts like a jackass, he just tells him to stop being such a dick. And they come to their senses and they both forget the issue and move on. Supposedly. He doesn't understand why women (like me) when confronted (by people like Pippa) can't call someone out. That we need to obfuscate, deliberate, plant messages behind the enemy line. Or worse, that we debate whether someone else's bad behavior was somehow our fault because we weren't nice enough. I think of how we huddled in whimpering little circles outside the guesthouse, and only Sylvie had the nerve to deal with it bluntly. She was alpha mare enough to say to Pippa, "Which room are you vacating?"

My friend who is a divorce lawyer says, "Women never forget an insult. They remember *every* word." I can attest to this, unfortunately. Some insults don't register with me, but if an insult happens to hit a nerve, I remember every word and I remember it forever. I remember who said it and where it was said and if pressed, I can recall the time of day, the slant of the sun, and my usual mute response. "You had no comeback?" my husband would ask. "Why didn't you let them have it?"

And even long after I've stopped brooding on the insult, which I eventually do, even when I have regained emotional distance from it, I still have total recall of the incident. "How do you remember that?" my husband asks me when I bring up something hurtful someone said to me twenty years ago. "I don't even remember who those people were."

Was anyone surprised when the #MeToo movement exploded and women remembered everything? (See Hallgerd of Njál's Saga.) The women could quote verbatim what had been said ten, twenty, thirty years ago. The men who were called out were flummoxed. They had some vague memory, but could they recall a word that was spoken?

Eve tries to be the peacemaker. She quotes the Pema Chödrön line about anger only lasting ninety seconds and reminds us of the temporariness of the physical manifestations: the palpitations, the fear, the rise in blood pressure—all of which were exactly the responses we felt at the time as if we were a herd of horses surrounded by roaring lions, not the mild-looking older Englishwoman in sweater sets and the middle-aged gym rat in Spandex. Sometimes I can see why women's conflicts baffle my husband.

We don't tell Helga about our quarrel, because we don't want her to think we are troublesome guests. Helga is like Aud the Deep-Minded in the sagas, who was one of the earliest settlers, considered the first mother of Iceland and known for her wisdom and kindness. Aud was greatly respected—she captained a ship of twenty men and freed the slaves. If Helga is like Aud, we are more like Hallgerd clashing with Bergthora over a bench, or, in this case, baðstofa. We are ridiculous.

When the five of us are together, we tell ourselves we have to put this flare-up with Pippa aside. She can't ruin our time in Thingeyrar. We want to deflect her hostility and not escalate the conflict because, quite simply, it will take up too much of our precious time at the farm. Eve sets the tone, because she always does, and we follow her lead. We practice being more civil to them, especially in the barn, where Eve is very nervous about bad karma around horses. So, we say, "Could you pass the curry brush when you're done? Can I have that hoof pick, please?"

Cordiality reigns, but it's an uneasy peace. And it bugs me. What Pippa said questioned my whole being. It wasn't that she rejected my early gestures of friendship. I'm sure that over the course of my life I too have unknowingly or purposely rebuffed overtures of friendship. It's that she objected to my very presence at Thingeyrar. You reach a point in life where you feel pretty confident, and there's enough evidence supporting the notion that you're a genial, interesting, likable person. Then suddenly you're made aware that someone thinks otherwise. It happens and normally I would spend the rest of my life avoiding that person, and they would avoid me. But I can't here. And it's here I want to be. And it's here where she intentionally picked me (and Viv) out of the circle to kick out of the tribe.

I try to avoid Pippa and Karen when we're not in the barn. I direct all necessary social interactions to Madison, when she doesn't have her earbuds in. I can't blame her for wanting to tune us out. She walked into a minefield of unknown women having a spat. And her mother spends all her time working out.

No one who has ever traveled with us has been as dedicated to fitness as Karen. She gets up at six every morning to run eight miles, while we get up at eight and spend a good part of the morning over a leisurely breakfast. She spends most of her free time on the lawn trying out some odd looking, old-fashioned calisthenics with a timer, while we spend most of our free time soaking in the hot pot or sitting around the kitchen table snacking. Eve finds out that Karen is a Spin and Pilates instructor and is preparing a new class, one of those boot camps, which is what she is testing out on the grassy knoll while we gaze up at the skies in the steamy hot pot.

Sociologists talk about the influence of social networks and social contagion, that is, if you hang out with people who are overweight, you tend to put on weight, or if you're always with smokers, you start smoking. If you hang around people who are unhappy, you become depressed. Basically, this theory is heavily dependent on mathematical models of network formation, using statistical analyses of large observational studies. I've seen the PowerPoint slides the professors put up at a lecture—they have a circle with a large point in the center (the infector) that radiates out with clusters of smaller points (the infected), which tells us that our behaviors are not individualistic, but instead socially contagious. A rather long-winded, heavily researched, and costly way of saying what our mothers used to tell us for nothing: "Birds of a feather flock together."

I've noticed our physical activity in Iceland reflects our social network: we ride, we walk, even strenuously at times, we do yoga—and we snack and soak a lot in the hot pot.

Karen doesn't rest or indulge. She runs, spins, lifts, pushes, pulls, jumps in place, and eats only vegetables. To us, she is an alien, and we hope her behavior isn't contagious and will infect us. And it sure doesn't look like she will adapt her behavior to be more like us.

Out on the trail, I ride a handsome gelding named Mokkur. He is the color of a portobello and his mane has blonde tips. He's a big boy for an Icelandic, fourteen hands, with a thick head and neck and a stocky body. But he trips often. I ask Frieda what I am doing wrong. She says, "He may be a little heavy in the front. If he starts to trip, pull his head up immediately. You need to help him balance." For a long time when I rode, I thought every problem the horse had was caused by my faulty riding skills. But there is rarely a perfect horse. No horse has perfect confirmation, perfect gaits, perfect balance, and perfect attitude. All horses have weaknesses, and all riders need to figure out what those are and work on it. Training is ongoing with horses; they are not done at any age.

Mokkur has a smooth tölt, but we're very crowded on a narrow path heading toward the Greenland Sea, and as the sand gets deep, I let him trot. He trips so badly he goes down on his knees. I get tossed out of my seat, hit the saddle's pommel hard, lose my stirrups, but manage to bring Mokkur's head up sharply while hanging onto his neck, and pop myself back into the saddle, avoiding disaster.

Pippa is riding right behind me, close to Mokkur's tail, and doesn't alert the others to slow the pace down as I am half hanging off the saddle. She expresses no word of concern for me, though she couldn't have missed my near catastrophe. When I regain my balance, she passes me and she's grinning. Eve is worried about bad karma in the barn; I'm worried about bad karma out on the trail. Horses are sensitive to moods. What if they pick up our antagonism toward each other? I've read that some Native American people believe you should never ride a horse when you are angry. Even if you are going to war.

But nothing makes the five of us tighter than a common foe. While we are walking in the fields after dinner, down by the drainage ditches with the massive dandelions and cotton grass, Margot poses this question: "And what's wrong with being ridiculous?"

"I don't know. I kind of like it."

"I think we should claim it, own it: The Sisterhood of the Ridiculous Women."

"It's subversive."

"It's who we are, what we are."

"It's how we roll."

In Which We Order, Dish Out, and Leave

We are driving around the town of Sauðárkrókur. Helga told us to remember it as "soda cracker." We are looking for a fish skin museum. Yep, it's one we haven't been to yet. Iceland seems to make every product they've ever made or every hardship they've ever endured into a national museum. Complete with entrance fees and a summer staff that dusts off the cash register when we enter, surprised that anyone, particularly tourists, have shown up. We've made a dent in most of them: textile museums, the saga and folk museums, the horse history museum, whale museum, seal museum, the phallus museum, witchcraft museum, the sea ice museum, half a dozen turf house museums, and our current destination.

Eve has gotten it into her head that she wants to buy a fish skin wallet. Don't we all. Over the years, enamored of all local crafts, we have collected stores of such items: lamb skin shoe liners, buttons made of sheep bones, combs from ram's horn, earrings made out of lava rock.

Sauðárkrókur translates as "sheep-river-hook" and Route 75 goes through it at the north end, right along the crook of the bay that features the town's livelihood: fish processing plants. Off the main road, the town has more roads than most Icelandic towns, with shops and cafés, even a few hotels. The buildings are brightly painted and we hit the town in sunny weather, so it sparkles with the light bouncing off the bay onto the blue-, green-, and yellow-painted houses.

At a stoplight, a crossing bar comes down in front of our car, as if a train is going to pass. We know there are no trains in Iceland, so we wonder what's up. Not too far ahead of us, the air tumbles with clouds of dirt and dust, out of which emerge three riders leading a herd of horses.

"Oh, look," Eve says.

Hundreds and hundreds of horses trot down the path along the edge of the bay; a mesmerizing sight that leaves us speechless, except for excessive sighing. Swooning over horses is what we do. It is a long, long line of horses, more horses than I've ever seen at once, even in Iceland. After fifteen or twenty minutes the end of the herd trots up with three people riding sweep, leaving the dust to settle.

"Don't you want to do that someday, be part of a horse roundup?" I ask everyone. They hardly jump all over it the way Holly did when I mentioned the sheep and horse roundup to her last year.

The women in the car sit in silence, digesting this horse roundup suggestion of mine. Even though, or maybe because, they are all better riders than I am, they tell me how easy it looks but how difficult it is to escort a large herd of horses down the street. Still, I dream of doing this and want to ride sweep behind hundreds of horses. Lots of people specialize in a particular form of riding, whether its barrel racing, polo playing, steeple-chasing, cross-country jumping. I am thinking horse and sheep herding may be my calling.

The horses of this district, the valley of Skagafjörður, have a particular bearing that is imperceptible to the ordinary eye. But Icelandic horse people in the know can immediately tell the horses that come from this area: their heads are shaped differently and often their eyes are two different colors or both are blue. I've seen Icelandic trainers look at an old horse in a riding clinic in Massachusetts and name the farm it came from in the Skagafjörður valley. "It's like magic," Eve says. "They look at a horse and tell you who their father and who their grandfather was."

Eve drives up and down every street in town until we find the fish skin museum. It is closed, and I am relieved I don't have to spend $14 to see how fish skin is tanned. But the restaurant next door that Helga recommended is open. We bustle into a booth, and immediately order beer.

That's the easy part for us. Margot, Sylvie, and I are beer aficionados. And lately we like this Icelandic stout, Lava, with 9.4 percent alcohol. Viv orders tea, because she never drinks. And Eve has recently developed an allergy to gluten, and therefore certain beers, and orders coffee instead.

The waitress comes over and explains the daily special, which is a local fish with the choice of three different sauces: curry, onion, or a mustard sauce. This causes havoc in our group. Sylvie wants the curry sauce and the onion sauce on the side; Margot doesn't want any sauce, but wants it broiled. And Eve wants the mustard sauce on the side, broiled, too, if they can, or baked. Viv isn't having fish, but wants to make sure the vegetable dish she orders doesn't have onions in it. And I tell the waitress I just want the fish 'regular'—the way it's described on the menu—with curry. And to differentiate mine from the difficult orders, I further explain, "The fish with curry sauce on top of the fish, not on the side."

In my effort to make matters simple for her, to distance myself from my picky compatriots and simply order something from the menu, I have confused her more. She looks irritated, too.

"Maybe this is confusing her," I say to the group. "I'm guessing that 'sauce on the side' may not translate."

"Do you know what sauce on the side means?" Sylvie asks the waitress, making her hands round like a little bowl. "It means you put it in a little dish, a sauce on the side, in a saucer."

This confuses the waitress even more. Almost all Icelanders speak English now, but the degree of expertise depends on the particular rural setting. I'm sure she knows the words for bowl or dish. But saucer? It must sound as if we're asking for our sauce in a sauce.

Eve steps in with cheerful diplomacy. She's like Glinda the Good Witch, always calm, smiling: the only thing missing is her magic wand. "She wants the fish with the curry sauce, and with the onion sauce on the side, in a saucer. She wants her fish broiled, no sauce whatsoever. I want my fish broiled or baked with mustard sauce on the side, you know, in that saucer, and . . ." She turns to me as if I'm the troublemaker, "And she wants the fish, how? Regular? The fish 'regular' with the curry sauce on top of the fish, not in a saucer."

Viv pipes up because Eve left out her order. "And no onions in my vegetable dish, please."

The waitress backs up from us and goes over to the bartender to confer with him. She comes back minutes later to make sure she has it right. But by that time Sylvie has changed her mind. "I don't want the curry sauce any more, just the onion sauce. On the side. In the saucer."

Second to invading countries to enforce democracy, this is my least favorite thing about being an American. This insistence upon persnickety, tailor-made meals in restaurants. In the States, this is de rigueur, and all waitstaff know the drill. But in other countries, it is baffling at its best, rude at its worst. And it all starts harmlessly enough with a simple request with our stated preference or choice: Can I have this dish but without that in it? We believe in choice and all the many variations of choice. But beware: pretty soon we're invading your foreign restaurant, enforcing menu democracy.

We drain our first beer fast, as is our way. It hits me between the eyes, that 9.4 ABV. It affects Sylvie quickly, too. With her volume cranked up, she starts with her signature parrot's screech. "Do you believe her!?"

And we are back to dishing about Pippa. Because what's starting to really bother us is that after the flare-up, instead of leaving and making herself scarce, she's been sitting around the guesthouse and in the common rooms with us, staring us down with malice.

Without her with us, malice begets malice. I come up with the nasty idea that Pippa probably paid for Karen and Madison to accompany her this year, that they didn't seem particularly friendly to Pippa, the way they split off from her and went into their separate bedrooms, not even coming out to have dinner. "It's like they don't really know her."

Eve says, sadly, and I know this does make her sad, "I thought it would be great to have Madison here, you know how I like having teenagers with us, like the years when Britt used to ride with us. It adds new life. But I don't think she wants to be here with us."

Eve's regrets only slow us down momentarily.

"Karen is so programmed. She gets up at six every morning to run eight miles."

"And the rest of the time she spends doing crunches and squats. The woman never sits still."

"Is that even admirable?"

"Means she's a control freak."

In truth, I don't care if Karen is a control freak or not really friends with Pippa. I only care that as a complete stranger to us, and after lashing out at us during the original skirmish with Pippa, she has made no attempts at peacemaking. We have dealt with difficult women on the trip before, but it was their quirky personalities we dealt with, not their hostile takeovers.

Pippa had challenged our inveterate social bonds. She disrupted the ethos that we had consciously or unconsciously agreed upon. Our protective cap said, "We're in Iceland for a week, leave all shit behind at the airport gate."

And usually it was Eve who kept us on course. If people got too negative, if conversation wasn't humanely understanding, she would fall back and sigh. "Oh, let's not go there. We're here. In Iceland."

But now, go there we do, even Eve. Waiting for the fish and the saucers of sauce, we go there full throttle, trashing Pippa and her entourage—when low and behold, they walk in.

Our conspiratorial huddle freezes. "Oh," Eve says. "Oh, you found us," which somehow conveys we are trying to hide from them. We are.

To be civil, we make a halfhearted attempt to make room for them in the booth. And they, to be civil, take the booth next to us instead. Karen orders coffee and nothing else. Pippa orders from the vegetarian menu and Madison orders a salad. In their defense, they don't make ordering difficult for the waitress. They are better customers than we are.

I ask Madison what she thought of the horse she rode today. She says, "I think it has balance issues."

"He does. Yesterday when I rode him he kept tripping on me."

"That means it has balance issues."

"You know a lot about horses, don't you?"

Madison nods, as if to say, of course. She is at heart another horse girl, like Britt and Mel, quiet and resolute, self-assured when it comes to horses. The rest of the world can fall around them, but they have their focus—the horses.

We finish our meal in a rush to get away from them and get to a horse show. Frieda and Helga are competing in a regional competition. For Helga, it's no big deal. For Frieda, a Holar student, it means a great deal. We've watched her practice all week. We need to cheer her on.

As we get up to leave, Pippa says all cheery-like, "We'll see you there." We part from them with a series of fluttery goodbyes.

Once in the car we launch into the discussion: "Why is she following us?" We are so involved in this question that we drive around in circles trying to get out of town.

"Does anyone remember the directions?" Eve says.

"Helga said it's minutes out of town."

Viv gets out of the car and says, "I'll try to find directions. Come back for me." We agree to meet her on the corner in five minutes.

Eve pulls up to a man on the next corner. "Excuse me, we're looking for the horse show. It's supposed to be nearby. Would you know where it is?"

The guy is white-haired, bowl-legged, craggy-faced. He sticks his head close to Eve's window and looks in to see who all is asking.

"Horse show? I don't go to horse shows. I eat horses. I don't have any other use for them." He rubs his tummy and laughs at his joke.

"Okay, nevermind," Eve says, and quickly drives away. "That was not funny."

"That was not funny."

"That was disgusting."

"I know they eat horsemeat in Iceland, but he didn't have to put it like that."

"Can we just forget he said that? It's making me sick," Margot says.

"How do we get out of here?"

"There's a road sign up ahead that looks like a campground symbol. That would be a likely place for a horse show."

One or two of these signs pop up along the way so we know we're on the right route. We're rolling along, looking carefully at every sign, when I realize there are only four of us in the car.

"We forgot Viv."

With a deep intake of air, Sylvie says, "Don't tell her."

Viv is on a corner waiting for us on the same street we left her on. "You forgot me, didn't you?"

"No, no, we didn't."

Raptured

The horse show arena is set deep in a green valley ringed by snow-topped mountains. Like Holar, it is another Shangri-La place, conveying peace, serenity, enchantment. We arrive at eight at night. It's bright and sunny with a cold, brisk wind that rattles the car. It's colder than usual this June. An

Arctic air inversion, we've been told. We wear parkas, hats, and gloves, and decide to watch the competition from our car.

Eve backs into a parking space and, being a cautious driver, looks over her left shoulder. And, because we are participatory passengers, we all look over our left shoulders, too, which is how we all notice him at the same time. In a group of men, he stands out because he is darker than the usual Icelander.

"That guy is handsome."

"The dark-haired guy?"

"Yeah. With the gray in his beard."

"Yeah. I thought so, too."

"Margot, there's your guy."

"Your fortune cookie guy."

"It wasn't a fortune cookie; it was her horoscope," Sylvie says.

"That's better, that's more accurate," I offer.

"Oh, look, Margot. He's so handsome!" Eve says, as if it's a done deal. "Lucky you."

Margot's got her hood up, but makes a weak effort to peak out and get a look at Handsome. "I'm in no shape to meet anyone. I'm coming down with a cold, my stomach hurts. I can't take all this conflict with Pippa; it has weakened my immune system." She sniffles and retreats back into her hood, taking out her Kindle to read *Game of Thrones*.

As we watch the horse show, we mindlessly pass around chocolate McVitie's and pretzels that were left in the car. Viv takes out some seed and nut concoction from her backpack and says, "These are full of protein." Except for Margot, we all partake in these nuggets as if we have been starved of protein less than an hour after finishing our fish dinner.

Every time Frieda and Helga have their turn in the show, we pop out of the car. We listen to what the judge says about them in Icelandic, clap our mittened hands together every time their names are mentioned, understanding nothing in the language but their names. Then we rush back to the car, turn it on, turn the heat on, and watch all the riders we don't know. We take particular notice of one rider dressed all in black on a big dark bay.

Sylvie recognizes him first: "Hey, that's him, with the beard."

And there he is—Handsome—putting a black beauty of a horse through tölt, trot, and canter. "Wow, he rides, too." Margot looks up from her reading briefly, momentarily impressed, sniffles, and goes back to the world of Westeros.

The night goes on like this, watching the riders, getting in and out of the car to cheer along Frieda and Helga. The sky is tumultuous with swirly clouds as if it's trying to send forth a message. It's the perfect setting for, oh, I don't know, the Rapture?

When it comes time for us to leave, Eve turns the key and the car just makes a weak *click-click-click* sound. "The car's dead," she says. We're a garrulous group, but we turn mute at this news. We can't bother Frieda during competition and Helga left for home a while ago. But Eve sums up the situation and quickly takes charge. She digs up the car rental number, calls up the guy in Reykjavík (a seven-hour drive away) and explains the situation.

"We're in Soda cracker," she says. "No, so-da crack-er," she says slowly, as if she's the native explaining how the word should be said.

I interrupt her, "I think its pronounced soda croak-er."

She says in the phone, "Soda crock-er."

I pipe up from the back seat again, "No, soda croak-er."

She says in the phone, "Soda-crack-er." She holds the phone away from her face, "He doesn't understand; he's going to put his wife on."

Eve goes through the "Soda cracker, Soda crock-er, croak-er" thing again with the wife, and then says, "It's near Holar." Pause. "No, we're not in Holar, we're near Holar, in Soda cracker. Okay, I'll find someone here who speaks Icelandic."

Viv is out of the car in a flash, asking a group of men on the hill. "Does anyone speak English? Our car seems to have died."

From a distance, no one looks eager to help us. But finally, one guy stands up and comes down the hill with Viv. Eve holds the phone out to him. "Can you talk to this person and explain where we are?"

I knock Margot's knee. "It's him! Handsome! Margot, this is meant to be. Get out of the car!" I'm thinking destiny, but she isn't feeling it.

"I can't just go out there and talk him up. I'm not like that."

But I convince her to get out of the car and hover around him. While he is on the phone explaining our situation in Icelandic to the other end, Eve turns the key on and off and says, "Hear the *click-click-click*?"

As if I am the only mechanic in this helpless gaggle, I point to the hood. "It's the battery, the battery is dead."

"But the horn works, see?" Eve toots the horn.

"Maybe it's the alternator," Viv says.

He nods politely to us as he tries to continue his conversation on the phone. We've exhausted our car knowledge and we've left Margot outside beside him, politely crossing and uncrossing her arms and legs, looking longingly at her Kindle in the car.

Finally, he gets off the phone and tells us, "I have a friend in town I'll call. He has cables. He'll get here faster."

We thank him profusely. He goes back to his friends on the hill and we sit in the car and wait. And wait. Though the competition is still going on, the place begins to empty out, and without being able to turn the heat on the car is cold. Sylvie asks, somewhat irritated, "Where is he?"

Margot is getting paler and sniffling louder, sinking deeper into the hood of her jacket. "Guys, I'm really not feeling well. It's freezing, too."

Viv jumps out of the car to look for Handsome. She's quickly back with the news. "Can't find Handsome. And Frieda has left. But Pippa and her friends are here, down at the other end."

"Did you tell them our car is broken? Can she take a couple of us in her car so we're not all stuck here?" Eve asks.

Viv hesitates. I know she doesn't want to talk to Pippa.

Eve presses. "Just say we need her help. She can't say no."

Viv, against her better judgment, scampers away to find Pippa. She has taken up the role of scurrying messenger seriously, leaving the rest of us to issue orders from our cold car. She returns from Pippa's car with the news, "She can take one person in her car, she says. She's leaving soon."

"Margot, you have to go with them. You're chilled and not feeling well." We are sending her into the belly of the beast, with the people who caused the stress that caused her illness.

Viv sprints back and delivers the message and soon Pippa pulls up, driving super-fast for a parking lot and stopping so abruptly next to us that her wheels spit up gravel and dirt. Once again, she expresses her emotions with aggressive driving.

It's as if we're passing Margot off to the other side of the Berlin Wall as we watch her get into Pippa's car and drive off. But within a few minutes, we see Margot, walking back to us, hunched over and looking sicker.

"What happened?"

"She kicked me out of her car. She asked me how did we choose who got to go with her? I said, everyone decided I should go because I wasn't feeling well. And that did it. She jerked the car around and said, 'You're sick? Get out!'"

"She kicked you out in the cold for being sick?"

"Oh, they're mean. When I first got in, they asked what we were doing about the car. So I told them about Handsome and how we were fussing about how good-looking he was, and you know what Karen says? She's says, 'Why would a guy like that be interested in a bunch of women your age? He'd be more interested in Madison here, she's young and beautiful.'"

This gets us going again. We are aghast, apoplectic about their meanness. Insult upon insult. To say nothing about inappropriateness. "She's bragging a 45-year-old guy would be interested in her 15-year-old daughter," Viv says. "What does that say?"

Margot keeps repeating: "I couldn't believe she said 'get out' like that. Just 'get out'!"

We rehash this until we're tired of it. Twenty minutes pass and we're back to "Where is he? Where is Handsome?" And Viv is out of the car before we ask her, looking for him. We marvel about how tireless she is. "Look at her go," Eve says.

Eve says to me, "Why don't you go out there, put the hood up so we look distressed and get some attention." But before I can even get out of the car, a pickup truck pulls up and Handsome comes down the hill to meet it, as if he had been keeping an eye on us the whole time up there on the hill. He and his friend attach the jumper cables and the battery starts recharging.

Eve revs the engine, Margot reads in the back seat, Sylvie intermittently groans out her angst, and Viv has disappeared down the road. Since everyone else is preoccupied, I feel the need to be friendly with Handsome, so I get out of the car.

"Did you ride in the competition?" I ask, even though I know he did. Yes, he says.

"Do you have a horse farm?" This is not an unusual question, giving where we are. And yes, he does. "A few miles away," he says, and points to the mountains and tells me the name of the town.

I try to keep up the patter of conversation, which isn't difficult. He seems willing to talk, even friendly, and I realize that he is more than handsome—he is kind, with kind eyes. And he is a horseman with a horse farm. I am stalling for Margot, who is hiding out in the car and not accepting that this is meant to be. My attention is drawn up to the hill and his friends are watching us and laughing. "Your friends up there are laughing at us." He looks amused, waves at them, shakes his head, and reassures me, "It's nothing."

Viv is walking back to the car and I summon her over. She immediately asks his name. "Baltasar," he says, which doesn't sound Icelandic to me. I can tell this occurs to Viv, too, so she asks his last name. He hesitantly says something that sounds like Cormico. I think, *that doesn't sound Icelandic*. But what I think, Viv says—"That doesn't sound Icelandic. It doesn't end in 'son.'" He tells us his mother is Icelandic, his father is Spanish.

Soon the car battery is charged. Eve tries to tip Baltasar, and leans out the window holding a couple thousand kronur (about $20). "Please, please, take this for all your trouble. You saved us. We would have been stuck here all night." He looks embarrassed and refuses. She holds it out again, "For your friend in the truck then?" He refuses for his friend in the truck. And there we are at the awkward tipping standoff: Eve holding the cash out the window with it flapping in the wind and him backing away from it.

So we thank him profusely and theatrically. Viv does a deep salaam-style bow and Eve does a yogi-style bow from the driver's seat. "Namaste," she says. And we're off.

Back in the car, Viv and I relay all the information on Handsome, the most relevant first. "He has a horse farm around here."

Sylvie shakes her head. "Margot, that was it. You missed your chance. A handsome Icelandic man with a horse farm."

"There's nothing better than that in the whole world."

"He wasn't interested in me. Karen is right, I'm too old."

"I bet you're the same age."

Viv tells everyone that he's half-Spanish and half-Icelandic and that his name is Baltasar. When Eve hears that she screams, "I know his father! He's a famous artist in Iceland. His name is Baltasar, too. I have his painting in my living room. Jack and I went to his house in Reykjavík to buy it. Years ago. He was such a lovely man, and his wife put out strawberries and Champagne for us. It's got to be his son. It's the law of attraction! We have to find him."

Suddenly, we are charged with this mission. We must find him! Why? Ostensibly, to tell him Eve knows his parents and had Champagne and strawberries with them.

Baltasar. His name suddenly means everything to us: handsome, gallant, rescuer, equestrian, car charger. It's as if a collective hormonal rush comes over us and we are all atwitter, squealing like lovelorn thirteen-year-old girls. Who knew we had that much estrogen left in us?

"Where is he? Baltasar. We have to find him." We can't seem to find our way out of the parking lot, let alone locate him. "Wait, where's the road?" Eve asks.

We're giving Eve directions all at once. "Here. No here. Turn around. Try that lane. Down there."

We back up, turn around, the tires squeal. Eve jumps a curb that bounces us high in the air, alarming people nearby. Then she has to back up over the curb again, which requires gunning it in reverse. A horse going into a trailer skitters and neighs. We get dirty stares from the horse handlers.

In the end, we can't find Baltasar, and it is nearly midnight as we drive away, antics over, emotionally depleted. Margot sleeps. The rest of us stay up to keep Eve company as she drives. We lose the sun on the horizon for a brief moment and then it's back up again.

It's one in the morning when we get back to the farm. Helga is up and we tell her our story all at once—we're jumping all over each other about Handsome rescuing us and Eve's connection to him.

Helga knows him. "Ah, yes," she says, "that's Baltasar Kormákur. He is the son of the painter. But he is also a very well-known actor and director in Iceland. He has an American movie coming out, an action movie." She is matter-of-fact about this because Icelanders aren't impressed with fame. It is, refreshingly, not a celebrity culture.

We explain between yelps and sighs how we were trying to set Margot up with him.

"Oh, no, no, he is married to a beautiful Icelandic woman. She is one of the richest women in Iceland."

"Rich and beautiful, what did you guys put me up against?" Margot jokes, color back in her face, pressure off, sniffles gone.

But the new information about Baltasar sets us reeling again. "He's a movie star and director!" We can't help it, he's like the George Clooney of Iceland.

We Google his name and his work and his new movie, *2 Guns*, that is coming out. We're sitting in the big bunk room, each on our own bunk bed. We're probably waking Pippa and company up, but they are insignificant to us now. There is no place for petty meanness anymore.

We recap the night and it gets more and more ridiculous in the retelling, with each of our roles in the plot producing bellyaching laughter. It's like we are back in college dorm rooms, debriefing with roommates after a night out. It's like all those youthful nights that were made thrilling with romantic possibility, the more far-fetched the better. We're so wired we will never sleep. Any chance of us simmering down is dashed when Eve gets out between gasps, "And . . . I tried . . . to . . . tip him!"

That does us in. We burst out in a delirium, it rumbles forth from our gut, registering audibly in the stratosphere. It's no longer about Baltasar; it's about us, our laughter that we can't seem to stop. It's so intense our bodies shake like jackhammers; our voices caterwaul out to the sunlit night, in release and relief. It sweeps us up with such force that we are temporarily lifted up and out of this world. We are raptured.

BOOK V
THE PACE (SKEIÐ)

—∞∞∞—

The "fifth gear" in Icelandic horses, also known as the Flying Pace (Flugskeið). It is a lateral two-beat gait, during which both legs on one side of the horse simultaneously touch the ground, but also at one interval all four hooves are suspended off the ground, thus giving it the feeling of flying.

2014

—⊶⊷—

The Road to Thingeyrar

It's our eleventh year in Iceland. "Eleven," Eve declares, "is a magical number."

Margot is back this year, along with the regulars: Eve, Sylvie, Viv, Allie, me. Pippa *did* email Sylvie asking if she could "reserve" a bedroom for the trip this year; Sylvie ignored the question and Pippa never pursued it.

I have not seen Viv since March when I met her in a New York and we went to an exhibit at the Native American Museum on "The Horse." I have not been up to the Berkshires to visit Margot and Sylvie since the winter. And I have not seen Eve since last year at a fund-raiser. We have a lot to catch up on. As soon as we get in the car, there is the immediate, almost ceremonial, unwrapping and passing of cookies, pretzels, licorice.

There is a discussion about the Martha Beck workshop Margot and Sylvie attended, and what she means when she used the Chinese term "soul sister."

There is new life to talk about: Viv had a grandson in April. "Now I really worry," she says. "I worry about having boys these days. I think this world doesn't favor little boys with ADD who can't sit in a classroom. I think they have it harder than girls." She has told me this before, and I don't disagree. "Girls rule these days."

And there is continuing life. "How are your kids?" Eve asks me.

"My daughter graduated college and has moved to Manhattan with a bunch of friends. And my son came home in May. He's one of those 'boomerang kids,' as they are called."

That's how my husband and I have decided to put it. He's another boomerang; one of many in our neighborhood that is rapidly refilling with returning children. He came home a month ago after losing his apartment, girlfriend, and temp job. We don't understand it all or why he's starting his adult life with such a bumpy ride, but we are grateful that when down, he at least comes back to us. After years of being a guy of few words, he now talks all the time to me. He paces the kitchen, telling me all the stuff that he has held in. For so many years his relationship with me was mute and recalcitrant. Now he's filling in the blanks on who he is and where he's been. Until I hold up my hand and tell him, "I don't need to know everything. I want to sleep at night." And I do. It's no different than it was seven years ago—when I smell his cigarette smoke wafting up from the patio to my bedroom window, I tell myself he has time to tackle the smoking. As for now, he's home, he's safe—and I can sleep.

Allie tells us she was in China earlier this year, her usual business trip.

Sylvie, who used to travel all the time, doesn't travel anymore, except to Iceland. "I have three horses now. It's hard to find someone to take care of them when I go to Iceland. I can't go to Asia anymore."

There are health worries: Allie is driving this year, because Eve has sight problems, a hereditary type of glaucoma that limits her vision. She says it should be temporary. "We've found a specialist in New York. I'm having laser surgery when I get back." And while she has some loss of peripheral vision, she assures us she should be fine riding. "I'm not worried," she says, "It's only a little blurry in the corners."

Margot says, "Horses have good peripheral vision because they have such wide set eyes, so they'll take care of you when you ride. And their range of vision is four times greater than ours. Of course, their short distance vision is not so good. They can't see right behind their ears."

"My friend had macular degeneration starting at forty-five," Viv says, "and she rode her horse till she was almost completely blind. Her horse was a saint."

"Okay, I'll keep that in mind," Eve says, sounding less optimistic and not completely comforted by the inspirational goal of riding blind.

There are dreams of a new Monterey farm: Sylvie and Margot are planning on making their adjoining property a horse farm. They have received the town permits needed to build the barn. Margot has started clearing the land, but one of her neighbors has disputed the zoning approval. He is trying to stop their barn from being built. "I can't take conflict; it makes me sick. These nasty letters this neighbor writes me, you wouldn't believe it. It's really hard on me. But that's why, guys, I'm so happy to be here. The whole neighbor thing was getting to me. But I'm not going to think about that. I'm in Iceland, it's so great to be back."

"I second that." I am with my friends, my girl pack, my band of merry travelers. I'm in my element, in Iceland. Allie bought a mug in the airport that read "Happiness is here and now," and Eve declared, "That should be our motto!"

By the time we get to the turn off to Thingeyrar, we are so wrapped up in each other's lives, we miss the turnoff from the Ring Road to the dirt road for the first time ever. We turn into a farm down the road and back up in the driveway to turn around. "Remember when we used to stop here?" Eve says.

The farm used to belong to a friend of Helga's. And in the early years, we would use the old-style cavernous barn as a pit stop before we crossed the Vatnsdalsá River. We would put our horses in the paddock and the farm couple would bring out coffee and donuts for us and talk to Helga for a while.

None of the horses we rode on the first trip are still at Thingeyrar. They have either been retired, have died, or have been sold. Even old Thoka is gone. She aged out of usefulness and was put down. Everything changes. Even in Iceland, especially in Iceland. A decade ago it was a more traditional country and less traveled; it never made the news cycle and wasn't the go-to locale for filming TV shows or movies. You could tell people you were going to Iceland and they'd think you were wildly adventurous. Even the REI sales clerks.

But our guesthouse on the farm remains the same, and one of the reasons I love returning is for the sameness, even if in the beginning what so entranced me was the newness. Part of the pleasure of being on a farm, even one with modern amenities, is the way it builds on and opens a door to the past. The agricultural life represents the not-so-distant lives of our farming ancestors. It's something I can hold on to—it is matter. The opposite of our digital world is this: dirt, mud, grass, horseflesh, all the things that ruffle your senses.

My aunt Ruthie used to say that when you get older, you're you, still the same you, but you become more you. I used to think that meant that the older you got the freer you were to stop capitulating to others' demands, and you got to a distilled sense of self, the more likely you. But lately I think it's less insular, and more expansive. The "more you-ness" comes from our recollections and connectedness. Our minds and hearts become fat and swollen with experiences and memories of places and people, and this makes us "more."

How long can our trips go on? I used to think there was a time limit. That every trip could be our last one. But we don't talk like that anymore. We forge ahead with next year's plans before we even leave the farm on the last day. Thingeyrar is here for us. I remember that first year with Sylvie, sitting in the bar on the wharves, when she said, "This is what I'll do for now."

This is what I'll do for now. This is where I'll be.

Of course, each trip marks the click of another year passing: memory is time, time is loss, loss is life. But these trips are the antidote to loss, and a reprieve from aging. As we drive past the gates of Thingeyrar, we squeal at the first sight of Helga's horses in the fields. "Look at the foals! So many mares pregnant! Is that the stallion?" We pull up to the farm, tumble out of the car, rush to the fence, and gush over the horses. We're like a pack of unrestrained girls, full of nerviness and excitement, blissfully unaware of anything but the horses. It never gets old. And, in the moment, neither do we.

Wild River

We call it "the wild river ride" because we trek along the banks of Vatnsdalsá and it always gets hairy. This is due mostly to the herd of about twenty young horses from another farm that graze there and rush us. They like to play, these young'uns, and see us as an irresistible curiosity. Helga forewarns the farmer who owns them that we will be on his property and asks if he would put his young horses in another field, but either the farmer forgets, or he doesn't care. So each time we ride on the path they come running down the hill to greet us. They see our steeds as playmates and friskily gallop beside us.

We are used to this, expect it, and try to prepare for it. But still.

Helga rides up front on a tall, gray dappled horse, a horse that looks like the gray charger Cate Blanchett rode as Queen Elizabeth when she urged on her soldiers into battle. Unlike the Queen of England, though, Helga gives us all several chances to turn back without threatening to have us shot as deserters.

From almost the moment we head out of the farm's gate, Helga starts with, "Anyone want to turn back?" No one takes her up on it. Then, when we get to the end of the road where we cross the bridge, Helga gives us another opportunity. "Last chance. Anyone want to go home? Speak now or forever hold your peace." But, no, we all voice our eagerness to continue.

And all goes as planned and unplanned. We stop after we cross the bridge, and Allie wants us to dismount and line up for pictures. We oblige her. On one hand, I hate doing this because it magnifies whatever jitters I have. On the other, when she emails these pictures to us months later, I open them up at my desk at work and am transported back to my friends, my horse, and that river, jitter-free.

As we stand for pictures, I wonder whether the farmer has put the young herd in another pasture. While there is always a hope that we won't run into them, if we didn't, I might be slightly disappointed. It would be just another river ride at fast speeds for a deliriously long time, and then a splash into the river and a scurry up to the island in the river, a fast tölt to the end of the island, and then a splash down and across the river again. That would be challenging on its own, but without the frisson of any real danger we can't control.

As we start out, Gauper is barking at the birds in the grass, and generally being a beloved nuisance. We spot the herd of young horses on the hill, but trot on, trying to stay the course. If we can spot them, they can spot us, and, more importantly, our horses know they are there. Their nostrils are flaring as they pick up the chemical messages of the other herd. Even before we are anywhere near them, the pace picks up.

As we get closer to the young herd, our horses start to race against each other. And it is only a minute before the young ones come at us full force: they invade our line, darting in and out of our formation, riling up our saddled, bridled horses.

"Don't let your horses gallop," Helga warns us. "Hold them back."

Helga attempts to divert the young horses, riding on the outside of the line to ward off the infiltration. She snaps her fingers at Gauper, who understands the cue to bark and nip at the young horses' heels. Frieda shouts, "Hup, hup," when the wild horses get in our way, and tries to drive them off.

I take this up with great enthusiasm: "Hup, hup!" I love yelling this, it makes me feel like a cowgirl, and it's the closest I'll get to a sheep or horse roundup. "Hup, hup!"

I am on an older, sturdy mare who is on autopilot. But she's not part of Helga's herd, she's from the Steinnes farm, and as an outsider she's making every effort to prove herself, and out race the other horses.

The pace quickens, and Frieda, who was the sweep, our safety check at the back of the line, becomes the leader. Then a horse's shoe is thrown up in front of me, making a quick arc in the air.

"Someone threw a shoe," I shout.

The news travels up and down the frantic line of riders, and everyone has an opinion:

"Sylvie's horse lost a shoe."

"Queenie, your horse lost a shoe."

"What?"

"No, nevermind, it was Allie's horse."

"Whose?"

"Allie's."

"No, I think it was Viv's, it was Viv's horse."

"Mine?"

"Yes. Or maybe it was Eve's."

Margot shouts out, "Forget about the shoe, guys, there's a stampede going on!"

Gauper, Helga, and Frieda are driving the young horses off our path and making every effort to herd them back up the hill. Which leaves the rest of us on the loose, unsupervised, and on the run. Allie is in front and I am right behind her. Though she is the least experienced rider, she is the most confident, and confidence counts a lot with horses.

During the stampede, she finally put her camera away and now she lets her horse go into a canter, and I let mine follow. Then her horse kicks it up another notch to a gallop, and my horse tries to catch up. Allie's flying and I'm right behind her and Margot is right on my horse's tail. The path is snaking along the river, so my horse shifts her weight frequently and I have to as well, in order to stay in balance. The feel of a gallop is different from a canter; it's not simply faster. A canter is a three-beat gait with one hoof always in contact with the ground, and you can convince yourself you are in control. But with the gallop, there is no such illusion of control. It is a four-beat gait with a moment of suspension combined with the feeling that the horse's engine has exploded. It is those moments of galloping and losing control while trying to keep my seat and doing everything to stay balanced, when I feel most utterly free.

Eventually Allie slows her horse down to a trot, then a walk, which slows my horse down to a trot and a walk.

"That was fun," I tell Allie.

"I couldn't hold her back anymore, I just had to let her go."

"That was really fun, guys! There was no way my horse was gonna get left behind," Margot says.

We are a half a mile ahead of the rest and we wait for them to catch up. Everyone has survived, and Helga returns to the front and we tölt swiftly, peacefully along the soft trail edging the fast-moving river.

When it comes time to cross the river, Helga leads us in. Allie follows, then Margot, then me. Sylvie is supposed to be following me, but she and Stulka hesitate. The river is deep from all the rain during the year, and the river's banks are soft and crumbly, giving way quickly as we enter. If it isn't done fast, if the horse doesn't have momentum, it'll get stuck in the deep mud. A large gap is forming between me and Sylvie as I hear her try to convince Stulka to get in.

There's a commotion behind me, then a splash, followed by an Sylvie shout, "Argh."

"Sylvie fell," someone yells. "Sylvie's down!" The news travels from the shore to me, to Margot to Allie to Helga. Sylvie has popped back up, but she went completely underwater. She empties her helmet of water.

Helga, though midway out in the river with us, turns around to rescue her. "Keep your horses here, don't cross alone, there may be eddies and sinkholes in the river."

The horses aren't going to stand still in the river, so we turn them in tight little circles.

"Guys, I have to be honest, I have a fear of water," Margot says, "I'm not a good swimmer." Margot wasn't with us all the times we crossed Lake Hóp. "I'm just putting that out there," she says.

"This river has never been this deep before," I say. "It must be all the rain they've had. I didn't tape my Wellies and my boots are filling up with water. I'm afraid that if I fall off, the weight of my boots would drag me down."

"That was not helpful," Margot says, "to tell me that. My boots are filling with water, too."

Allie says, "Everything will be fine. Let's just keep turning the horse in circles."

We turn the horses in circles in the middle of the river, but they are pushing us to go on and cross. Turning them in circles is making them nervous.

On shore, we can see that everyone else is gathered around Sylvie and asking her if she's alright. "Sylvie seems to be fine," Margot says. "Thank God she fell really close to the shoreline. She could stand when she got up. And Eve's got hold of Stulka."

We keep making circles in the middle of the river, but the circles are getting larger and we are separating a little more from each other. I fear we are drifting down the river a little. And I'm trying not to stare too long at the water, which might cause me to lose my balance, but I have to watch out for eddies.

I hear Helga ask Sylvie if she's alright.

"Yes, but I'm annoyed," Sylvie says. "I was feeling so good about my riding today, so proud of myself. You know what my mother used to say, 'pride cometh before the fall.'"

Everyone who's left on shore is laughing and yukking it up, discussing the fall that cometh after Sylvie's pride—while we are continuing our circles in the middle of the river. The water is getting deeper, but I keep that to myself, not wanting to alarm Margot.

"They do know we're still out here, don't they? They haven't forgot about us, have they?" Margot asks.

"I was wondering the same thing."

Finally, we can hear Helga ask Sylvie, "So, Queenie, are you ready to get back on?"

Margot says to herself, "C'mon Sylvie, get back on."

"I suppose," Sylvie says, not in any hurry to curtail our agony. But it takes a while, an eternity to us in the middle of the river, as Sylvie finds something near the riverbank to stand on, a sturdy rock, to give herself a boost to remount.

When she gets back on the horse, everyone lets out a cheer. It's like they are having a celebration on shore while we are close to drowning in the river. Then there is even more discussion and laughing among them with very little forward movement.

Allie says, "Do you think we can continue across now that Sylvie's back on? These guys are getting awfully fidgety."

Margot yells across the water to Helga, "Can we go across now?"

Helga yells to us to wait for her. "There's a tricky part up ahead. Don't do it alone."

"Guys, I'm getting vertigo," Margot says. "I'm feeling dizzy and light-headed."

"I am, too," I say. "I can't help looking down. I have to look where I'm going. How do you not look down?"

Allie says, "She's almost here, hang on."

Helga finally reaches us with everyone else behind her, and we continue on. But instead of going straight to the shoreline of the island as we would have, Helga first leads us down the middle of the river before turning in toward the shore. She knows the river well, but her horse knows the river better. She trusts her horse to pick the route. She gives him full rein, tactilely listening to the horse, as he cautiously, intuitively finds the best footing, and we follow behind them single file, avoiding the sinkhole that would have taken us down if we had gone on without her and pushed the horses to take the quickest route to the shore.

About Those Ghosts

No one has heard from the ghosts for a while. The kitchen window in Thingeyrar looks out on the circle of old gravestones, but they are just part of the scenery. Normally inquisitive types, we have sat at the kitchen table and looked out on that mini skyline of gravestones for the last few years without questioning it too much. In fact, we have become rather ho-hum about the sight, like, Oh, there is the church, the laundry line, the gravestones. "Pass the skyr, please."

Sometimes an Icelander, like a Holar intern who has spent the winter here, will remind us that our guesthouse is indeed haunted. "Right there is where there are ghosts," one said, pointing to where we hang our coats up in the hallway. And we feel obliged to bring up the times we've seen them (Allie), felt them (Eve), and heard them (me).

They have not come back. Why is that? I wonder. Are we not worthy of being visited? Is it because we are not Icelandic? Is there a language barrier? Or are we no longer receptive to them? While the idea that the guesthouse is haunted has never been an impediment to our staying here—every year we greet our rooms in the guesthouse with giddy excitement, "We're he-eere!"—I am not actually eager to see, hear, or feel them. I did not embellish one bit of my ghost story, and I am assuming the others didn't embellish theirs, either.

But this year we are armed with new information. This year we know that all those headstones were moved when our guesthouse was built, and they all belonged to the people who witnessed the beheading of Agnes Magnúsdóttir in 1830. And this year we know who Agnes is. We did our homework—we read the new novel about Agnes before we flew to Iceland. So these ghosts are no longer nameless, generic ghosts that visited us. Now they are ghosts with a past and a purpose.

Sitting at the kitchen table, looking at the headstones, we are left to wonder: "What does it mean that they were *moved* exactly?"

"Were the graves all left underneath this house?"

"Were only the headstones moved? Is this a poltergeist situation?"

In all fairness to Helga, she had tried telling us the story of Agnes a few times over the years. She started telling us out on the trail the year of the horse flu but was repeatedly interrupted by horses thought to be coughing and riders too nervous to be riding. She tried again to tell us last year and brought over a CD with an aria from an opera written about Agnes. She put the music on, and I remember her saying, "This is a very sad story that happened around here." And she looked sad as she listened to it, as she translated some of the Icelandic words from the song for us.

But after the song was over, our follow-up chatter took a different turn. It wasn't about Agnes and her lover, it was about our old loves, and how some of them still haunt us. Helga wanted to know why we chose the husbands we did, what was the defining characteristic that made each of us think, *this is the one*. I was quick to speak up: "Humor. He can always make me laugh." Eve seconded the humor reason, adding that Jack always made life exciting. Allie simply said, "Trust." Sylvie said, "To get out of my mother's house—I was nineteen!" When we asked Helga why she married Gunnar, she paused as if really thinking about it and said, "Dependability. I knew he'd make a good father. So many Icelandic men run around and have children with lots of different women. I knew he was trustworthy, a Steady Eddie."

So every time the Agnes story was raised in the past it got usurped by our own emotional lives and loves. Until one day this past winter, I was standing in the Yale New Haven bookstore and I picked a book on the featured table, *Burial Rites* by Hannah Kent, and had a "hold on, I know this story" moment. I dashed off an email to my fellow travelers. "This book is about *that* story that Helga was talking about, *that* song she played for us, *that* opera she mentioned." We passed a flurry of emails back and forth. We all agreed to read the book about the life and death of Agnes Magnúsdóttir, who started out with every strike against her: a poor, illegitimate daughter of a tenant farmer, orphaned at an early age and sent from farm to farm to work since the age of seven. A character straight out of Dickens, she hit the tragic trifecta: hard luck, hard life, awful death.

Hearing from all of us over the winter about how much this story finally resonated with us, Helga scheduled a full day of sightseeing for us through Vatnsdalur, Agnes Magnúsdóttir's home turf. Thirty minutes south of Thingeyrar, Agnes was born; thirty minutes to the northwest, she lived with Natan in Illugastaðir; twenty minutes inland in Kornsa, she stayed with a family before her execution; and ten minutes from our guesthouse she was put to death in Þrístapar. (Travel distances are measured by today's cars, not by the horses Agnes and her contemporaries rode.) And in Thingeyrar itself, Friðrik, the farmhand convicted of murder along with Agnes, was held before his execution. We were at the epicenter of this tragic tale. Not to mention, the witnesses were buried beneath us.

The night before we set out, Helga brings over the 1995 Icelandic movie *Agnes*, where actor, director, and our personal Samaritan, be-still-my-heart Baltasar Kormákur, plays the lead role of Natan, Agnes' lover. When we see him in the opening scene we sigh like thirteen-year-olds. "That's him, that's our Baltasar," Eve says, stressing the possessive. "Was it just a year ago?" Viv says. We ogle him in the steamy—literally, in hot springs—love scene. But it is not a swooning type of role for long and we have a hard time separating the Natan character from the Baltasar we had met last year. In the movie, he plays Natan as a self-promoting sexual healer.

"Uh-oh, he's doing her, and her, too?" Sylvie comments, when he moves from woman to woman. It reminds me of the stallion we watched one summer.

"What a womanizer," Allie says. "Sheesh." But she wasn't with us the night we met Baltasar, so she doesn't know his real soul.

"How could he do that, our Baltasar," Eve says, sounding personally so disappointed.

I'm a little more forgiving of his character. "Yeah, but it's Baltasar," meaning that obviously it's more like free love than womanizing. More obvious, at least to me, is that I am no better at distinguishing character from performer than my grandmother was when she watched her soap opera, *One Life to Live*. She'd twist her hands: "I'm so mad at Charles."

When we set out the next day, our first stop is at the church at Tjörn where Agnes's head is buried, or, er, reburied. I am first out of the car, charged with this mission. "Where's her head?" I feel as if we are on a Dan Brown mystery-history-literary tour and this is our Rosslyn Chapel. We spread out across the graveyard, impatiently scanning the names of each tombstone. Finally, Helga finds the marker, which looks like it is carved out of new marble. The grass is thick and long with a sprinkling of dandelions. But wait, what's this? Agnes and Friðrik—Friðrik?—share the site, like a marriage bed. The marker has just their two names, birth dates, and the same date of death. There is nothing indicating the story behind their deaths, or that it is just their heads buried there. If it is just their heads.

For me, Agnes is the central character in the story. Poor Agnes, wrongly put to death for her love and lust by the Danish colonial overlords to teach the wild Icelanders a lesson. The Danes thought they were a semi-feral northern tribe, who secretly worshipped pagan idols more than the Christian God. One prevailing thought about the case is that the Danes wanted to teach Icelandic women a lesson: stay chaste.

Because I am caught up in the story between Natan and Agnes, I forget that Friðrik was also beheaded in Þrístapar, only minutes before Agnes. And we pay little attention to two other women who played a part in the tale—Rosa, a famous poetess, who was Natan's real love and intellectual equal, and sixteen-year-old Sigríður, another maid in Natan's house who he easily seduced. This wasn't just a love triangle, one needs a Venn diagram to figure it out.

But they only sent Friðrik and Agnes to the chopping block. After the beheadings, their bodies were quickly disposed of and their heads were put on pikes facing the road, which sounds more like bloody old England than Iceland.

Helga tells us how their heads happened to find their way to this churchyard in Tjörn, a ghost story within a ghost story. Back in 1932, a woman in Reykjavík, a psychic type, was "summoned" by Agnes, who expressed her desire to have her head and Friðrik's buried in the churchyard at Tjörn. A picky, demanding ghost, this Agnes. She apparently told the psychic exactly where their heads were buried in Þrístapar, though they were buried secretly in the middle of the night. With the psychic's excellent directions, the heads were dug up, complete with the wooden pikes embedded in skulls, and reburied in Tjörn.

We spend the rest of the time in Tjörn looking to see if Natan is buried here, too, figuring maybe that's why Ghost Agnes chose this as her final resting spot. But there is no headstone that reads Natan Ketilsson.

We drive over to where Natan had his farm in Illugastaðir, on the northern coast of the Vatnsnes peninsula. The sky is overcast. The tide is out. Seaweed is thick in the tidal basin. It's a wild, moody place, and it's easy to imagine a mad love affair gone deadly wrong. A new house stands where Natan's house once stood, where a destitute Agnes came to him, hired as a housemaid, and stayed as his lover. The remnants of his workshop where he made his medicine and potions are nothing but fallen planks and broken sticks of wood, what nature has left after 180 years of abandonment.

The land itself is now a nature preserve for eiders. There is a car park, a restroom, and a well-maintained path where the ducks nest, protected in the grass by old tires. The path ends at a point where there is a bird lookout with a sign-in guest book. Looking west there is a spit of land where the seals are trying to sun themselves on the rocks. The sun shoots out in brief intermittent flashes of light. And beyond that, across the fjord, are blue-and-white snow-capped mountains, a sparkling winter land in great contrast to the green summer land we stand on. It hovers almost as a mesmerizing mirage. Helga points to that blue, wintry coast, which looks for all the world like something out of a fairy tale, and tells us that is where her mother was born.

Then we head to Þristapar, where the execution took place. It's marked by a green post on the side of the road, signifying a historical event, that we have passed for eleven years without stopping to look around.

It is warm and rainy as we walk to the site of the executions. We don't engage in our usual chatter. We walk solemnly, as if in a funeral procession, as if we are paying our respects to a woman executed almost two centuries ago. The three hills are only small mounds, only about ten feet high, not exactly grand gallows. Standing there, I'm not thinking of Agnes and Friðrik as we walk to the site; I'm thinking of the neighboring farmers who were forced to witness the event, the ones who haunt our guesthouse, the very ones who were kicking the muddy snow off their boots while I was trying to sleep that first night at Thingeyrar. I don't imagine they were thrilled about being buried together just because they happened to witness a couple of beheadings.

I was once on a jury for a personal injury case. I had lunch with my fellow jurors, we cracked some good jokes, and we had a two-week camaraderie based on being stuck together every day and wanting to get the trial over with. But I would not have wanted to be buried with them.

And why was the guesthouse built on top of the graveyard anyway? Why not move it a little to the left? They have 8,000 acres of open land. They couldn't have reconfigured a parcel of pasture?

Icelanders think nothing of having ghosts around, but this seems as if they were asking for ghosts. Maybe that's the point, maybe they like their ghosts; they always have a piece of history whispering in their ears.

At the top of the mound, the Þristapar marker is weathered, pocked with lichen and moss. It looks a thousand years old. I can't make out the letters and it's not much to look at. But the views are vast in this part of Iceland. Look one way and there are the hills of dry dirt left behind by a landslide from the Ice Age. And inland from there is Kornsá, a deep lush valley. Look the other way and the land opens up to the rolling green farmland that gives way to Lake Hóp. I can easily make out the black basalt of Thingeyrarkirkja, and the low building that is our guesthouse.

At dinner that night, we pepper our Icelandic hosts with questions about the details of the execution. We, who come from a country that just bungled a supposedly foolproof chemical execution in Texas—it took three tries! We are fascinated with the idea that Icelanders rejected capital punishment almost 200 years ago.

It is our last dinner together, since we leave tomorrow. We put together two dining room tables to seat everyone: Helga and Gunnar, Oli and Gita, Frieda, plus the six of us.

Oli has grilled lamb chops, baked potatoes, and sautéed mushrooms for our dinner. When we express admiration that capital punishment was banished after Agnes and Friðrik were beheaded, Oli reminds us that the Icelanders didn't have a say in the matter; they were a colony under Denmark's rule. A reprieve would have had to come from the King of Denmark. And capital punishment wasn't officially off the books in Iceland for another hundred years. Iceland wasn't independent from Denmark until 1944.

I ask Oli, "Did Agnes kill Natan out of mercy after Friðrik bludgeoned him, like in the book, or do you think it was like in the movie, when she finds him dead already and pulls him out from the burning wreckage?"

Before anyone has a chance to answer, I follow up quickly with another question. "Do you think Natan emotionally abused her and she lost it when she found him with Sigríður?"

My questions cause a flood of inquiries from the rest of us:

"Did women from her station of life have no rights?"

"And did Agnes have a child with him or not?"

"Rosa had a child with him, right?"

"And why were Agnes and Friðrik buried in the same plot? Was it assumed they had an affair and they killed Natan because of it?"

"And where is Natan's body buried?"

"Yeah, where is Natan's body?"

"And where are Agnes and Friðrik's bodies? What did they do with them after they put their heads on pikes?"

"Was the poet Rosa jealous of Agnes?"

"Was it Rosa who wanted Agnes blamed for the murder?"

"Why wasn't Sigríður also accused of murder?"

"And why, why, did they bury the witnesses together? What was the point of that?"

"And did they really just move the grave markers and not the bodies underneath this house?"

We throw out so many questions that we're talking over each other. The Icelanders sit back and take a breath.

What more can they tell us?

No one could have anticipated—either in 1830 or 2014—this sympathy for Agnes, the historical novel written by an Australian, or a bunch of American women newly obsessed with a love-murder tale that took place so long ago, a tragedy spawned on this island long forgotten by most of the world, now suddenly worthy of a Hollywood movie.

Who could have seen this coming?

But we have been here, sleeping on these ghosts each year at Thingeyrar, looking at their grave markers every morning over breakfast without giving it much thought. And now that it has finally aroused our curiosity and our compassion, we can't stop thinking about it. We have so many questions that the Icelanders can't, or don't want to, answer or revive the story. Helga tells us that this is still a touchy story in these parts, that old people remember their great-, or great-great-grandparents' parts in the execution or trial, or witnessing the beheading. In other words, we should back off or at least tread more carefully. The Agnes story has never fully died around here. History in Iceland is ever present. The ghosts are still active at Thingeyrar. It's personal for them.

My Iceland Thing

As we leave Helga's farm we have the dates for our return trip the following June.

Sylvie says, "It's not that we're returning and repeating this trip every year, it's that we're recreating the trip and ourselves each year."

"This was a great year," Eve says. "Some years come together better than others."

"It was the right mix of people," Viv says. "That matters."

"You never know how it is going to turn out," Eve says. "That's what I like about these trips."

"You never know what people are going to bring," Margot says.

"Most of the time, people bring something good here, and leave with something better," Eve says. "I like to think of it that way. But I'm done trying to save people by bringing them here. I'm over that. It got too messy."

Margot says, "You have to be open to the possibilities. Otherwise you can't be saved."

"Every trip has saved me in some way," I tell them. "Not that I think of myself as needing salvation. It's more that I think of myself as needing to get lost. It's the opposite of that youthful obsession of 'trying to find yourself.' I need to lose myself, and more often. Sometimes I lose myself with the horses, and sometimes I lose myself just being in Iceland."

Eve says, "I get that."

"It's like personal emancipation."

We stop at a bakery in Borgarnes. After coffee and cake, we stop in a gift shop to buy last minute presents for friends and family. I have difficulty making choices. Does my daughter need another wool hat? Would my son use a package of Icelandic herbs? I am mindlessly humming to a song that is on, before realizing it is the well-known song by Of Monsters and Men, "Little Talks," but sung in Icelandic. The others are rushing about saying we have to leave soon. I feel antsy and melancholy leaving Iceland, overwhelmed that I am leaving it too soon. I want to hang back, stay longer, remain in this country for at least a few more days. Everyone else is eager to leave, though. We have to be in the airport in two hours.

———

I arrive home on a Friday and two days later I am at a party, looking for someone to talk to. The party has a DJ, a sushi chef, a pizza truck, a crepe stand—soon to be followed by oysters and lobsters. A young waiter circulates on the lawn offering mojitos. I swipe one off his tray. It's a swanky lawn party at a friend's beach house that sits on the Connecticut Sound, and I can't help but add up the costs of this event and note that it would fund at least ten of my trips to Iceland.

Iceland is still with me. I carry in me a leftover sense of peace, and a residual exhaustion from a week of midnight sun insomnia. I still have the gravlax and smoked lamb that I bought at Keflavík airport waiting for me in my refrigerator. And I still feel as if I don't want to reenter my regular life, not quite yet. This party is a perfect go between.

There is something about this particular part of Connecticut that reminds me of the coastline in Iceland. Maybe it's the dark green and black of the moss and seaweed on the rocks during low tide. Maybe it's the dark pebbly sand and the big craggy rocks that tumble disorderly into the blue-gray sea. Or maybe it's that the New England coastline is a gateway to the more northern waters.

Finally, someone starts talking to me and my lonely mojito, a woman I haven't seen in a while. "Oh, did you do your Iceland thing?" she asks me.

"Yes, I just got back."

"How was it?"

"It was great," but I don't offer up anything more. She's being polite, but I find it slightly reductive to sum up my trip when, three days before, I was spinning my horse circles in a river with Allie and Margot. My Iceland thing is more suitable for the late at night heart-to-hearts, and then only with certain people, preferably the people I travel with.

"Did you ride the ponies?"

"They're horses, and yes."

She's nodding her head and smiling. I'm nodding my head and smiling. She's looking for a conversation and I am not being very forthcoming. I could stand to be more friendly. "They are small, but strong and really fast. And they roam free all over the countryside. And Iceland is almost all rural." I am giving it a try, but I can tell she's not interested in horses.

I have been tuning out the music the DJ is playing because it's mostly trilling songs by warbling pop divas. And I'd rather listen to the gulls screech.

But then I hear trumpets and a folk music chorus yell, "Hey!"

"Oh, Of Monsters and Men, this is their song, 'Little Talks.'" The woman looks confused.

"They're an Icelandic band," I offer up, as if that might arouse some interest. "And this is their most popular hit. I heard it in an Icelandic gift shop in this small town before I left." I see her interest fade again.

On our way north and then again on our way south, we always stop at the bakery in Borgarnes and, as we eat our pastries, look out on the fjord. We always seem to get there at low tide and the mudflats stretch way out and strand the fleet of small boats in the harbor. Like elsewhere in Iceland, the town has has grown in population and number of businesses, and looks slightly changed from our last visit. But that first stop on the way up signals the beginning of our trip and we're full of chatter and expectations. And the stop on the way back signals the end of our trip and we're wrestling with quiet reluctance and anticipated anxiety. I want to skid my feet on the ground, slow the ride down, stop the world. Better yet, I want to start it all over again.

<hr />

It's nice here—the party, the setting, the drink, the sun shining off the water. It induces a rest-assured benevolence, a brief bulwark against hurrying time. But the party will be over in a few hours and tomorrow morning I will be back at work and the images of Iceland will quickly fade. Another year will pass in a dormant state of expectation, before I'm sitting at that bakery again, looking at the mudflats, eager for our arrival at Thingeyrar. My Iceland thing.

I've left a very long pause in the conversation and I worry the woman is figuring out how to politely escape my company. She's surveying the crowd around the sushi chef, making excuses about getting something to eat. I don't know her all that well, but I know she had a tough time a year ago when her nine-year-old daughter needed surgery to remove a tumor; and I know the woman who hosts this party spends too many days in bed suffering from an autoimmune disease. And I know that life has a way of beating you up with one thing or another: ill health, sick kids, too many bills, broken hearts, bad jobs, or too much complacency. At some point you lose whatever it is that makes your heart beat wild. It doesn't have to be a horse, or a particular country, but we all need our Iceland thing.

Looking around at the other women on the lawn, I wonder who would be a good fit for Loki, who would tumble like Sylvie into the river, who would have some Pippa in her, who would have Allie's confidence in the saddle, Eve's cheerfulness, Viv's walking speed? I ask her with genuine interest where she plans to travel this summer. "I haven't thought about it till now," she says.

2015

—∞∞∞—

Getting Iceland

Reykjavík grows larger and larger. It's recovered from the 2008 crash and the suburbs spread out for miles. New roads, new apartment buildings, an entire rebuilt section of the wharves that were once fish processing plants have been reconstructed into unaffordable shops and restaurants. Parts of Reykjavík feel like parts of millennial-inhabited Brooklyn.

About 20,000 tourists a year came to Iceland when I first started visiting in 2001—now its 1.5 million a year. Immigration was 1 percent, now it's 12 percent. Unemployment is practically nonexistent, so the Icelandic business owners have to hire foreign workers to do the menial labor—the hotel housecleaning or the factory work at the fish processing plants. Iceland has become a very rich country, importing poorer people to clean up their shit—always a depressing measure of success. A supermarket in downtown Reykjavík has signs in Icelandic, Polish, and English. I have been told that in nursery schools the teachers have to encourage the children to speak Icelandic to each other, otherwise they will default to English.

Years ago I came to Iceland to get away from the world. I had no idea the world would come to Iceland.

How long will this last? This sweet spot of access and discovery, growth and openness? Like elsewhere, the changes are rapid. Some people welcome the changes, others mourn their lost world. The politics reflect the usual mix of grievances and opportunity-seeking expansion. I used to marvel at the country's solipsistic innocence and self-protectiveness. But it has caught up to the modern world with all its attendant problems.

Eve's eyes are healed. The surgery was a success. She can see again and is driving. "Isn't it funny," she says, "all these years we came here, everyone thought we were crazy. Now everyone I know is coming here."

"Now everyone is crazy."

Eve laughs. "I remember people asking me, why are you . . . where are you going? And why do I keep coming back? No one got it."

"We got it. We just didn't think anyone else would get it."

"Iceland was like our secret place," Sylvie says.

"It was the horses," Eve says. "We came for the horses first, Jack and I did, and then we connected with Helga and Thingeyrar."

Sylvie interjects that it was her friendship with Helga that brought us all here.

Eve eagerly agrees with her and continues, "And there was nothing here when we first came." Her hand sweeps the windshield to the view of the new downtown. "There used to be one main street and it was full of T-shirt shops. This place is a city now. It's actually got things to do."

"Even my daughter wants to come here," I say. "She used to laugh at me for going. Now she wants to spend a week in Reykjavík with her friends."

Talking about all the changes in Iceland makes me realize we've been coming here long enough to reminisce, to feel the melancholy of nostalgia. We can't help it and don't want to help it.

"Remember that empty bar we went to down by the wharves, ages ago? We were the only ones there," Sylvie says.

"I do remember. I think of that place often, Sylvie."

I know I have no right to be nostalgic; it's not my country. But nostalgia isn't a right, it's an expression of loss. As Sylvie (and Buddha) says, "Life is about letting go."

We talk about the changes when we meet up with Sibba at a bakery outside of town. Her eyes widen as she intakes with that breathy affirmative. "Yeow. Iceland has changed so much, I don't even recognize my little country. I don't know how it happened. I can't get over it. It's so crowded. We have to go to the West Fjords to find our country."

Eve changes the subject with a bright question: "How is your grandchild?" Sibba shows us the pictures on her phone of her new granddaughter. We remark how much she looks like Sibba, who seems unsure of the resemblance. "It's the dimples," we point out, as if the dimples are a particular Icelandic trait.

On the drive up to Thingeyrar, Margot and Sylvie fill us in on how their farm is taking shape. Unexpectedly, the old neighbor who had been giving them all the problems with zoning and trying to stop or slow down their plans, died.

"I know, it's sad, but he died two weeks ago," Margot says, "he *was* eighty-nine."

"When he was alive he was *so mean* to us," Sylvie says.

"But then he died," Margot repeats. "Sadly, but . . ."

Sylvie interrupts, "That's what happens when people are mean to me. They die." I give Sylvie a look. "It's true! People wind up dying when they're mean to me."

Margot continues. "So his children are selling off parcels of his property and Sylvie and I put an offer on a twenty-acre piece of land just before we left. If our bid is taken, we'll have a twenty-four-acre farm—with Icelandic horses. We will recreate your farm, Eve."

"We are manifesting this farm," Sylvie says.

While most people Sylvie's age, or younger, are downsizing their lives and saving money for real old age, Sylvie is expanding her life, buying more property, more horses, starting a farm. As Sylvie gets older, she's still Sylvie, only more so, Sylvie at the peak of her Sylvie-ness.

"That's great," Eve says. But I can tell it's not great for Eve. She doesn't like to be reminded of losing her farm five years earlier, even if Sylvie and Margot's farm will be only half the size of hers. The idea that this is a replacement farm probably hurts her. At some point, she gave up on owning horses again. Jack gave up saying he was going to buy her horses. And the only riding she does is at Helga's once a year with us.

Eve changes the subject and asks me how my son is doing.

"He's really good. He has a girlfriend and they are making a life together. They've moved in together."

"Do you like her?" Sylvie asks.

"Yeah, what's she like?" Eve asks.

"She's one of these big, bold, robust young women who's full of life. You know the type? Full of life. And she brings all this good energy to the relationship and she's woken him up. He's back to being that kind, sweet kid he used to be."

Eve claps. "That's so wonderful. I love to hear it." She shouts, "Love cures all!"

"That's beautiful, it really is," Sylvie says.

"Women civilize men."

"We really do," Viv says.

Viv knows all this already. We talk once a week. Usually on the same day, same time, when I go grocery shopping at 5:00 on Thursdays, which is usually the time she is cleaning out the barn, bringing her horse in from the pasture. While I'm putting yogurt in my cart and she's forking up the manure, we catch up on everything. If I have any news about the Berkshire group, I tell her, since I keep in touch with them more than she does. And she tells me all about her horse's Cushing disease. We know each other's family members, though we've never met them: "How's mom?" she always asks. And I ask, "How's your father-in-law?" Though our friendship started all those years ago during those long sunlit walks at midnight, bonding over our sons' problems, we've gone way beyond that; in fact, our sons usually, finally, come up last in our long conversations. My son, and her son, Jonathan, have both found girlfriends and that has brought them back to us. They have survived themselves. And we have survived through it. "It must be because of the votive lighting in the church and the red rocks of Thingeyrar," Viv says. "It must be."

Learning to Fly

D o you realize how lucky we are to have this place?" Sylvie says, as we pull up to Thingeyrar. She sighs, and we all sigh.

"I love this place," Margot says.

"I love this place more than any other place on earth," I say.

Getting out of the car, we stand at the fence and Allie takes pictures. She is the only one who still carries an actual digital camera. The rest of us use our phones.

It is a bright sunny day, but there is a brisk chill to the wind. I know we are on the edge of the Arctic circle at 66 degrees latitude, and while I don't expect it to be balmy, this feels colder and brighter than normal.

Helga comes out of her house in one of her brightly colored housedresses, wrapping a sweater around her shoulders. She greets us in the driveway. "I didn't think you'd show up the first year, and now here you are on your twelfth."

"Am I sensing regret you ever came to know us?" Sylvie prods.

"No, what would I do without you all in my life," Helga laughs. "My life would not be complete."

We drag our suitcases into the guesthouse and there is an older woman there—small, gray-haired, and frail looking. She is coming down the stairs from the spooky bedrooms. She appears very shy and when Helga introduces her, she nods her head hello to us, and quickly leaves the house.

"She is a very special person to me," Helga explains. "She was my teacher in college and she is very well-known for writing books on Icelandic plants, botany textbooks. She wrote this very important book on medicines that can be derived from Icelandic herbs." Helga taps her fist to her heart. "She is a very special friend of mine. She is one of those women I feel honored to know."

And then, switching the subject, Helga says, "I have the names of the horses you will ride today up on the blackboard in the barn. Frieda is down there, waiting for you. When should I tell her you'll be ready?"

"Give us an hour," Sylvie says.

"Okay. And Oli has made dinner for you. He's made coq au vin, and he's very proud of it." Helga leaves us to our unpacking.

"Do you believe how lucky we are?" Sylvie repeats. "I can't stand it," she squeals.

"This is all I want in life," I say. "A horse waiting in the barn for me to ride; a meal waiting for me after the ride."

"This is happiness," Eve says, "the best karma in the world."

I bring my luggage into my small bedroom, which I now consider mine. After Pippa demanded but didn't get it, it became my bedroom, and I make it my home.

Soon everyone is in the kitchen, making tea and munching on the bowl of dried bananas and chocolate-covered raisins that has been left for us on the kitchen table. Eve goes into the fridge and brings out cheese, *rúgbrauð*, and currant jam. Sylvie finds the smoked salmon. It's four in the afternoon. We'll ride for an hour or two, come in at seven. Dinner will be at eight. We know the rhythm of our days here, and our rides will get longer as the week goes on, and our last ride will be the most challenging.

My first ride is on Moldi. In Icelandic, the horse's name sounds nice. The "d" has a soft "th" sound, the "l" is basically dropped. Of course, the subtleties of pronunciation are lost on us. We call out his name like a fungus: "Who's riding Moldy today?" He hasn't held that against us, though. His name means earth-colored and Moldi is a robust dun gelding with an eel stripe and a black and white mane, which nicely shows off the Norwegian Fjord DNA of Icelandic horses.

I was originally scared of Moldi. He was one of Disa's horses and she trained primarily competition horses. Moldi was not one of those, but the second year we came to the farm, he was a five-year-old and hence not completely trained. Now he is twelve and Frieda has assigned him to me, and I am happy to ride him in his more mature years.

Frieda takes us out to the lupine trail, but the lupine has not bloomed yet. The ground is hard, as if we are tölting on frozen tundra. Frieda tells us it has been the coldest spring, and now the coldest recorded summer, in history. And the wind is brutal. I've got on my merino wool buff and I've pulled it up under my helmet, but the wind is cutting into my ears. My eyes are tearing. The flap of my helmet keeps whipping across my chin.

Frieda starts us at a fast speed, and keeps it going fast. She's cold and this is the best way to warm up—have the horses work hard and the rider benefit from their warmth. Now no one says, slow down, let's walk, not even Sylvie. It's taken her many years to get over her need to go slow, and now, well into her seventies, she's more than willing to go fast.

Allie, of course, is riding a spiffy competition horse. Helga now gives her higher end horses, since Allie needs very little instruction, except to be told that the horse is very sensitive and to be light in the hands. Allie is the only one in our group who spends no time with horses outside of these Iceland trips. And yet she rides well, better than most of us. She is unfazed and fearless when she is on a young spirited horse. When the horse spooks or acts flighty or rude, she says to it, "Oh, c'mon now," or, "Sheesh, what do you think you're doing?" That's it. No trepidation, no fight, no tense shoulders. Just that Midwest pragmatic patter. And the horses listen to her. It is a lesson in how much confidence plays into horse-rider communication.

Frieda moves back and forth in the line making sure everyone is okay. We are. When we get to a slight incline in the path, Allie asks if we can canter up it. Frieda answers her, but I can't hear the answer. The wind is making a racket in my ears. Allie canters though, so I'm guessing the answer was yes.

I want to catch up to Allie and I ask for canter from Moldi. Not that out on the trail these horses need much encouragement. Once my horse sees the lead horse canter, all I usually have to do is adjust my seat slightly and place my reins on his neck to give him enough room to move his head. But that is not working with Moldi. When I give him the aids, he trots faster. I know some horses don't like to canter; it's too much work for them, but they all can do it.

Frieda rides up beside me and gives me instructions that are partly obscured by the wind howling in my ears. She calls out my name in her German accent, but I miss the other words. "Tauwri, do . . . bring him . . . Tauwri . . . then he'll be . . . Tauwri."

"What???" I am reminded of the dog in the Gary Larson cartoon—the human gives him a list of instructions and all the dog hears is her name, Ginger, over and over again. I am ripping through the not-yet-bloomed lupine trail and have almost caught up to Allie.

I just want to canter with Allie, and keep asking it from Moldi, but he keeps trotting faster and faster and it's a weird mixed gait. I can't post to it and it's too fast to sit to. I try my arsenal of riding tricks: leg on, leg off, sit forward, sit back, tighten reins, loosen reins, give and take reins. And then suddenly it feels strange and I don't know what to do. Moldi increases his speed again without going into a canter. The gait is smoother than a trot, but it's not a tölt and I am zooming.

Frieda canters up next to me and says, "Tauwri, he's pacing. You've got him in a pace!" She's excited I got him into this gait; she thinks I meant to. The gait is better left to expert riders and I would have never purposely tried to pace. But Moldi offered, and I unknowingly accepted.

Pace is the fifth gear in the Icelandic horse, the horse's feet leave the ground laterally at once and the horse is suspended briefly in the air, flying over the ground. Pacing clocks in at 30 miles per hour. On a horse, it feels like flying.

Not every Icelandic horse can pace. A lot of Icelandics are only four-gaited. This has always been a given with horse owners and breeders, and recent research has shown why. In order to be truly five-gaited, the horse has to have a specific gene, known as the AA genotype. This gene gives the horses' limbs better coordination in lateral movements, so a horse with this gene would score high in tölt as well. And though 75 percent of horses born in Iceland have this genotype, they still need to be trained in pace.

The other horses are mostly the CA genotype and only four-gaited. The CA gives the horses' limbs more coordination in diagonal movements, and, hence, better suspension in trot and canter. Tölts in these horses tend to be somewhat trotty.

There are many horse breeds that are four-gaited, generally referred to as the ambling gait. Think of the American Saddlebred and Tennessee Walking Horse with their rack, or the Paso Finos with their paso largo. In medieval days, light horses that were gaited were called palfreys. These horses all share the same genetic mutation, the DMRT3, that allows it the extra gait. DNA testing on ancient horse bones traces this mutation back to a horse breed found in northern England about 1,200 years ago. Coincidentally, the spread of gaited horses happened around the same time as the Viking age of expansion, so it's very possible these two events are inextricably linked.

And that is why Moldi doesn't like to canter. He's an AA genotype with a very smooth tölt and a natural pace. He could be trained to canter, but his training was cut short because Disa moved away, and there was no real reason to teach him to canter. He is the perfect trail horse. One could ride him at a tölt all day and even, by accident, get him to pace.

"Þetta Reddast" (Life Will Work Out)

Helga comes in one evening during our cocktail hour. Eve and I are sitting in the kitchen drinking beer and eating banana chips. Allie is drinking wine. Viv is reading *Veterinary Medicine*.

"I have an announcement to make," Helga says. Her announcements can mean anything from "Stulka is pregnant" to "there is a new exhibit at the Sea Ice Museum." Except that Helga has a bottle of Champagne in her hand.

Eve yells, "Helga has an announcement!" Sylvie and Margot come out of the living room, where they have been hovering over their laptops.

Helga waits for everyone to join her in the kitchen. "Well, I thought you all should know that I am now the owner of a house in Selfoss. I have just signed the papers."

She looks so happy, exuberant, but our reaction doesn't match hers. We don't cheer or clap like we would normally. I don't think any of us knew she was looking for another place to live. And even if she was, that it would be down south in a suburban town like Selfoss.

Sylvie says, "You're going to leave Thingeyrar?"

"Not immediately. It will probably take another year to get everything together and make the move."

"So you'll be here next summer?" I ask, after an awkward pause.

We're deflating her good news bubble. "Yes, I think so. I think you can depend on coming back next summer."

"How did this come about?" Viv asks. "I mean, I didn't know you wanted to move."

───

"You know that woman you met the other night? My old friend who was staying here? It's her house in Selfoss. She wants to move into Reykjavík; she is getting old and she doesn't want to drive. It's a very special house, built in the '70s, and she and her husband were the first to try reforesting Iceland. So, there are many trees on the property protecting the house, keeping it warm from the wind and even extending summer for another two months.

"And she is selling me the house for a reasonable price. She wants the house to go to someone who would appreciate it."

"Wow, what an opportunity!" Margot says, finally stepping up to be the first one to congratulate her. "Helga, that's wonderful. I'm so happy for you."

"See, the universe provides," Eve says.

And the universe takes away.

"You know I was looking for some place closer to Reykjavík where we could move. And then this house was offered to me and I'm ready to move. I've been ready to move for a while."

"Will you bring all your horses to this place?"

"No, it's not a farm. I might keep a few of my horses down the street, but horses won't be my life anymore."

But horses were her life. For the last twenty years, she had built up her bona fides in the Icelandic horse world as a trainer and breeder. She had established a brand name, a horse that was "fra Thingeyrar" meant it was sure to be of good confirmation, temperament, and training. Not only that, when she entered the training world twenty years ago, it was a man's world. She was the first woman trainer and breeder of any note. And her training techniques were now being taught in equine schools. Helga was a big deal in the Icelandic horse world. And she was giving it all up.

"What are you going to do in Selfoss?"

"I'm going to take it easy for a while and see what interests me. I have this idea for a children's book; and I might design knitting patterns. But I am not going to worry about making money, I am not going to worry about anything. I am going to start something new in my life. *Þetta reddast.*"

Þetta reddast is an often used Icelandic saying, meaning life will work out somehow. It expresses a national come-what-may attitude toward fate and I can't help but wonder if it doesn't contain vestiges of the three wyrds of the old Norse faith.

Eve says, "Helga, this is your next incarnation. You are recreating yourself."

"Yes, I believe that."

"Well, we have a big announcement to make, too," Margot says, beaming nervously. "Our offer for the property has been accepted. We just got the email. Sylvie and I are the proud new owners of twenty more acres and now we will have a proper Icelandic horse farm."

I muster up a belated, but I hope genuine, congratulations to Helga on her new house, and a heartier congratulations to Sylvie and Margot on their new horse farm. Now there will be another Icelandic farm in the Berkshires. The three of them are giddy with their choices and fortunes, all talking about how they are all "transitioning" into the next phase of their lives, and how they "manifested" the good outcomes.

"And we've already got a name picked out. Because today is the solstice and I got the email today," Margot says, "so it's preordained, I'm going to name the farm 'Solstice Icelandics.'"

Eve adds, "This is meant to be! The universe is coming together!"

Not for me, I think. It's falling apart.

"Yes, it's meant to be," says Helga. "And you can all come visit me in Selfoss. It's a big house with room for all of you. And it's got lots of greenhouses and gardens. It's almost tropical compared to here."

"That's it then. We will all go to southern Iceland instead," Eve says.

We can, I think, and it will be treed and gardened. It will be tamed and civilized. It will be warmer and busier. But it will not be the windswept wild north of Thingeyrar.

When all the toasts are made and the bottle of Champagne drunk, I walk outside by myself. I hike up to the church grounds where I have a clear view of it all: the farmland to the south and east, Lake Hóp and the Greenland Sea and the place where the rivers converge and Helga had her birthday bash, the whole vast valley with its endless sky on this day with its endless sun. I am losing Thingeyrar, the end is being written.

———

We were forewarned, if we had been listening. Helga was ready for a change of life, and she was hatching a plan. Two years earlier, when she was visiting us in New York, she told us that she was giving up her position at Holar. "Yeah, it is time to leave. I am done teaching, and I am done with the long commute."

We were standing in line behind a rope to the Egyptian wing of the Met, when she said, "My sons are settled, they both have work and partners and children on the way. I no longer have to work full-time."

It was hard to pay attention to what she was saying because Helga was causing something of a commotion. Men were walking into the ropes to get a better look at her. Rich-looking men, with rich-looking wives on their arms, tripped over their own feet as they stared at her, mouths ajar. One man craned his neck around us, and impatiently motioned for us (Viv, Eve, me) to "step aside, step aside," corralling us away from Helga, like Gauper nipping at the hooves of stray horses, all so he could see her better. I thought perhaps he worked as a guard there, the way he pushed us out of the way with such twitchy authority, but no, he was dressed business casual with a metal admission MMA tag bent on his lapel.

All this was distracting me from what she was saying. I was aware that Helga was a momentary phenomenon in New York City, as if the aurora borealis had suddenly flashed over the tomb of Thebes on the Upper East Side. The people staring at her were not subtle, but they weren't ogling her, either. The look was more quizzical, more of a sense of wonderment, "What is she?" "Who is she?" "She must be somebody."

She was fifty-three that year, wearing simple clothes: a red sweater, a leather bomber jacket. She had her jeans rolled an inch or two below the rim of her black lace-up boots. Her white-blond hair was cut bluntly and short to her chin; she pulled it back haphazardly with barrettes. She wore no makeup. It was unexpectedly hot—80 degrees and humid—at the end of October and her face was red from the heat and the sun. Her skin was flawless, unlined, as if the cold clean air of Thingeyrar neutralized the aging process. She was outstandingly beautiful and unusual looking, especially by New York standards. She seemed oblivious about the fuss she was causing. And if she were aware, she didn't care.

We were all there. It was one of our rare New York reunions: Allie was up from Georgia, looking at NYU for her son. Margot and Sylvie came in together on the train from the Berkshires and me from Connecticut. Viv came in from New Jersey. Eve was already in the city. We met at the Met, walked to midtown for lunch, and then took a cab to Soho for drinks.

"I just figure it's my time to move on," she said over cocktails at Fig & Olive. The woman bartender was staring at her and continued looking at her when the rest of us gave our drink orders. She didn't pivot to us once.

And Helga tried to put the question to us, too. "Are you satisfied with what you're doing with your life?"

The question went unanswered by all of us; we took it as rhetorical.

On reflection, she said, "I've never cared about money. I've never wanted that to guide me. I figure that part of my life will just work out."

We were listening to her, but at the same time we weren't. What I heard was that she was dissatisfied, but I assumed that she had found an easy fix—she was going to stop teaching at Holar, because it was a long commute and she was tired of that age group. But she was talking about something larger. If we had been listening closely, we would have realized she was testing out some ideas on us, thinking out loud and revealing the kind of questions that you share only with certain friends like us—long distant friends that don't figure into her day-to-day life in Iceland. She was done being the horsewoman of northern Iceland. She was telling us that, but I couldn't hear it because it didn't make sense to me—why would she leave what I saw as a perfect life in a perfect place?

I had always asked myself, *how long will our trips go on?* The other question I should have asked was, *how long will Thingeyrar be there for us?*

Finding Our Way

We are heading out to Lake Hóp. I am riding Skjoni, and because he is a tall gelding the water doesn't come as up as high on him, and the lake is low anyway. The horses can walk the last part. Skjoni is the perfect horse, an easy tölter, a sturdy, thick horse. He seems to intuit my needs, and I don't have to focus much on giving him cues. The entire ride so far has been quiet and dreamy, as if I am being led by a collection of memories.

While we eat our lunch on the other side of the lake, Helga looks concerned watching the sky and the lake. "We should get going, I don't like the way things look," and she hurries us to saddle up.

A misty spritz of rain and a light fog descend on the lake as we enter it. We get through the deeper part fast enough, but that is the short part. Helga is riding fast, leading us to the shore as quickly as she can. But the fog becomes denser and I lose sight of Helga. Everyone else, horse and rider, become a smudge in this great white expanse. I only see Eve, who is closest to me. Helga tells us to slow down, and then to stop. We can hear each other's voices, but I lose sight of even the horse and rider smudges.

I even lose sight of Eve. "Eve, are you there?"

"I'm here." She doesn't sound far away.

"Is everyone okay?" Helga asks. There is no panic in her voice, but I can tell this is not good. I hear everyone's voice say, "I'm okay."

We've lost all sense of direction. We could be heading out to the sea. Allie's voice says, "Wait, I have my phone in my pocket and it has a compass." I hear her jacket pocket unzipping, the fumbling, the swearing. "It's dead. Did anyone else bring their phone?"

I can hear Margot and Allie discussing the merits of "sitting it out" in the middle of the lake, waiting for the fog to lift. "But what if the fog is here for hours? And the tide comes in quickly?"

Sounds are magnified: the horses breathing, the plop of a horse's hoof lifting and then dropping in the water. Since we are stalled, the impatient horses are stepping in place.

I'm not worried yet, but I remember Ljotur saying, "Iceland is a safe place in town, but the countryside is different: people fall off cliffs, they get swept away by a single wave. Nature is dangerous here."

With every air molecule fat with water, the edges of the world are gone. I am suspended in this place, as if time has stopped. I have come to expect otherworldly moments in Thingeyrar, and especially in Lake Hóp, the thinnest place in this world. If there is a crack where the light gets in, this is one such crack, but instead of a metaphorical beam of light, it is a pause in time, a temporary hold. In the fog, in the middle of the lake, on my horse Skjoni, with no up or down, north or south, no east or west, I sense myself floating in the world and filling up on it—it is enough, all, everything—it is the essence of an oceanic oneness.

The spell is broken, and I am awoken when someone calls out, "Sylvie, are you alright?"

For what seems like a very long time, there is silence. Then finally, "Yes." Her tone is gruff and unhappy.

Helga says, "Let's all get very close to each other, within sight of each other." And by call and response, we find each other and cluster together.

"Look," Helga says, "My horse is very good in the water and he will lead us out, I trust him. But don't lose sight of me."

She is riding her gray dappled horse. In the sagas, gray horses are endowed with special powers, able to run through the air and over the sea. In the Eddas, gray horses are water horses, they emerge from rivers and lakes; water is often in itself a liminal element and gray horses are the connection. Odin's horse, Sleipnir, was a gray stallion, and capable of passing through divine places.

Heroes ride horses, gods and goddesses, kings and queens ride horses—in so many myths they are the transport, the medium, the carrier between the worlds, and in so many cultures are buried with their masters when they die to carry them into the next world. We need our myths.

Helga urges her gray horse on with the slightest forward motion, to pick out the course, the same way she did when we crossed the river after Sylvie fell. The horse is cautious at first, and we follow her very slowly, careful not to lose sight of each other.

But then there is more surety in her horse's step, as he senses the ground growing firmer beneath him. The water gets shallower until it is only inches deep.

"I see the shoreline," Helga says, and the fog is lighter along the edge of the lake. "Take it slowly though." We let out a collective breath and compliment Helga's horse.

Sylvie, relieved, says, "Okay, next time, Helga, don't cue the fog machine. Leave that part out."

Once on land, the fog is light, and disappears completely away from the lake. We are quiet riding home, taking it slowly. I don't know whether it's the experience of the fog or if everyone is wondering the same thing I am: whether this will be our last ride together across the tidal lake, our last trek back to Thingeyrar.

The Golden Summerland of Thingeyrar

On our last night in Thingeyrar, we throw a big dinner party. Oli cooks as we prepare the table. Allie cuts and arranges large bouquets of lupines, dandelions, and buttercups as centerpieces. Sylvie, Eve, and I go to the vínbúðin in Blönduós and buy bottles of Pinot Noir and Pinot Gris and six-packs of specialty beers—the microbrewery industry has exploded in Iceland. Helga brings over appetizers of wood-smoked salmon and small pieces of halibut dry-cured in salt and herbs. Oli's main course is sea trout in onion sauce, potato gratin, roasted mushrooms, and arugula salad with blue cheese. For dessert, blueberry skyr cheesecake.

These dinners on the last night have become grand affairs and get larger and last longer each year. This time it is the six of us, plus Oli and Gita, Helga and Gunnar, the ambassador and his wife, and Frieda. We set aside time to perform skits, read poems, and tell our jokey faux medieval sagas chronicling our mishaps and adventures, starring Sylvie the Red, Eve the Cheerful, Viv the Unweary, Allie the Assured, Margot the Eager-Hearted, Helga the Deep-Minded, Frieda the Thoughtful, and Oli the Woman Fattener. I am the Scribe, who writes and reads aloud these sagas. Each ends with: "And so it was, year after year, Queen Sylvie and her merry band traveled to their favored golden summerland of Thingeyrar." We need our myths.

After dinner, we walk up to the church for a concert Helga has arranged with two of her nieces, vocalists in the music conservatory in Reykjavík. The girls, accompanied by a pianist, sing a dozen songs that range from Paul Simon's "El Cóndor Pasa" to a traditional Icelandic riding song to the Beatles "In My Life" to an aria from the opera about Agnes Magnúsdóttir.

After the concert, the six of us go back to the guesthouse and sit around the dining room table. We stay up late, long into the sunlit night, watching our horses gamboling in the grassy tussocks under the midnight sun. As if we know there will not be another summer at Thingeyrar, we talk about stories of years past, with one story reminding us of another: the horses we rode and loved and didn't love; the rivers we crossed and got stuck in; the first time in Lake Hóp when our horses plunged in and swam; how we fell in love with the sound of the hooves cantering in the shallows of the lake; how the horses pranced in place while we prepared ourselves for the ride along the riverbank; how the band of frisky young horses ran alongside us; the daylong trips to the Greenland Sea; and the years when Disa rode with us with a flask of cognac, and the day she made herself big, and bellowed and scared the bulls away.

These were our tales, these were the times, these were the women, and this was the place.

EPILOGUE

LOCKED GATES AND LOST PLACES

⎯⎯⎯⎯

As it happened, Helga moved out of Thingeyrar in November, 2015. She sold most of her horses, keeping only a few near her new home. Her horses were bought by people from the Netherlands, Germany, and Sweden, countries where Icelandics have been popular for years. Three buyers were from the States, Margot being one. She bought Freyr to join the new herd at Solstice Farm. On the transport plane to New York, Helga's three traveled in the company of forty other horses being exported from Iceland. The population of Icelandic horses in the States is inching up to 5,000.

The next time we see Helga, it's June 2016, and Eve, Allie, Sylvie, and I have come to visit her in Selfoss. In Thingeyrar, I don't remember even seeing a plant in a flowerpot, but here the yard of her new home is lined with raised garden beds full of growing vegetables. Tomatoes and herbs grow in her greenhouse. Flowering trellises grow against the southern side of her house. Her property is tree-lined and leafy with mossy little streams hidden in between patches of grass. It reminds me of Ireland.

Helga sends us to a nearby mega-farm to ride. We join a group of about forty people we don't know, some of whom have never been on a horse before. The guides give instructions in English, German, and French. "This is how you steer; this is how you stop; this is how you make it go."

Sylvie says, "It makes me cry to think how good we had it all those years at Helga's." Within fifteen minutes of riding on the trail, she bails. "I am not comfortable riding this horse at all," she tells the guides. She turns to us, "It's not Stulka. It's not Thingeyrar." Eve eagerly offers to get off with her and walk the horses back to the barn.

Allie and I continue with the group and when the guides ask who wants to split off into slower or faster groups, we go with the fast group. Our guides are not Icelandic, but young German and Norwegian girls, who tell us stories of Iceland—about elves and trolls, and about an argument in a saga that took place nearby. They assume that we are all new to Iceland.

After a few days in the south, we meet up with Sibba and Ljotur and head north to Siglufjörður. We visit yet another one of Iceland's quirky museums, The Herring Era Museum, commemorating the fishing industry that disappeared about sixty years ago when there was a sudden dearth of herring in the North Atlantic.

We walk up the planks to the old boats and enter the cramped quarters of the decks below; we watch a video of life at sea projected against a wall. Next door is the station house, another museum requiring a separate entrance fee. Downstairs are the shipping offices, kept perfectly in the 1940s decor. Upstairs are the apartments that once housed the "herring girls," farm girls who came to the town to spend their summers working on the piers, rinsing and salting the fish when the boats came in. It was a way to get off the farm and meet men to marry. Their living quarters are cozy, dusted, and clean; the beds are made, an iron and ironing board left out, skirts and bathrobes hang in the closets. In the kitchen are the coffee and teapots, the flour and sugar tins, mugs, a toaster, a painted-metal roll-top bread box, the wall calendar turned to the month of August 1941—as if the girls are coming back, their rooms waiting for them. You can almost hear the herring girls' laughter in the hallways, the bustle of movement and the clatter as they run downstairs when the ships' horns blow.

After the week with my group is over, my husband comes to Iceland for the first time. He flies into Akureyri Airport. We spend time at Lake Mývatn, go whale watching in Húsavík, and stop in on the horse competition at Landsmot that is being held at Holar this year. We sit on the hill overlooking the parades, eating dried haddock and drinking beer that Eve recommended so many years ago. We stay overnight in Blönduós in a barn that has been transformed into a luxurious inn. The next morning, we head out on Route 1 going west. Ten minutes out of Blönduós at a crest in the road, I point down to the black basalt church in the valley. "See the church and the farm below it? There's Thingeyrar. That's the farm."

It feels odd to be saying that to him—"there's Thingeyrar"—as if pulling back the curtain on my secret place, where I lived a part of my life that didn't include him or anyone else back home. I am conflicted about sharing it with anyone, as if showing it will cause me to lose my secret self, or more importantly, to trivialize everything the place has meant to me.

"Do you want to drive up the road and see it again?" he asks.

He knows I do.

At first, I play the tour guide as we drive up the dirt road to Helga's farm, faking a lighthearted mood. "There's the Steinnes farm where we stopped for coffee and donuts; there's the barn pit where we corralled the horses; there's where Dora fell off when the horse wasn't moving; and over there is where the terns attacked me and Viv, very Hitchcock."

When we get to the gate of Thingeyrar, I get out to open it, but it is padlocked. It has never been locked before—there's never been any reason to lock it. I know from Helga that the dissolution of her business at Thingeyrar with the ambassador was quicker than either had anticipated. And I know that the farm won't be used for horses anymore. Helga told us that once she moved out and the horses were all sold, the grass was poisoned with weed killer to kill all of the dandelions. It is unfit for horses to graze there now.

We drive up to the farm's church and get out of the car. On the hill, I point out the sights in the valley below to my husband: "That's Lake Hóp that we used to cross, that's the Greenland Sea, there's the Vatnsdalsa River." Facing the other way, and still in my tourist guide mode: "There's the house and the barn and the guesthouse. And there, you see the headstones clustered together and fenced in?" It occurs to me that I never told him the ghost story. "Well, there's a long story about a woman named Agnes."

It is early July and unusually warm for Iceland. There is no wind, the lupine have gone to seed. The structures are all here—house, barn, fields—but no horses, no people or life. Thingeyrar is another Iceland museum, patiently and lifelessly waiting for us, for the girls who will never return.

Back in the car, my husband says, "You're tearing up, aren't you?"

I nod mutely. I'm tearing up and trying not to. I can't speak or I will burst.

Couples, if they're lucky, transition as they age together. My husband originally thought these trips with the girls, to what he considered a godforsaken place, were a kind of fling, that I would get over wanting to keep coming here. But then he began tolerating my week of horses and friends with a close facsimile of good cheer, which then one day morphed into a true pride. "My wife, she rides horses in Iceland."

Now he is here with me, overlooking the fields of Thingeyrar, and when he sees me tug on the locked gate, he gets what I kept in abeyance for years.

"You really miss this place, don't you?" he says softly.

I break, sobbing at the loss, but also at his understanding of my loss, because once someone names your grief, you can no longer pretend it isn't real.

⁂

Thingeyrar means "place where the assembly (the thing) meets at the sand-bank (eryar)," referring to the early parliament meetings of Iceland's first settlers and to Lake Hóp's tidal beaches, those long stretches of black lava sand that gave our horses a soft but firm, steady footfall. If history has marked itself like a palimpsest upon this land, from the island's first settlers to the Benedictine monks to the ghosts of the witnesses of Agnes Magnúsdottír's death to the recent Holar interns, did we as frequent visitors leave a faint smudge on the parchment of Thingeyrar? Did I leave my imprint on the history of the land the way it has left its imprint on me?

On winter mornings at home, I look out at my hemmed-in New England forest of a backyard and picture Thingeyrar covered in snow, with its vast vistas, open, treeless, and desolate. Though the guesthouse is empty now, I like to picture the students from Holar who interned there, living out their hard eighteen-hour workdays, most of it in polar darkness, training horses, cleaning the barn. I imagine them sitting in the kitchen, making coffee, and talking about the horses or about their young lives and loves. How lucky they were to be there. As the days got longer, they would get ready to go, clean up the house for the next guests, for us.

And I knew my small paneled bedroom at Thingeyrar would be waiting for me in June: the comforter folded in half on the bunk bed, Icelandic style, the bedside table with water stains where I spread out my books, the casement window with the single plaid curtain that partially blocked out the constant sunlight, the church and the graveyard of witnesses within my view. I could depend on the cry of the skua and the kria, the beating of the snipes' tail feathers in the grass, the barking of Helga's dog, the sound of the clotheslines snapping in the brisk Arctic wind, and the sounds of the horses so close to the window that I could hear them exhaling, their short yips and neighs as the sudden urge of the herd made them trot to the other end of the field.

Sometimes I would open that window a few inches and the whole wild north would whistle in my bedroom, straight from the glacier, fresh from the clean oxygenated polar cap. And it would make my heart quicken. How wind can do that! And the persistent summer sun low on the horizon would keep me awake, receptive and enthralled to this bright green earth.

ACKNOWLEDGMENTS

Sometimes the stars align and a constellation of luck appears. At a lunch in Los Angeles my good friend Connie Brown (brilliant mapmaker) mentioned my Iceland book to her good friend Mona Edwards (famed courtroom artist), who later mentioned it to her good friend Deborah Ritchken (literary agent extraordinaire). My thanks to Connie for Mona, and to Mona for Deborah.

Deborah gave me the confidence to actually take seriously the idea of publishing this book, and as my agent played the dual role of guiding shepherd and dedicated champion. Thoughtful editor and publisher Jessica Case at Pegasus Books then tended it carefully through to publication. Heaps of gratitude to these stellar, tenacious women who came into my life at just the right moment.

Without another group of women—all my traveling companions—there would be no stories to tell, no rivers to cross, no 'in' to Iceland. Because there were many more women who I traveled with than are mentioned in the book—for the sake of brevity, privacy, and readability—I mashed up a few scenes, changed names and some identifiers, but kept the spirit of our tales and adventures true. Fellow riders, you have no idea how much you all meant to me.

Takk fyrir to all the Icelanders in this book. To Sibba and Ljotur who caravanned with us around Iceland with ceaseless bonhomie. To Helgi, who not only fattened us with healthy Icelandic food, but always welcomed us with unwavering bigheartedness. And most importantly to Helga, who opened up to us her guesthouse and the Golden Summerland of Thingeyrar, and was our guide, host, horse whisperer, friend.

When I needed time and space to finish this book, the artist residency at Gullkistan provided me with a room, a desk, and solitude. It was a dream of a place to write, with bonus views of Mt. Hekla and Mt. Katla.

For years my writing self has been buoyed by many encouraging friends, who probably don't realize how much I hang on their every word. Particularly longtime friend, Tina, a true seeker, who has an uncanny knack for saying the right thing at pivotal moments ("Move, and the way will open").

For new young friend, Grace Valentine, whose exuberance for this book and for all things in life was, frankly, irrepressible. I couldn't let you down.

For Bev, expert horsewoman, who was only a call away with either emotional support or an answer to an equine question. May the *midnight sun* shine on you.

For Mikey, whose persistent interest ("What are you writing, when can I read it?") kept the pressure on. A blessing on your head.

For my mother, who taught me to explore with delight and astonishment. I only wish I wrote this earlier so you could have read it.

And finally, for my family, my ballast—my children David and Anna, the very beat of my heart, and my husband and life mate, Matthew—first reader, first responder, first star I see tonight.